R0083155929

05/2015

W9-AHX-610

PALM BEACH COUNTY
LIBRARY SYSTEM
3650 Summit Boulevard
West Palm Beach, FL 33406-4198

The Pilgrim Chronicles

The Pilgrim Chronicles

*An Eyewitness History of the Pilgrims and
the Founding of Plymouth Colony*

ROD GRAGG

REGNERY
HISTORY

Copyright © 2014 by Rod Gragg

All rights reserved. No part of this publication may be reproduced or transmitted in any form or by any means electronic or mechanical, including photocopy, recording, or any information storage and retrieval system now known or to be invented, without permission in writing from the publisher, except by a reviewer who wishes to quote brief passages in connection with a review written for inclusion in a magazine, newspaper, website, or broadcast.

Except where taken from the 1611 King James Bible, all scripture quotations are from the Geneva Bible, printed in London by Robert Barker in 1606.

Library of Congress Control Number: 2014950137

ISBN 978-1-62157-269-5

Published in the United States by
Regnery History, an imprint of
Regnery Publishing
A Salem Communications Company
300 New Jersey Ave NW
Washington, DC 20001
www.RegneryHistory.com

Manufactured in the United States of America

10 9 8 7 6 5 4 3 2 1

Books are available in quantity for promotional or premium use. For information on discounts and terms, please visit our website: www.Regnery.com.

Distributed to the trade by
Perseus Distribution
250 West 57th Street
New York, NY 10107

Author is represented by the literary agency of
Alive Communications, Inc.
7680 Goddard Street, Suite 200
Colorado Springs, CO 80920
www.alivecommunications.com

For
Kylah, Cody, Sophia, Jaxon,
Ashlyn, Gracie, and Jate.
May they all have Pilgrim hearts.

CONTENTS

CHAPTER ONE

"Who Shall Separate Us from the Love of Christ?"

In the soft fresh light of a new dawn they peered over the railing of their ship and studied the distant shoreline. Before them lay a long stretch of towering sand dunes and farther to the west they could see a long line of forested hills. "And the appearance of it much comforted us," one of them would later recall, "it caused us to rejoice together and praise God...." It was November 9, 1620. They were the people who would become known to history as the Pilgrims, and they were looking for the first time at their new home—America.

Almost ten weeks earlier they had left England aboard the *Mayflower,* bound for a new life in the New World. The voyage across the fierce Atlantic had been stormy and perilous. To some of them, the dangerous passage may have seemed symbolic of their history as Pilgrims—a stormy, perilous quest for freedom that had begun decades earlier in Old World England.[1]

In 1620, the *Mayflower* brought the Pilgrims to the forested shores of what would become New England. The voyage across the Atlantic had been stormy and perilous, much like their quest for freedom in England.

LIBRARY OF CONGRESS

"Many More Came Forward with Fresh Courage"

Early Pilgrim Attempts to Flee England Result in Arrest and Persecution

Soldiers hurried through the marshy lowlands toward the shore of England's North Sea. It was a sizeable force, composed of horse dragoons and infantry. Some carried firelock muskets; others were armed with bills, deadly-looking polearms equipped with ax-style blades and spiked points. The troops presented a fearsome appearance to their target—a body of unarmed civilian men, women, and children huddled on the deck of a masted coal barque anchored in the shallows at water's edge.

The advancing troops were English militia, dispatched by local authorities to stop the shipload of civilians from leaving England without an official license to travel. It would have been easy for authorities in the nearby town of Grimsby to learn of the group's attempt to flee the country. Grimsby was located on England's northeast coast at the mouth of the River Humber, and several days earlier the ship *Francis,* a fifty-ton masted coal hauler, had come downriver from the river port of Hull.

The *Francis* carried more than coal: aboard ship were approximately eighty men, women, and children desperately hoping to make passage from England across the North Sea to sanctuary in Holland. By the time the *Francis* had moved downriver to await the outbound sailing tide on the coast—May 12, 1608—news of a coal barque taking on so many passengers with their baggage had quickly reached English authorities in Grimsby.

The would-be exiles were Puritan Separatists—a sect of Christians who felt called to separate themselves from the Church of England, the official government denomination, which they believed was engaged in worldly ways they could not accept. As Separatists, they were deemed "dissenters" by the rule of England's King James I, and they were forbidden to leave the country without official licensed permission—which they did not possess. Awaiting them just offshore was a Dutch ship—a sloop-like single-masted hoy—which was anchored in deep waters within easy sailing distance of the *Francis.* The coal barque, however, had gone

"The poor men already aboard were in great distress for their wives and children"

With sails raised, Dutch hoys line the docks of a European port.

WIKIMEDIA COMMONS

aground at low tide, and the ship's crew had begun to transfer passengers to the Dutch ship. The men had been sent first, and already more than a dozen had been rowed to the Dutch vessel aboard the *Francis*'s longboat.

More were preparing to board the longboat for transfer to their getaway ship when the militia appeared, hurrying through the coastal flats toward the grounded *Francis*. Seeing the troops approach, the captain of the Dutch ship ordered anchor up and sailed away—with the dozen Separatist husbands and fathers still aboard. On the *Francis*—probably by a prearranged plan—most of the male members among the passengers jumped ship to escape arrest and imprisonment. Left aboard the grounded coal ship to face the armed troops were the group's women and children, who began to sob aloud as their men folk scattered or disappeared over the ocean horizon, bound for distant Holland.

They were ordered off the *Francis*, then marched into town and jailed until the local court could determine their fate. Most of them were members of illegal Separatist congregations in the town of Gainsborough and the village of Scrooby, which were located to the west in England's East Midlands region. One of their principal leaders, Thomas Helwys, an affluent lawyer, landowner, and local Separatist, faced the authorities with them. While local authorities pondered their sentencing and sought advice from England's Privy Council, an advisory body that administered the king's policies, they were moved from jail to jail. Most had no other place to live, because they had sold their homes to raise money for their escape to the Netherlands.

For many of them, it was not their first attempt to escape from England to Holland, where—unlike England—they could freely worship as they wished. Several months earlier, some of them had bought passage on a ship from the nearby port of Boston, Thomas Helwys among them, but the ship's English captain betrayed them, keeping their money and belongings and turning them over to local authorities. English law ordered that all adult citizens who failed to worship in the Church of England for one month—or who attended a worship service outside the official Church—would be classified as a "non-conformists" and jailed. If they did not agree to conform to the Church of England within three months, they would be given the option of death or exile. Exile was what they were seeking, but non-conformists were forbidden to emigrate—so they were left in a legal no-man's-land: expected to flee England, but denied official permission to do so.

Eventually, after months of imprisonment in various places, they were released. Meanwhile, the husbands and fathers who had sailed for Holland made their way back to England and rejoined their families. Undeterred, the Separatists from Scrooby and Gainsborough began to make new plans to escape to the Netherlands. Eighteen-year-old Separatist William Bradford, who would later become the most famous Pilgrim leader, recorded the group's desperate, doomed attempt to obtain freedom of faith in 1608.

They heard of a Dutchman at Hull who had a ship of his own belonging to Zeeland, and they made an agreement with him, and acquainted him with their plight, hoping to find him more reliable than the English captain [at Boston] had been; and he bade them have no fear. He was to take them aboard between Grimsby and Hull, where there was a large common a good way from any town. The women and children, with all their effects, were sent to the place at the time arranged in a small bark which they had hired; and the men were to meet them by land. But it so happened that they all arrived a day before the ship came, and the sea being rough, and the women

"What weeping and crying on every side"

An early seventeenth-century infantry musketeer brandishes his matchlock musket. So armed, a company of English militia could present a fearsome appearance to civilians.

WIKIMEDIA COMMONS

very sick, the sailors put into a creek hard by, where they grounded at low water.

The next morning the ship came, but they were stuck fast and could not stir till about noon. In the meantime, the captain of the ship, seeing how things were, sent his boat to get the men aboard whom he saw were ready walking about the shore. But after the first boatful was got aboard and she was ready to go for more, the captain espied a large body of horse and foot, armed with bills and guns and other weapons—for the country side had turned out to capture them. The Dutchman, seeing this, swore his country's oath, "sacraments," and having a fair wind, weighed anchor, hoisted sail, and away! The poor men already aboard were in great distress for their wives and children, left thus to be captured, and destitute of help—and for themselves, too, without any clothes but what they had on their backs, and scarcely a penny about them, all their possessions being aboard the bark, now seized.

It drew tears from their eyes, and they would have given anything to be ashore again. But all in vain, there was no remedy; they must thus sadly part.... But to return to the rest where we left them. The other men, who were in greatest danger, made shift to escape before the troops could surprise them, only sufficient staying to assist the women. But it was pitiful to see these poor women in their distress. What weeping and crying on every side: some for their husbands carried away in the ship; others not knowing what would become of them and their little ones; others again melted in tears, seeing their poor little ones hanging about them, crying for fear and quaking with cold. Being thus apprehended, they were hurried from one place to another, till in the end the officers knew not what to do with them; for to imprison so many innocent women and children only because they wished to go with their husbands, seemed unreasonable and would cause an outcry; and to send them home again was as difficult, for they alleged, as was the truth, that they had no homes to go to—for they had sold or otherwise disposed of their houses and

livings. To be short, after they had been thus turmoiled a good while, and conveyed from one constable to another, they were glad to be rid of them on any terms; for all were wearied and tired of them. Though in the meantime, they, poor souls, endured misery enough. So in the end, necessity forced a way for them....

I must not omit, however, to mention the fruit of it all. For by these public afflictions, their cause became famous, and led many to inquire into it; and their Christian behavior left a deep impression on the minds of many. Some few shrank from these first conflicts, and no wonder; but many more came forward with fresh courage....[2]

In May of 1608, Separatist families attempting to flee England were overtaken on the coast by armed militia troops.

A POPULAR HISTORY OF THE UNITED STATES

"The Person So Offending... Shall Suffer Imprisonment"

Dissenters from the Church of England Face Severe Punishment

A Puritan was "a Protestant frayed out of his wits." So declared a crude but common joke among England's ruling class in the early 1600s, which referred to the brutal beatings sometimes administered to dissenters from the Church of England. Why did so

"Their Christian behavior left a deep impression on the minds of many"

If caught and arrested, English Separatists who tried to flee England in search of religious freedom could be imprisoned as dissidents from the Church of England.

WIKIMEDIA COMMONS

many English leaders dislike Puritans and, especially, the Puritan Separatists who would become America's Pilgrims? The answer: many in power viewed the Puritans, and especially the Separatists, as threats to authority. Originally a term of ridicule, the name "Puritan" was given to English Christians who wanted to purify the Church of England of practices they considered to be unbiblical. Their concerns were rooted in the Protestant Reformation.

In 1517, Martin Luther, a Roman Catholic priest in Germany, had ignited the Reformation by calling for the Church to return to key biblical doctrines that many believed had been distorted or abandoned in the early Middle Ages. Personal salvation came through God's grace through faith in Jesus Christ alone, Luther and other Reformers proclaimed, rather than by a combination of faith and human works. They preached the "priesthood of believers," which held that any believer should be allowed to read the Bible without the oversight of a minister or priest. They upheld the authority of the Bible over Church tradition and papal rulings, and they denounced the Church for "selling indulgences"—a practice that promised less

English Puritans—including the future Pilgrims—were influenced by sixteenth-century German theologian Martin Luther, the Catholic priest who sparked the Protestant Reformation.

WIKIMEDIA COMMONS

punishment for sin in the afterlife in exchange for a donation.

Although Church leaders in Rome rejected Luther's call for reform and excommunicated him, the Reformation had flooded western Europe, producing both a spiritual

In this satirical engraving, King Henry VIII, who broke with the Roman Catholic Church, sits on the throne of England with his foot atop Pope Clement VII.

NATIONAL AND DOMESTIC HISTORY OF ENGLAND

revival as well as dramatic political change. While the renewed emphasis on the Gospel transformed hearts and minds and produced countless believers, it also promoted the belief that everyone was of equal value to God, whether a pauper or a prince, and that all people were subject to the Higher Law of God as revealed by the Bible—even royalty. The poorest peasant felt empowered as a child of God. This Bible-based notion of equality unnerved many European monarchies, perhaps even more than the Reformation's challenge to the theology and practices of the Catholic Church. At the orders or acquiescence of the monarchy, tens of thousands of Protestants were executed in Spain, Portugal, and France—but in England, the Reformation flourished.

It came to England during the reign of King Henry VIII, who initially persecuted the Protestants as a Catholic ruler. Then in 1534, after being refused a marriage annulment by Pope Clement VII, he broke with the Church in Rome, and set up the Church of England with himself as its head. His motives were self-serving, not faith-based, but many people in England were ready for a change, seized the opportunity, and embraced the Reformation. After years of attempting to suppress the printing of the Bible in English, King Henry begrudgingly reversed course, and officially sanctioned an English language Bible. Following his death in 1547, the

"The whole nation became a church"

Queen Mary I attempted to restore Catholicism as England's official state denomination, but she sickened and died before she could succeed. Her persecution of Protestants earned her the nickname "Bloody Mary."

LIBRARY OF CONGRESS

English Reformation flourished during the reign of his young son and successor, Edward VI, who assumed the throne at age nine under the oversight of Protestant advisors. Despite the opposition of devout Catholics, the Church of England and Reformation theology appeared to be generally accepted in England—until 1553, when Edward grew ill and died at age fifteen.

After a foiled attempt by Edward's advisors to have him succeeded by his young Protestant cousin, Lady Jane Grey, King Henry's daughter Mary became Queen of England. Devoted to Catholicism, she aggressively attempted to roll back the English Reformation, executing Lady Jane Grey and several hundred other Protestants, and earning the nickname "Bloody Mary" from her opponents. After only five years of rule, however, Queen Mary I also sickened and died. She was succeeded by her half sister, Queen Elizabeth I, who would establish England's national identity as a world power—and who was a professing Protestant. To bring stability to the nation, she established what became known as the Elizabethan Religious Settlement.

Through the Act of Supremacy and the Act of Uniformity, Queen Elizabeth's Settlement solidly established the Church of England as the nation's official government denomination. It was a compromise of sorts: the Church of England would retain its Protestant doctrine, but it would also keep familiar, Catholic-style worship ceremonies and traditions. The publication of English language Bibles, once outlawed in England, now proliferated, and commoners and gentry alike eagerly purchased personal copies.

"The street, the tavern, the ale-house, the church and every company were the scenes of earnest dispute or holy zeal."

More than three hundred Protestants were executed during Queen Mary's reign. Many of them were burned at the stake at an execution site in London's Smithfield neighborhood, where a butchers' market had been located in Medieval days.

NATIONAL AND DOMESTIC HISTORY OF ENGLAND

Learning and sharing Scripture became the rage in England. "Everywhere might be heard the eager conversation of minds enlightened by the truth, speaking those wonderful words which the Most High had spoken unto men," reported nineteenth-century church historian Edward B. Underhill. "The street, the tavern, the ale-house, the church and every company were the scenes of earnest dispute or holy zeal [as] scripture was compared with scripture and its sense closely scrutinized." By the early 1600s, the common people of England were awash in a flood of faith. "The whole moral effect…was simply amazing," observed renowned English historian John Richard Green. "The whole nation became a church."

While Queen Elizabeth's compromise solidified Protestant doctrine in the Church of England, it also placed requirements and restrictions on Protestants as well as Catholics. The English people were required to abide by the standards and policies of the Church of England as stated in the 1559 Book of Common Prayer. Pastors and preachers were forbidden to publicly "preach, declare or speake any thing" that was not sanctioned by the Anglican Church. Disobedient pastors could be

Queen Elizabeth I implemented what would become known as the Elizabethan Religious Settlement in England, which reinforced Protestant doctrine in the Church of England while retaining some Catholic-style worship elements.

NATIONAL PORTRAIT GALLERY

discharged from their salaried positions in the Church and even imprisoned for life. The punishment for any minister who deviated from Church policy was outlined in the Book of Common Prayer:

And that if any manner of parson, vicar, or other whatsoever minister, that ought or should sing or say common prayer mentioned in the said book, or minister the sacraments, from and after the feast of the nativity of St. John Baptist next coming, refuse to use the said common prayers, or to minister the sacraments in such cathedral or parish church, or other places as he should use to minister the same, in such order and form as they be mentioned and set forth in the said book, or shall willfully or obstinately standing in the same, use any other rite, ceremony, order, form, or manner of celebrating of the Lord's Supper, openly or privily, or Matins, Evensong, administration of the sacraments, or other open prayers, than is mentioned and set forth in the said book (open prayer in and throughout this Act, is meant that prayer which is for other to come unto, or hear, either in common churches or private chapels or oratories, commonly called the service of the Church), or shall preach,

"The same person shall for his second offence suffer imprisonment by the space of one whole year"

declare, or speak anything in the derogation or depraving of the said book, or anything therein contained, or of any part thereof, and shall be thereof lawfully convicted, according to the laws of this realm, by verdict of twelve men, or by his own confession, or by the notorious evidence of the fact, shall lose and forfeit to the queen's highness, her heirs and successors, for his first offence, the profit of all his

In the mid-sixteenth century, English-language Bibles were made available to the common people for the first time. By royal order, English-language pulpit Bibles were distributed to churches, where they were chained to the lectern.

NATIONAL AND DOMESTIC HISTORY OF ENGLAND

spiritual benefices or promotions coming or arising in one whole year next after his conviction; and also that the person so convicted shall for the same offence suffer imprisonment by the space of six months, without bail or mainprize.

And if any such person once convicted of any offence concerning the premises, shall after his first conviction soon offend, and be thereof, in form aforesaid, lawfully convicted, that then the same person shall for his second offence suffer imprisonment by the space of one whole year, and also shall therefore be deprived, ipso facto, of all his spiritual promotions; and that it shall be lawful to all patrons or donors of all and singular the same spiritual promotions, or of any of them, to present or collate to the same, as though the person and persons so offending were dead.

And that if any such person or persons, after he shall be twice convicted in form aforesaid, shall offend against any of the premises the third time, and shall be thereof, in form aforesaid, lawfully convicted, that then the person so offending and convicted the third time, shall be deprived, ipso facto, of all his spiritual promotions, and also shall suffer imprisonment during his life.[3]

— ✦ — ✦ —

"Who Shall Separate Us from the Love of Christ?"

English Puritans Embrace a Bible-Centered Theology

In England, no group of believers was more committed to living according to the biblical worldview than the Puritans. Like the Presbyterians in Scotland and England, the Huguenots in France, and the Dutch Reformed in Holland, the Puritans were followers of the sixteenth-century French-Swiss Reformation theologian John Calvin, whose systematic theology, they believed, faithfully reflected biblical truth. Queen Elizabeth's compromise of Protestant doctrine and Catholic-style ceremony was generally acceptable to much of the English population, but it deeply troubled England's Puritans. The Puritan movement included large numbers of laborers, farmers, tradesmen, and merchants, but much of its early development occurred within the faculty of England's Cambridge University. There Christian intellectuals contended that the Roman Church had long before veered off course by equating man's tradition with God's Word, and had thus burdened believers with unbiblical, man-made dogmas.

They and other Puritan leaders argued that worship should be Bible-based, emphasizing simplicity instead of ceremony and biblical doctrine rather than Church tradition. The focus of true worship, they held, should be God-centered, and they feared much in the Church of England was man-centered. Despite their deep concerns, however, mainstream Puritans wanted to reform the Church, rather than replace it. Their goal was to bring it closer to what they believed was the model of the New Testament church. The Bible alone, Puritans believed, was the revealed Word of the Triune God, and was therefore inerrant and authoritative.

England's Puritans, including the Separatists, accepted the systematic theology of French-Swiss Reformation leader John Calvin as accurately reflecting biblical truth.

WIKIMEDIA COMMONS

Puritans treasured Scripture, and loved deep, meaty sermons, which became a trademark of their preachers. Puritan theology consistently stressed salvation through personal faith in Jesus Christ rather than by good works. Saving faith, Puritans generally believed, was not merely belonging to a church, intellectually accepting a belief system, or engaging in religious practices. It was an undeserved gift, an act of grace, given by a loving and sovereign God to those who personally surrendered their hearts and lives to Jesus Christ as Lord and Savior. Such saving faith in the life of a believer, Puritans held, was marked by repentance of sin, a desire to live as a disciple of Christ, and a belief that salvation from God is eternally secure. "This truth is perceived...," wrote seventeenth-century Puritan theologian William Ames in *The Marrow of Theology*, "by a certain spiritual sense in which the grace of God now present becomes known and evident to the believer."

"Also we know that all things work together for the best unto them that love God."

The faith and focus of Puritanism was based on Bible passages such as the following, which are excerpted from chapters eight and ten of the New Testament book of Romans:

In the sixteenth century, England's Cambridge University became the center of Puritanism, as Christian professors there promoted a movement to purify the Church of England of what they deemed to be unbiblical worship practices.

WIKIMEDIA COMMONS

"Who shall separate us from the love of Christ?"

Now then there is no condemnation to them that are in Christ Jesus, which walk not after the flesh, but after the Spirit.... Also we know that all things work together for the best unto them that love God, even to them that are called of his purpose.

For those which he knew before, he also predestinated to be made like to the image of his Son, that he might be the firstborn among many brethren.

Moreover, whom he predestinated, them also he called, and whom he called, them also he justified, and whom he justified, them he also glorified.

What shall we then say to these things? If God be on our side, who can be against us?

Who spared not his own Son, but gave him for us all to death, how shall he not with him give us all things also?

Who shall lay anything to the charge of God's chosen? it is God that justifieth.

Who shall condemn? It is Christ which is dead: yea, or rather, which is risen again, who is also at the right hand of God, and maketh request also for us.

Who shall separate us from the love of Christ? Shall tribulation or anguish, or persecution, or famine, or nakedness, or peril, or sword?

As it is written, For thy sake we are killed all day long; we are counted as sheep for the slaughter.

Nevertheless, in all these things we are more than conquerors through him that loved us.

For I am persuaded that neither death, nor life, nor Angels, nor principalities, nor powers, nor things present, nor things to come, nor height, nor depth, nor any other creature, shall be able to separate us from the love of God, which is in Christ Jesus our Lord....

For if thou shalt confess with thy mouth the Lord Jesus, and shalt believe in thine heart that God raised him up from the dead, thou shalt be saved.

For with the heart man believeth unto righteousness, and with the mouth man confesseth to salvation. For the Scripture saith, whosoever believeth in him, shall not be ashamed.

> ❧
>
> "For thy sake we are killed all day long"
>
> ❧

The pastor's pulpit was the central focus of a Puritan worship service. From the pulpit, Puritan ministers preached long, meaty sermons that were intended to "expose" Scripture as God's revealed truth.

THE STORY OF SOME ENGLISH SHIRES

By the early seventeenth century, the Puritan movement had attracted a steadily growing cross-section of the English population. Even so, Puritans were often mocked by many for their devout ways and criticism of the Church of England.

LIBRARY OF CONGRESS

For there is no difference between the Jew and the Grecian: for he that is Lord over all, is rich unto all that call on him.

For whosoever shall call upon the Name of the Lord shall be saved.

But how shall they call on him, in whom they have not believed? And how shall they believe in him, of whom they have not heard? And how shall they hear without a preacher?

And how shall they preach, except they be sent? As it is written, How beautiful are the feet of them which bring glad tidings of peace, and bring glad tidings of good things![4]

"She Stood the Fiery Ordeal without Flinching"

Memories of Public Executions Linger in Late Sixteenth-Century England

G od would have our joys to be far more than our sorrows," proclaimed a popular Puritan saying. Contrary to the modern negative stereotype of a Puritan—"a gaunt, lank-haired killjoy, wearing a black steeple hat"—English Puritans were generally outgoing, optimistic people who loved life. Their perspective on life was based on biblical teachings such as Psalm 16, verse 11: "Thou wilt shew me the path of life; in thy presence is fullness of joy; at thy right hand are pleasures for evermore." They generally understood and appreciated Reformer John Calvin's attitude when he wrote, "Shall the Lord have imbued flowers with such beauty, to present itself to our eyes, with such sweetness of smell, to impress our sense of smelling; and shall it be unlawful for our eyes to be affected with the beautiful sight, or our olfactory nerves with the agreeable odor?" They believed that God's creation was meant to be explored, examined, and enjoyed. Typical of the English people of their day, they loved field

Contrary to the later stereotype that would depict them as grim-faced killjoys, Puritans were known for their zest for life and enjoyed English field sports such as bowling.

LIBRARY OF CONGRESS

sports such as bowling, archery, fishing, hunting, and even horse-racing. Such zest for living in Puritan families led Quaker leader George Fox to criticize them, not for grim legalism but for their appreciation of "ribbons and lace and costly apparel."

Whether it was work, play, the arts, education, law, government, family life, or worship, they believed that everything should be done in a manner that honored God. They saw the family as the bedrock of society, and marriage and children were seen as gifts from God. Husbands and wives were intended to enjoy physical intimacy for the purpose of reproduction, they believed, but also to strengthen an unbreakable bond of marriage. Puritan teaching held that husbands and wives were to approach the marriage bed "with good will and delight, willingly, readily and cheerfully." As the leader of his family, Puritans believed, the husband was commanded by Scripture to love his wife "even as Christ also loved the church," and to "train up a child in the way he should go" by modeling morality and providing biblical instruction.

As a movement that arose among university educators, Puritanism understandably placed great value on education, and Puritans were well informed for their day—on cultural and political issues as well as the content of Scripture. Illiteracy was viewed as almost sinful because it blocked access to the Bible. "So faith comes by hearing," advised the New Testament, "and hearing by the Word of Christ." Puritans considered

England's Puritans came from all sectors of English society, including many who were prosperous members of the nation's middle class.

THE STORY OF SOME ENGLISH SHIRES

"Puritanism… corresponded in many points with the most absolute democratic and republican theories"

Bible study to be essential to the Christian life, and responsible believers were obliged to read, write, and learn. "The Puritan scholar studied all history, heathen or Christian, as an exhibition of divine wisdom," twentieth-century Puritan expert Perry Miller would observe, "and found in the temporal the unfolding of the divine plan…."

It was Puritan politics that rankled and unnerved the ruling class even more than Puritan theology. "Puritanism was not merely a religious doctrine," the famous nineteenth-century political observer Alexis de Tocqueville would conclude, "but corresponded in many points with the most absolute democratic and republican theories. It was this tendency which had aroused its most dangerous adversaries." In an age when many European rulers held to the divine right of kings—that royalty was established by God and therefore should never be challenged—Puritans were viewed suspiciously by some rulers because they believed that every person was equal before God.

Although numerous Protestant dissenters were fined or imprisoned during Queen Elizabeth's reign, comparatively few were actually executed, Puritans included. The Queen viewed the Puritan movement as more of an aggravation than a genuine threat to her throne. Even so, the horror of fiery executions at the stake was still as much memory as history in late sixteenth-century England, kept afresh by the immensely popular work *Actes and Monuments of These Latter and Perilous Times*

> "He told the people to bear witness that he was about to suffer in a just cause"

by Puritan minister and author John Foxe. Better known as *Foxe's Book of Martyrs*, the book recorded the grim martyrdom of numerous Protestants, including many under the reign of Queen Mary I. Critics denounced the work as sensationalistic and one-sided, although *Encyclopedia Britannica* would judge it to be "factually detailed" in the twenty-first century. At the height of Foxe's fame, his study of martyrdom led him to boldly—but unsuccessfully—petition Queen Elizabeth to spare the lives of several Anabaptists and Catholics who were scheduled for execution. Such executions lessened during Elizabeth's reign, but some still occurred, and accounts such as these from *Foxe's Book of Martyrs* were a reminder of what could befall any dissenters who roused royal displeasure:

In the year 1557…Rev. Mr. John Hullier was…brought to the stake. While undressing, he told the people to bear witness that he was about to suffer in a just cause, and exhorted them to believe that there was no other rock than Jesus Christ to build upon. A priest named Boyes then desired the mayor to silence him. After praying, he went meekly to the stake, and being bound with a chain, and placed in a pitch barrel, fire was applied to the reeds and wood; but the wind drove the fire directly to his back, which caused him under the severe agony to pray the more fervently. His friends directed the executioner to fire the pile to windward of his face, which was immediately done.

A strong family was central to the Puritan lifestyle, which followed the biblical admonition that a husband should love his wife "as Christ loved the Church" and that parents were obligated to "train up a child in the way he should go."

LIBRARY OF CONGRESS

A quantity of books were now thrown into the fire, one of which (the Communion Service) he caught, opened it, and joyfully continued to read it, until the fire and smoke deprived him of sight; then even, in earnest prayer, he pressed the book to his heart, thanking God for bestowing on him in his last moments this precious gift. The day being hot, the fire burnt fiercely; and at a time when the spectators supposed he was no more, he suddenly exclaimed, Lord Jesus, receive my spirit! And meekly resigned his life….

"She stood the fiery ordeal without flinching"

Simon Miller received the crown of martyrdom. Miller dwelt at Lynn, and came to Norwich, where [the bishop committed him] to his prison, where he remained till the 13th of July, the day of his burning.

Elizabeth Cooper, wife of a pewterer of St. Andrews, Norwich…was taken from her own house by Mr. Sutton the sheriff, who very reluctantly complied with the letter of the law, as they had been servants and in friendship together. At the stake, the poor sufferer, feeling the fire, uttered the cry of Oh! upon which Mr. Miller, putting his hand behind him towards her, desired her to be of good courage, for, said he, "good sister, we shall have a joyful and a sweet supper." Encouraged by this example and exhortation, she stood the fiery ordeal without flinching, and, with him proved the power of faith over the flesh.

Agnes Bengeor and Margaret Thurston were doomed to the fire at Colchester, Sept. 17, 1557. Humbly they knelt to pray, and joyfully they arose to be chained to the stake, uttering invocations and hallelujahs, till the surrounding flames mounted to the seat of life, and their spirits ascended to the Almighty Saviour of all who truly believe!

John Noyes, a shoemaker, of Laxfield, Suffolk, was…led to the stake, prepared for the horrid sacrifice. Mr. Noyes, on coming to the fatal spot, knelt down, prayed, and rehearsed the 50th psalm. When the chain enveloped him, he said, "Fear not them that kill the body, but fear him that can kill both body and soul, and cast it into everlasting fire!" As one cad placed a fagot against him, he blessed the hour in which he was born to die for the truth; and while trusting only upon the all-sufficient merits of the Redeemer, fire was set to the pile, and the blazing fagots in a short time stifled his last words, "Lord, have mercy on me! Christ, have Mercy upon me!" The ashes of the body were buried in a pit.…

Mrs. Cicely Ormes. This young martyr, aged twenty-two, was the wife of Mr. Edmund Ormes, worsted weaver of St. Lawrence, Norwich. At the death of Miller and Elizabeth Cooper, before mentioned, she had said that she would pledge them of the same cup they drank of. For these words she was brought to the chancellor, who would have discharged her upon promising to go to church, and to keep her belief to herself. As she would not consent to this, the chancellor urged that he had shown more lenience to her than any other person, and was unwilling to condemn her because she was an ignorant, foolish woman; to this she replied, (perhaps with more shrewdness than he expected) that however great his desire

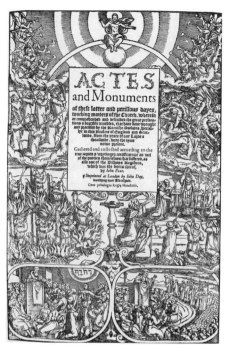

The title page of the 1563 edition of John Foxe's *Actes and Monuments of These Last and Perilous Days* featured a montage of images. Popularly known as *Foxe's Book of Martyrs*, it was widely read in England during the late sixteenth and early seventeenth centuries.

WIKIMEDIA COMMONS

Two Protestants die for their faith in this engraving from a sixteenth-century edition of *Foxe's Book of Martyrs*. Foxe's hugely popular book was a reminder of what could potentially befall anyone who incurred royal displeasure.

WIKIMEDIA COMMONS

might be to spare her sinful flesh, it could not equal her inclination to surrender it up in so great a quarrel. The chancellor then pronounced the fiery sentence, and, September 23, 1557, she was brought to the stake, at eight o'clock in the morning.

After declaring her faith to the people, she laid her hand on the stake, and said, "Welcome, thou cross of Christ." Her hand was sooted in doing this, (for it was this same stake at which Miller and Cooper were burnt) and she at first wiped it; but directly after again welcomed and embraced it as the "sweet cross of Christ." After the tormentors had kindled the fire, she said, "My soul doth magnify the Lord, and my spirit doth rejoice in God my Saviour." Then crossing her hands upon her breast, and looking upwards with the utmost serenity, she stood the fiery furnace.... Her courage in such a cause deserves commendation—the cause of Him who has said, "Whoever is ashamed of me on earth, of such will I be ashamed in heaven."[5]

CHAPTER TWO

"Rather than Turn, They Will Burn"

Q ueen Elizabeth I called him her "little black husband." His name was John Whitgift, and he was the archbishop of Canterbury during the later years of Elizabeth's reign. The unmarried queen trusted the black-robed clergyman so much, court gossips claimed, that she listened to his opinions as a wife would listen to her husband. And John Whitgift did not like Puritans. As the archbishop of Canterbury, he was the senior pastor in the Church of England, with a junior archbishop presiding in the city of York, and he wielded immense power over the lives of the English people. Whitgift had risen through the ranks of the Church, serving as vice-chancellor of Cambridge University and bishop of Worcester, attaining the post of archbishop of Canterbury in 1583, at the height of Queen Elizabeth's reign. He had gained the queen's notice and favor as a bishop, and when promoted to the top position in the Church, he became Queen Elizabeth's principal minister and chief confessor. To Whitgift, it was said, the queen shared "the very secrets of her soul."[1]

———◆◆———————————◆◆———

"Yea, He Will Be with Us in Fire and Water"

Puritan Separatists Accept Persecution and Death for Their Faith

Archbishop Whitgift was determined to rein in the Puritans and other "non-conformists"—and if they resisted, he intended to punish then. Although he shared the fundamentals of the Puritans' Protestant doctrine, he fiercely disagreed with their criticisms of the Church of England. As archbishop of Canterbury and the Church's top official, it was his charge to bring all of England into conformity with Church doctrine, policies, and practices. In 1583, with the queen's blessing, he officially prohibited preaching, teaching, and Bible training in private homes—a favorite practice of some Puritan ministers. The queen also allowed him to establish the Court of High Commission within the Church of England. The Court outlawed the publication of any literature it considered to be critical of the Church, and was granted authority to arrest, imprison, and punish anyone it deemed to be a threat—including ministers who preached without an official license or anywhere besides an Anglican church. Whitgift considered his three main enemies to be Catholics, the fledgling Baptist or Anabaptist movement, and what he called "wayward persons"—which included Puritans and Separatists.

Whitgift's repression apparently intimidated some Puritans, and made others more careful about calling for reforms. "Our Puritan brethren," observed a Church official, "are lying in concealment, partly silenced by a most able [archbishop], and partly terrified by the authority of our queen...." Puritans believed the Bible commanded all Christians to submit to authority—but not if forced to choose between man's law and God's law. At such times, Puritans believed, the Christians' first obligation was to God's higher law. "In that obedience in which we have shown to be due to the authority of rulers," wrote John Calvin, "we are always to make this exception, indeed, to observe it as a primary: that such obedience is never to lead us away from [God], to whose will the desires of all kings ought to be subject...." The Puritans, therefore, responded to Whitgift's repression by remaining submissive to the queen and the Church except on issues for which they felt called to obey a Higher Authority. Not so the Separatists—who saw Whitgift's persecution itself as a violation of higher law and further justification for worshipping outside the Church of England.

Adding to the queen's suspicions of Puritans, Separatists, and other dissenters were attempted revolts by England's repressed Catholics. Earlier, in 1569, Catholic noblemen from northern England had attempted to forcibly overthrow Elizabeth and replace her with Mary, Queen of Scots, who was Elizabeth's cousin and the Catholic ruler of Scotland. The uprising, known as the Rising of the North, was defeated by Queen Elizabeth's forces, and hundreds of its supporters were executed. Eventually, in 1587, Mary, Queen of Scots, was also executed for plotting Queen Elizabeth's assassination. As a result of the uprising and repeated attempts on her life by Catholic radicals, Elizabeth's official policies toward Catholicism hardened, and English Catholics would not obtain full religious freedom for centuries.

While the reforms they sought were mainly church-related, the Puritans undoubtedly wondered if they too might sometime face the same fate as England's Catholics, even though they threatened no violence against the queen. After all, Elizabeth I was the head of the government denomination that they so earnestly wanted to reform. And they had numerous complaints. They opposed kneeling for communion, for example, which they considered to be worshipping the elements rather than the Lord. They resisted the Church of England requirement to bow at the church altar, which they viewed as misplaced devotion. They were

Press operators proof the first draft of their latest publication. Separatist writers such as Robert Browne produced a steady stream of theological pamphlets and books—and works that harshly criticized the Church of England.

LIBRARY OF CONGRESS

offended by liturgical ceremonies, which they saw as man-centered and prideful, and they opposed the requirement that ministers in the Church of England wear a surplice (a Catholic-style priestly tunic that Anglican officials considered to be an indispensable symbol of ministerial authority). One Church official reportedly had declared that it was less sinful to have "begot seven bastards than to have preached without a surplice." To Puritans, the surplice was a man-centered adornment that detracted from humble, Bible-based worship.

While Puritan attempts to "purify" the Church of England were generally ecclesiastical in focus, they nonetheless challenged the authority of the official government denomination. Anglican officials were constantly aggravated and often infuriated by the repeated appearances of Puritan pamphlets and books that were critical of the Church of England. Eventually, Queen Elizabeth also grew weary of Puritan criticism of the state Church, and therefore was willing to give Whitgift the authority to force them into conformity with Church policies and practices. It was a severe repression. Puritan publications were deemed seditious, and their authors and printers were arrested and punished as traitors to the Crown. Countless Puritans were arrested and jailed alongside hardened criminals in notorious English prisons such as the Clink, the Bridewell, the Fleet, and the Gatehouse.

One of the most sensational cases of Puritan persecution was that of John Penry, a Welsh Catholic who became a Puritan while he was a student at Cambridge University. After graduation, Penry transferred to Oxford University, earned a graduate degree, and was officially licensed by the Church to preach to university students. In his late twenties, he returned to his native Wales, where he became an itinerant Puritan preacher and prolific Puritan writer. By then, the Bible had been translated into the Welsh language, but the Church of England was slow to supply an adequate number of Bibles to the churches in Wales. Increasingly frustrated by the lack of Bibles, Penry authored and published a series of pamphlets critical of Church officials. Archbishop Whitgift ordered him arrested, and he was briefly imprisoned. When released, he resumed publishing and continued to call for changes to the Church.

In 1590, Penry's home in Northampton was raided by Church authorities, but he escaped to Scotland. Two years later, he quietly returned to England and began preaching to a Separatist

Separatist preacher and writer John Penry is hauled to his execution site. In 1593, the thirty-four-year-old Penry was hanged in London for penning an unpublished manuscript that Church officials deemed disrespectful to the queen.

NATIONAL AND DOMESTIC HISTORY OF ENGLAND

Puritan congregation in London. In 1593, he was recognized by a Church official and was again arrested. Church officials searched his home for evidence to justify executing him, but found nothing worthy of a capital charge. After combing through his papers, however, they found a manuscript which they declared to be harshly disrespectful to the queen. It was an unpublished draft, but it was enough for Archbishop Whitgift: Penry was declared to be "a seditious disturber of her Majesty's peaceable government." On May 29, 1593, the thirty-four-year-old Puritan preacher was hanged. Before his execution, Penry had asked to see his wife Eleanor and their four daughters—Sure-Hope, Safety, Comfort, and Deliverance—but his request was denied. A month before his death, however, he did manage to get a farewell message to the members of his London congregation:

✦━•━━━━━•━✦

To the distressed faithful congregation of Christ, in London, and all the members... of this poor afflicted congregation, whether at liberty or in bonds: Jesus Christ, that great King and Prince of the kings of the earth, bless you, comfort you with His invincible Spirit, that you may be able to bear and overcome these great trials which you are yet (and I with you, if I live) to undergo for His name's sake, in this testimony.

Beloved! Let us think our lot and portion more than blessed, that are now vouchsafed the favor not only to know and to profess, but also to suffer for the sincerity of the Gospel; and let us remember that great is our reward in Heaven, if we endure unto the end....

Wherefore, my brethren, I beseech you be of like mind herein with me. I doubt not but you have the same precious faith with me, and are partakers also of far more glorious comfort than my barren and sinful soul can be. Strive for me, and with me, that the Lord our God may make me and us all able to end our course with joy and patience: strive, also, that He may stay His blessed hand (if it be His good pleasure), and not make any further breach in His church by the taking away of any more of us as yet, to the discouraging of the weak, and the lifting up of the horn of our adversaries.

I would, indeed, if it be His good pleasure, live yet with you, to help you to bear that grievous and hard yoke which yet ye are like to sustain, either here or in a strange land. And my good brethren, seeing as banishment with loss of goods is likely to betide you all, prepare yourselves for this hard entreaty, and rejoice that you are made worthy for Christ's cause, to suffer and bear all these things....

The Lord, my brethren and sisters, hath not forgotten to be gracious unto Zion. You shall yet find days of peace and of rest, if you continue faithful. This stamping and treading of us under His feet, this subverting of our cause and right in judgment, is done by Him, to the end that we should search and try our ways, and repent us of our carelessness, profaneness, and rebellion in His sight; but He will yet maintain the cause of our souls, and redeem our lives, if we return to Him. Yea, he will be with us in fire and water, and will not forsake us, if our hearts be only intent on serving Him, and especially of the building of Zion, whithersoever we go....

And here, I humbly beseech you—not in any outward regard, as I shall answer before my God—that you would take my poor and desolate widow and my mess of fatherless and friendless orphans with you into exile, whithersoever you go; and you shall find, I doubt not, that the blessed promises of my God, made unto me and mine, will accompany them, and even the whole church, for their sakes. For this, also, is the Lord's promise unto the holy seed; as you shall not need much to demand what they shall eat, or wherewith they shall be clothed; and, in short time I doubt not but that they will be found helpful, and not burdensome to the church.... Be kind, loving, and tender-hearted the one of you towards the other; labor every way to increase love, and to show the duties of love, one of you towards another....

Finally, my brethren, the eternal God bless you and yours, that I may meet with you all unto my comfort in the blessed kingdom of Heaven. Thus having from my heart—and with

"I humbly beseech you...take my poor and desolate widow and... fatherless and friendless orphans with you"

tears—performed (it may be) my last duty towards you in this life, I salute you all in the Lord, both men and women, even those who I have not named, as heartily as those whose names I have mentioned (for all your names I know not). And remember to stand steadfast and faithful in Jesus Christ, as you have received Him, unto your immortality; and may He confirm and establish you to the end for the praise of His glory. Amen.

The twenty-fourth of the fourth month April, 1593.

Your loving brother, in the patience and suffering of the Gospel,

JOHN PENRY
A witness of Christ in this life, and a partaker
of the glory that shall be revealed.[2]

"Rather than Turn, They Will Burn"

Despite Dangers and Threats, Puritan Separatists
Grow in Numbers

If Archbishop Whitgift's crackdown on non-conformists made England's Puritans uneasy, it was a genuine threat to the nation's Separatists. Despite their call for reforms, mainstream Puritans were still officially members of the Church of England, and in most cases their protests were not considered to be treasonous. That, and their growing numbers, encouraged even Archbishop Whitgift to show some restraint in dealing with them. So did the existence of prominent Puritans in almost all walks of English life, from academia to commerce to Parliament. England's Separatists, however, were an easier target. Like the Puritans, the sect also had a cross-section of the English population in its ranks, including members and leaders who were accomplished in their professional fields, but Separatists were few in number compared to the ranks of Puritans. And, unlike the Puritans, their principal goal *was* illegal—Separatists felt called by Scripture and conscience to worship outside the authority of the Church of England—and in their day *that* was a criminal act under English law.

England's Act of Uniformity required everyone to regularly attend church or be punished with fines, and any attempt to worship outside of the Anglican Church or in any manner that deviated from the Church's Book of Common Prayer was deemed to be a criminal act. Especially offensive to Anglican officials was the Separatist belief that every local church should be independent and self-governing rather than submitting to the Church of England's governing hierarchy. Like mainstream Puritanism, the Separatist movement traced its roots in large part to a theological movement at Cambridge University in the sixteenth century. There, a young ministerial student named Robert Browne came under the influence of Thomas Cartwright, a university professor and Puritan theologian who had gained attention for his outspoken criticism of the Church of England. Although he remained a member of the Church, Cartwright accused it of departing from the New Testament model of worship and government. By the time he graduated in 1572, at about age twenty-two, Browne was a committed Puritan who went beyond Cartwright's call for Church reform. He believed that local churches should choose their own leaders and should be autonomous, which meant separating from the Church of England.

He reportedly tossed his official Anglican preacher's license into the fire and took a job as a schoolmaster in London, where he became an open air preacher in defiance of the law. There, and in Cambridge and Norwich, Browne preached at outdoor venues and in private homes. He

Surrounded by the English countryside, the town of Bury St. Edmunds greets visitors with a peaceful appearance. In 1583, it was the site of a book-burning and a double execution of Separatists.

ST. EDMUNDSBURY CHRONICLE

also authored a string of books that harshly criticized the Church of England. His books were banned by the Church and burned by Church authorities, and he was repeatedly arrested and jailed. Undeterred, he continued to preach and write, and gained a growing number of followers—who were dubbed "Brownists."

In 1583, in the town of Bury St. Edmunds to the east of Cambridge, persecution of "Brownists" turned deadly. Inside the town church, someone had painted a Bible passage from the book of Revelation beside an image of the queen's coat of arms. According to an investigator from the Church of England, the graffiti implied that Queen Elizabeth was the false prophetess "Jezebel" of the End Times. In response, Church authorities launched a crackdown on Separatists and Puritans in the region, arresting several dozen church members and five Puritan ministers. Two Brownists—a cobbler named John Coppin and a tailor named Elias

Thacker—were hanged outside of town for promoting and distributing Browne's writings, and a pile of Browne's books were burned at the execution site. At their sentencing Coppin and Thacker reportedly told the presiding judge: "My Lord, your face we fear not, and for your threats we care not...."

By then, Browne and some of his followers had fled to Holland, where tolerant laws allowed them freedom of worship. Eventually, however, Browne's preaching and writing style became so fiery and unpredictable that scores of his followers turned away from him. He then left Holland and migrated to Scotland, but his confrontational ways alienated would-be supporters there as well. Apparently disgusted by his rejection in Scotland, he returned to England, where he was excommunicated from the Church of England—an act that seemed to undermine his resolve. Middle-aged and pressed by the need to support his family, he shocked the Separatists he had once inspired by renouncing Separatist practices and rejoining the Church of England. He was accepted back into the Church, and was allowed to serve as a schoolmaster and pastor until his death as an old man in 1633.

Browne's fiery and inconsistent ways eventually led many Separatists to denounce him, including the Pilgrims, who refused to wear the name "Brownists." Pilgrim leaders such as William Bradford would stress that the Separatist preference for autonomous, congregational government rather than the hierarchy of the Church of England was not based on Browne's writings, but on the model of the New Testament church. Despite his conflicted behavior, however, Robert Browne's original call to separate from the Church of England was the chief

Separatists John Coppin and Elias Thacker await execution at Bury St. Edmunds in June of 1583. They were executed for printing books critical of the Church of England and Queen Elizabeth's reign.

ILLUSTRATED HISTORY OF ENGLAND

35

spark that ignited the Separatist movement. By the early 1600s, Separatism had matured and stabilized into the belief system that would be characterized by the Pilgrims: a largely non-confrontational body of believers who held to Puritan doctrine, but sought to worship in independent, self-governing church congregations outside the Church of England.

Under Archbishop Whitgift's predecessor, English Separatists had generally been treated with begrudging toleration. When Whitgift became archbishop, however, he promptly launched a campaign to crush the Separatists. In 1588, Separatists and other "non-conformists" received an official warning: "And that from henceforth no person or persons whatsoever, be so hardy as to put in print or writing, sell, set forth, receive, give out or distribute any more of the same or such like seditious books or libels will answer for the contrary at their uttermost

English Separatists participating in a Puritan-style worship service. Separatists braved the threat of arrest and imprisonment for attending secret worship services in private homes, which was illegal in late sixteenth- and early seventeenth-century England.

LIBRARY OF CONGRESS

perils...." Despite Whitgrift's crackdown, Separatist leaders continued to preach and write, and Separatist congregations continued to assemble for worship in private homes. A rare, brief description of a secret Separatist worship service in an English house-church was recorded by an agent of the Church of England, who infiltrated the congregation and filed this report:

In that house where they intend to meet, there is one appointed to keep the door, for the intent, to give notice if there should be any insurrection, warning may be given them.

They do not flock together, but come two or three in a company; any man may be admitted thither; and all being gathered together, the man appointed to teach stands in the midst of the room, and his audience gather about him. He prayeth about the space of half an hour; and part of his prayer is, that those which came thither to scoff and laugh, God would be pleased to turn their hearts; by which means they think to escape undiscovered.

His sermon is about the space of an hour, and then doth another stand up to make the text more plain; and at the latter end, he entreats them all to go home severally, lest, the next meeting, they should be interrupted by those which are of the opinion of the wicked. They seem very steadfast in their opinions, and say, "rather than turn, they will burn."[3]

"In that house where they intend to meet, there is one appointed to keep the door ... to give notice"

"No person ... be so hardy as to put in print or writing, sell, set forth, receive, give out or distribute ... seditious books"

—◆—————————◆—

The King Would Come Forth to See "Pastimes and Fooleries"

England's New King Proves Himself No Friend of Puritans

In 1603, Queen Elizabeth I died. She was sixty-nine years old and had ruled for forty-five years. She was succeeded by the next-in-line: James VI, the king of Scotland. England's Puritans, including the Separatists, were hopeful that the new monarch would remove the threat of persecution that hovered over them like a dark cloud. Perhaps, they speculated, he might even agree to the Puritan calls to reform the Church of England—after all, the Scots Presbyterians of his homeland were Calvinists like the Puritans. The thirty-six-year-old monarch, who became James I of England, also fancied himself a Bible scholar and had even authored a commentary on the book of Revelation. Puritan hopes were soon crushed, however: King James I had no love for Puritans, Separatists, or other non-conformists.

James I was the son of Mary, Queen of Scots, and her second husband, Henry Stewart. His father had been murdered when James was still a baby, and his mother had been executed by Queen Elizabeth for plotting her overthrow. He had grown up under the wily manipulation of court advisors, some Catholic and some Protestant, but despite his mother's Catholicism, he had emerged a Protestant. Understanding that the line of succession potentially positioned him to be king of England some day, he shrewdly established a Scottish alliance with Queen Elizabeth when barely twenty years old—an alliance he kept even when the queen executed his mother. When he assumed the English throne, he took his duties seriously. He was an enthusiastic promoter of the arts, managed to keep England out of serious warfare for more than twenty years, and was generally popular with the English people. He reportedly believed that he had been called by God to unite England and Scotland, and he managed to maintain a fragile alliance during his reign. He also expanded English trade with the Far East, and under his rule England established its first successful colony in America at Jamestown in Virginia.

His personal life, however, tilted toward the bizarre. Although obviously intelligent, he was a complicated and conflicted man, who at times appeared to suffer from paranoia and severe depression. He was married to a foreigner—Princess Anne of Denmark—who bore him eight children, although only two lived to adulthood. Whispered rumors of his infidelity and immorality abounded in his court, and followed him all his life. He was a notoriously heavy drinker, and some claimed that he once injured himself when he drunkenly toppled from his horse. Court gossips described him as chronically anxious and easily frightened. "James was singularly effeminate," claimed one account, "he could not look at a drawn sword without shuddering...." If so, he was nonetheless a bold hunter who fearlessly raced through the countryside on horseback in pursuit of game.

"He could not look at a drawn sword without shuddering"

An early seventeenth-century jester entertains court visitors. Comedy skits were a favorite of James I, who was known for his notoriously "bawdy" humor.

NATIONAL AND DOMESTIC HISTORY OF ENGLAND

His physical appearance was unimpressive: his smile revealed gaps of missing teeth and he walked with an odd gait caused by a childhood illness. He was a man of average height, wore a thin auburn beard and moustache, was known to burp loudly even in public, and seldom washed his hands. Vain and self-indulgent, he spent lavish sums on royal functions, while the Crown's debts increased and the renowned English navy deteriorated for lack of funding. He insisted that the "Divine Right of Kings" endowed him with godlike authority, and he was frequently embroiled in divisive debates and controversies with Parliament.

While professing to be an astute scholar of the Bible, he was renowned for his crudity, even in public. A knowledgeable observer depicted him as habitually profane and notorious for his "words of perfect obscenity." Once, for example, he famously described a sensational comet that passed over England as "nothing else but Venus with a firebrand in her arse."

In his private chambers, he was said to have spent much of his time enjoying bawdy theatricals —"pastimes and fooleries" performed by his court jesters.

Aware of King James's irreverent sense of humor, His Majesty's jesters at one point reportedly staged sacrilegious mockery of the ordinance of baptism, dressing a pig in a baptism gown. The story was recorded by seventeenth-century English playwright Arthur Wilson, who had once frequented the king's court. King James promptly dismissed the farce as "blasphemy," according to Wilson, although the playwright claimed the king's displeasure was prompted less by his aversion to blasphemy and more by his dislike of pigs:

When James became melancholy in consequence of various disappointments in state matters, Buckingham and his mother used several means of diverting him. Amongst the most ludicrous was the present. They had a young lady who brought a pig in the dress of a new-born infant. The countess carried it to the king, wrapped in a rich mantle. One Turpin, on this occasion, was dressed like a bishop in all his pontifical ornaments. He began the rites of baptism with the common prayer-book in his hand; a silver ewer with water was held by another. The marquis stood as godfather. When James turned to look at the infant, the pig squeaked: an animal which he greatly abhorred. At this, highly displeased, he exclaimed—"Out! Away for shame! What blasphemy is this!"[4]

"When James turned to look at the infant, the pig squeaked"

"I Will Make Them Conform Themselves, or Else…"

James I Unleashes a Wave of Repression against Puritans and Separatists

When James I ascended to the throne, England's Puritans quickly realized he was not their friend. King James considered Puritanism to be a disease that threatened his rule. Puritans, he said, were "an evill sorte" who were "pestes in the Church." His opinion of England's Puritan community was reflected by one of his "bawdy" court comedies: a "Puritan" festooned in donkey ears loudly chastised the ruling class for "making

Upon Queen Elizabeth's death, the English throne passed to King James I, the former ruler of Scotland. Intelligent and well read, he considered himself to be a Bible scholar, but he was a heavy drinker whose personal life was clouded by rumors of infidelity and immorality—and he would prove to be no friend to Puritans and Separatists.

NATIONAL PORTRAIT GALLERY

41

King James I leads a royal hunt. The king was a bold hunter and a fearless horseman, but court gossips said his heavy drinking sometimes caused him to topple from his mount.

ILLUSTRATED HISTORY OF ENGLAND

merry" while Christians suffered persecution. In 1604—early in his reign—King James was presented with a formal petition by Puritan leaders detailing the reforms they felt were needed in the Church of England. Eventually known as the Millenary Petition, it reportedly included the signatures of one thousand Puritans. In response, the king agreed to hear a formal presentation from Puritan leaders at Hampton Court Palace near London. At what would become known as the Hampton Court Conference, Puritan leaders made their case for reform of the Church of England, asking for changes to Church government and the Book of Common Prayer—as well as the king's support for a new English-language translation of the Bible. James I granted little that the Puritans requested except for a new translation of the Bible. To that he readily agreed: he intensely disliked the Bible used in most English homes at the time.

It was known as the Geneva Bible because it had been translated into English by Calvinist scholars in Geneva, Switzerland, where many English Calvinists had fled during Queen Mary's persecution of Protestants. It was a favorite of the Puritans, but it was now a half-century old and Puritan scholars

and leaders wanted a new, even more accurate translation of the Scriptures. On the margins of its pages, the Geneva Bible featured a Calvinistic commentary—which King James detested. The commentary reflected Puritan thought and theology, which he believed challenged the practices of the Church of England. The English version officially sanctioned by the Church at the time—the Bishops' Bible—was only available as a pulpit Bible, so there was no suitable alternative to the Geneva Bible available for personal use in England.

James I was therefore quite willing to support a new translation. What emerged from the Puritans' petition at the Hampton Court Conference was the 1611 Authorized Version of the Bible. Superbly translated from Hebrew and Greek texts by forty-seven Church of England Bible scholars, it would become the most popular English-language Bible in history. Ironically, although it originated with a Puritan request for a new English translation, the Authorized Version would become famous for the ages as the revered King James Bible. Despite that single major concession to the Puritans, which served the king's self-interests, James I ended the Hampton Court Conference on an ominous note. Obviously aggravated and weary of Puritan calls for reform, he abruptly arose and closed the conference, muttering an implied threat against Puritans, Separatists, and other non-conformists. "I will make them conform themselves," he stated, "or else harry them out of the land."

> "I will make them conform themselves, or else"

Soon afterward, King James unleashed severe royal repression against the Puritans and Separatists. Leading the purge was Archbishop Richard Bancroft—a devoted enemy of anyone who dared to dissent from the Church of England. It was his efforts as chief investigator that had resulted in the hanging of John Coppin and Elias Thacker in 1583, and his zeal for persecuting Church dissidents had not lessened.

King James accepted none of the Puritans' principal requests at the Hampton Court Conference—except for one: he agreed to sponsor a new English-language translation of the Bible. The Authorized Version, as the new translation was officially named, would become the most widely used English Bible in history—popularly known as the King James Bible.

WIKIMEDIA COMMONS

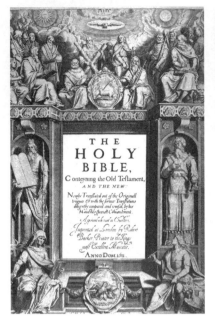

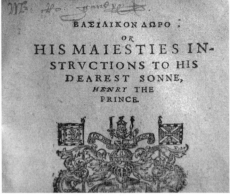

In a published work entitled *Basilikon Doron* or "Royal Gift" in Greek, King James I proclaimed his view that Puritans and Separatists were "brain sick" troublemakers who deserved "exemplary punishment."

HAROLD B. LEE LIBRARY

When Archbishop John Whitgift died in 1604, it was Bancroft who succeeded him—just in time to be King James's instrument of persecution.

The new archbishop conducted his purge with severe efficiency, "silencing, imprisoning and bearing down on the true and faithful preachers of the Word of God"—in the words of a Calvinist critic. Under King James, Bancroft banished approximately three hundred Puritan ministers from the Church of England, stripping them of their income and their pulpits. The banished pastors became known as "the silenced brethren." Puritan ministers and their followers who openly defied Church policies were jailed at the notorious Maiden Lane Prison, where they were whipped at times and forced to perform hard labor. The purge sent a chilling warning to the Puritan ministers who remained in the Church, and established an atmosphere of oppression within England's Separatist community. Increasing numbers of Separatist leaders and their congregations began to seriously consider escaping from England to

Holland. In a published work entitled *Basilikon Doron*—"Royal Gift" in Greek—King James revealed his view that Puritans and Separatists were "rash-headed" and "brain sick" troublemakers who deserved "exemplary punishment."

<hr />

The true practice hereof, I have as a King oft found in my own person, though I thank God, never to my shame, having laid my count, ever to walk as in the eyes of the Almighty.... To come then particularly to the matter of my Book, there are two special great points, which (as I am informed) the malicious sort of men have detracted therein; and some of the honest sort have seemed a little to mistake: whereof the first and greatest is, that some sentences therein should seem to furnish grounds to men, to doubt of my sincerity in that Religion, which I have ever constantly professed; the other is, that in some parts thereof I should seem to nourish in my mind, a vindictive resolution against England, or at the least, some principals there....

The first calamity (most grievous indeed) is grounded upon the sharp and bitter words that therein are used in the description of the humors of Puritans and rash-headed Preachers that think it their honor to contend with Kings, and perturb whole kingdoms.... [When] I speak of Puritans, it is only of their moral faults.... When they condemn the Law and sovereign authority, what exemplary punishment they deserve for the same.

First then, as to the name of Puritans, I am not ignorant that the style thereof does properly belong

Under King James, Anglican Archbishop Richard Bancroft directed a widespread purge of Puritan ministers from the Church of England, removing approximately three hundred from their pulpits.

NATIONAL PORTRAIT GALLERY

only to that vile sect amongst the Anabaptists, called the Family of Love, because they think themselves only to be pure and in a manner without sin, the only true Church, and only worthy to be participant of the Sacraments, and all the rest of the world to be but abomination in the sight of God.

Of this special sect I principally mean when I speak of Puritans; divers of them, as Browne, Penry and others, having at sundry times come...to sow their people amongst us.... I give this style to such brain-sick and headed Preachers their disciples and followers, as refusing to be called of that sect, yet participate too much with their humors, in maintaining the...contempt of the civil Magistrates, and in leaning to their own dreams and revelations; but particularly with this sect, in accounting all men profane that swear not to all their fantasies, in making for every particular question of the policy of the Church...

Judge then, Christian Reader, if I wrong this sort of people.... It is only of this kind of men that in this book I write so sharply; and whom I wish my Son to punish in-case they refuse to obey the Law, and will not cease to stir up a rebellion....

Take heed therefore (my Son) to such Puritans, very pests in the Church, and commonwealth; whom no deserts can oblige; neither oaths or promises bind; breathing nothing but sedition and calamities—aspiring without measure, railing without reason, and making their own imaginations (without any warrant of the word) the square of their conscience. I protest before the great God, and since I am here as upon my Testament, it is no place for me to be in, that ye shall never find with any Highland or Border thieves greater ingratitude, and more lies and vile perjuries, then with these fanatic spirits. And suffer not the principals of them to brook your land, if you like to sit at rest: except you would keep them for trying your patience, as Socrates did an evil wife.

And for preservation against their poison, entertain and advance the godly, learned, and modest men of the ministry, whom of (God be praised) there lacks not a sufficient number: and by their promotion to Bishops and Benefices... you shall not only banish their conceited party whereof I have spoken, and their other imaginary grounds, which can neither stand with the order of the Church, nor the peace of a commonwealth, and well ruled Monarchy, but also shall you reestablish the old institution of three estates in Parliament, which can no otherwise be done.... And to end my advice about the Church estate, cherish no man more than a good Pastor, hate no man more than a proud Puritan... [and] chain them with such bonds as may preserve that estate from creeping to corruption.[5]

> "Hate no man more than a proud Puritan"

CHAPTER THREE

"They Resolved
to Get Over into Holland"

It was a bomb built to kill a king—and its intended target was James I. Besides killing the king, the conspirators hoped to wipe out the English House of Lords—the upper chamber of Parliament—thereby overthrowing England's government. Their goal was to restore a Catholic ruler to the English throne. The plot was developed by a cell of renegade Catholics led by Robert Catesby, an affluent nobleman who had suffered prolonged persecution for his faith. Detonation of the bomb was set for November 5, 1605, when King James would deliver the opening speech to Parliament in the House of Lords. With the king dead and Parliament in chaos, the conspirators would kidnap King James's nine-year-old daughter, Princess Elizabeth, install her as a puppet ruler, raise her as a royal Catholic—and reinstate Catholicism as England's officially mandated faith.

To construct and detonate the bomb, Catesby had recruited a capable and fanatically committed triggerman named Guy Fawkes. A tall, bearded thirty-five-year-old professional soldier, Fawkes had left England as a young

By renting a house adjacent to the English Parliament, the plotters gained access to this cellar beneath the House of Lords, which they packed with thirty-six barrels of gunpowder. They planned to detonate the mammoth bomb while King James was making his opening speech to Parliament.

ILLUSTRATED HISTORY OF ENGLAND

man to serve in the army of Catholic Spain. Despite the loss of religious freedom that had befallen them since Queen Elizabeth's religious compromise, most English Catholics unquestionably would have been horrified at the assassination of their king. Not Catesby, Fawkes, and the other conspirators. Earlier attempts by Catholic radicals to assassinate King James and Queen Elizabeth had all failed, but the conspirators fervently believed theirs was well-planned enough to succeed.

The plotters managed to rent property adjacent to the English Parliament in London and broke through a wall to reach the cellar beneath the House of Lords. There, Fawkes oversaw construction of a giant bomb consisting of thirty-six wooden barrels filled with gunpowder. It was enough explosives to blow up the House of Lords—and perhaps bring down the entire Parliament building and a large portion of the surrounding neighborhood. The conspiracy went forward as planned, and as the opening of Parliament neared, Fawkes readied the massive bomb. Shortly before the planned detonation, however, authorities were alerted by an anonymous letter, and found it. Some of the conspirators, including Catesby, were hunted down and killed, and Fawkes and others were tortured and executed for treason. The king, his daughter, Parliament, and the Church of England all survived without harm, but the assassination attempt further fueled the king's royal suspicions toward all dissenters.[1]

In 1605, a ring of renegade Catholics attempted to assassinate King James I by detonating a bomb beneath the English Parliament. The conspiracy was led by Robert Catesby, pictured second from far right, and Guy Fawkes, third from right

WIKIMEDIA COMMONS

"A Rumor Was Spread … That the King Was Stabbed … with a Poisoned Knife"

After his attempted assassination, King James called for public calm and restraint against England's Catholics. In private, however, he remained fearful, and royal suspicions of the nation's Catholics increased, along with public hostility. English Separatists could only wonder if the royal displeasure toward Catholics would also descend on them. They had not plotted anyone's assassination, manufactured bombs, or engaged in treason, but worshipping outside the Church of England was a criminal act—and the Separatists knew they were guilty of *that*. They also knew that King James had placed restrictions on the Scots Presbyterians when he ruled Scotland. Now, in the wake of the Gunpowder Plot, he appeared determined to do the same to England's Puritans and Separatists. Opposing the Church of England and its hierarchy of bishops, the king believed, was the same as opposing him. "No bishop, no King," he reportedly declared. Would King and Church now begin to view dissent from the Church of England as treason—which was a capital crime?

"A rumor was spread … that the King was stabbed … with a poisoned knife"

51

The plotters intended to kidnap King James's nine-year-old daughter Elizabeth, install her as a puppet ruler, raise her as a Catholic, and thus restore Catholicism as England's official state denomination.

WIKIMEDIA COMMONS

Following the Gunpowder Plot, King James reportedly remained closeted in his royal chambers for a time, surrounded by none but his most trusted associates from Scotland. The entire nation was on edge, and the tension produced various rumors of successful assassinations, as reported in this period account:

✦━━━━━━━✦

A rumor was spread (by what strange means unknown) that the King was stabbed at Okingham, twenty miles from London, where he was hunting, with a poisoned knife. The Court at Whitehall, the Parliament, and City took the alarm; mustering up their old tears, every man standing at gaze as if some new prodigy had seized them. Such a terror had this late monstrous intended mischief imprinted in the spirits of the people, that they took fire from every little train of rumor, and were ready to grapple with their own destruction before it came....

The Lord Mayor gave forthwith precepts unto the warders to leave trained soldiers, and they to repair unto their known London captains. Sir W. Wade, lieutenant of the Tower, summoned his hamlets, drew his bridge, shut close his prisoners, charged [various] pieces of great ordnance, took all the keys from all inferior officers, being well prepared in all points to stand upon his guard. By reason for two hours space and more the news grew more and more,

"Whilst the terror of this terrible news lasted, all sorts of people were sore frightened"

that not only the King was slain, but with him, in his defense, the Earl of Montgomery, Sir John Ramsay, and Sir James Hay, which treason, some said, was performed by English Jesuits, some by Scots in women's apparel, and others said by Spaniards and Frenchmen. Most reports agreed that the King was stabbed with an envenomed knife, which bitter news was more grievous unto all sorts of people than can well be here expressed, great weeping and lamentation both in old and young, rich and poor, maids and wives.

Whilst the terror of this terrible news lasted, all sorts of people were sore frightened, the court gates being aforesaid strongly kept and strongly guarded, the Queen, the Prince, and the Lords of the Counsel and sundry other Lords and Gentlemen [were] assembled at White Hall, being all exceedingly amazed and full of sorrow, both in their hearts and eyes. [But] so soon as certain news came from the King unto them, that he was well and on his way towards London, they received new spirits [as] partakers of this most happy news of his Majesty's safety.[2]

"So soon as certain news came from the King unto them, that he was well…they received new spirits"

"Come Out of Babylon"

The Making of a Pilgrim Leader

John Robinson never saw America. Yet no one did more to put the Pilgrims there than he. In 1607, Robinson was acting as assistant pastor of an illegal Separatist congregation in the farming village of Scrooby, which was located in Nottinghamshire, about 150 miles north of London in the East Midlands. By then, cells of Separatists were firmly established in London and various regions of England. Most of the Separatists who would become known as the Pilgrims came from an area in England's East Midlands along the borders of three counties—Lincolnshire, Yorkshire, and Nottinghamshire. There, villages such as Scrooby, Gainsborough, Austerfield, Babworth, North Wheatley, and Sturton-le-Steeple were home to many Separatists.

John Robinson's boyhood home was there, in the village of Sturton, where he was born to a family of modest income in 1575. Despite his lack of finances, he had attended Cambridge University, studying for the ministry and working his way through school as a "sizar"—a student who earned his keep by doing chores. Bright and disciplined, he excelled at Cambridge, and—under the influence of some of the leading Puritan thinkers of the day—he embraced Puritan theology and became committed to reform the Church of England. He earned undergraduate and graduate degrees at Cambridge, and then was invited to join the university faculty. He spent seven years on the Cambridge faculty, rising to the post of dean, then left the university to marry Bridget White, a farmer's daughter from his hometown.

The Pilgrim exodus to New England was greatly inspired by the Reverend John Robinson, depicted here in later life, but the pastor never made it to America.

LIBRARY OF CONGRESS

The couple moved to the city of Norwich, which was located on the Wensum River about 115 miles northeast of London. There, Robinson took up the post of assistant pastor at St. Andrew's Church in Norwich. One of the largest cities in England, Norwich was an industrial center known for a growing population of Puritans at St. Andrew's and elsewhere.

Studious, empathetic, and gentle in nature, Robinson had a pastor's heart and a preacher's gift for exposing the Word from the pulpit. His assistant pastorate at St. Andrew's appeared to offer a promising ministry for young Robinson—but it was not to be. In 1604, Archbishop Richard Bancroft launched his purge of Puritan preachers from the Church of England, ordering all pastors to swear allegiance to the Church's new Book of Canons. Robinson disagreed with the Church's hierarchical government, and believed submitting to it would violate his conscience. Along with hundreds of other Anglican pastors with Puritan leanings, Robinson was suspended from the ministry, and lost his position at St. Andrew's Church.

It was his suspension from the ministry that apparently moved Robinson from Puritan to Separatist. In a heart-wrenching personal struggle, he prayerfully began to ask a life-changing question. Could he continue in good conscience to serve the Church of England if its leadership indeed held what he believed to be unbiblical positions on key issues? As with other Separatists, he realized that it was no small decision to leave the official government denomination. By now he and his wife had children, and separating from the Church was a criminal act that potentially placed the family in harm's way. All of them could be arrested and imprisoned, and as a former minister in the Church, Robinson knew that he could suffer an even worse fate. Still, Robinson believed he had to "find satisfaction to my troubled heart," as he put it—and he believed that he found direction in the New Testament book of Ephesians:

> *Be ye therefore followers of God, as dear children. And walk in love, even as Christ has loved us.... And have no fellowship with the unfruitful works of darkness, but even reprove them rather.*

As a student at Cambridge University, John Robinson worshipped at times in the King's College Chapel. Under the influence of Puritan professors at Cambridge, Robinson embraced Puritan theology.

ILLUSTRATED NOTES ON ENGLISH CHURCH HISTORY

In obedience to Scripture, he finally concluded, he could no longer serve the Church of England. The Reverend John Robinson thus became a Separatist.

As he explained his position to a Church official, leaving the Anglican Church, Robinson believed, was comparable to the Jews of the Old Testament escaping their captivity in Babylon:

"Break asunder those chains of unrighteousness... and come out of Babylon"

But let all them that fear the Lord and his righteous judgments, and...to whom the liberty purchased with the blood of Christ seems precious, break asunder those chains of unrighteousness, those bonds of Antichrist, and come out of Babylon, and plant their feet in those pleasant paths of the Lord, wherein they may make straight steps unto him, walking in that light, and liberty, which Christ hath dearly purchased for them...But for separation from a church rightly constituted...I do utterly disclaim it. For there is but one body, the church, and but one Lord, or head of that body, Christ, and whosoever separates from the body, the church, separates from the head, Christ, in that respect. (Ephesians 4:4)

But this I hold, that if iniquity be committed in the church, and...the church will not reform...she makes it her own by imputation, and enwraps herself in the same guilt with the sinner...and now ceases to be any longer the true church of Christ. (Titus 1:16, Proverbs 21:27) No church now can...depart from the Lord by any transgression, and therein remain unrepentant after due conviction, and will not be reclaimed, it manifests unto us that God also has left it, and that, as the church by her sin hath separated from,

and broken covenant with God, so God by leaving her in hardness of heart without repentance, has on his part broken and dissolved the covenant also....

For what doth your church represent,...binding men to subscribe to the hierarchy, service-book, and ceremonies...tying men to a certain form of prayer and thanksgiving; excommunicating men for the refusal and omission of these and the like observances of their laws? And what do you but loose and unbind the conscience in tolerating, yea, approving, yea, making and ordaining unpreaching ministers, and in binding the people under both civil and ecclesiastical penalties to their ministrations in their own parishes, and from others?... Are not these matters of conscience...?[3]

As a young assistant pastor at St. Andrew's Church in Norwich, John Robinson appeared to have a promising ministry in the Church of England ahead of him—until he was suspended by Church officials for his Puritan theology.

THREE CENTURIES OF A CITY LIBRARY

"We Seek the Fellowship of His Faithful and Obedient Servants"

The Separatist Movement Grows in England's East Midlands

"Are not these matters of conscience?"

Dismissed from the Church of England, John Robinson took his family and went home to Sturton in Lincolnshire, where the Separatist movement was growing in illegal congregations among the region's farmers, laborers, merchants, and land-owners. There, in the town of Gainsborough, another defrocked Anglican pastor, the Reverend John Smyth, pastored a growing congregation of Separatists. Smyth and his Separatist flock at Gainsborough, which numbered more than sixty members, were supported by the attorney and landowner Thomas Helwys.

In nearby Scrooby, another Separatist congregation of about a hundred members had arisen under the leadership of the Reverend Richard Clyfton. A white-bearded, fatherly-looking minister, Clyfton—in the words of a church member—"had done much good, and under God had been a means of the conversion for many." A native of the East Midlands, Clyfton had pastored an Anglican church at the nearby village of Babworth until he was defrocked for preaching Separatist doctrine. He had then established an illegal Separatist congregation in nearby Scrooby, presumably comprised of his former church members and others. Sometime in 1607, Robinson and his family joined the Scrooby congregation, where he assumed the duties of co-pastor with Clyfton. Witty, knowledgeable, and endearing, Robinson soon proved himself to be a powerful and magnetic preacher who ministered to the Scrooby congregation, and helped lead it in Separatist style worship.

England's East Midlands region was marked by small villages and pastoral countryside—and, in the early seventeenth century, it was also known as a seat of the Separatist movement.

THE STORY OF SOME ENGLISH SHIRES

For Separatists like the Scrooby congregation, a worship service typically lasted all day, from early morning until five or six in the afternoon, with a two-hour intermission at midday. Worshippers sang from a psalter, a collection of works from the Old Testament book of Psalms, and the musical worship was typically performed by the congregation rather than by a choir. Separatists thus followed John Calvin's advice to "sing some psalms in the form of public prayers…so that the hearts of all may be roused and stimulated to make similar prayers and to render similar praise and thanks to God with a common love." To Separatists, genuine prayer was not merely a public recitation led by a minister, but was instead a deeply personal and heartfelt act, which, in Robinson's words, was meant to "pour out the conceptions of a godly and devout mind unto God, from faith and feeling of our wants, by the Holy Ghost." A Separatist worship service was also an opportunity for worshippers to enjoy fellowship with each other, and to give God their tithes and offerings.

The central focus of Separatist worship, however, was the reading of the Word—the pastor's selected biblical text for the service—and the pastor's sermon, which would "expose" the theme and meaning of the selected Scripture. Following the sermon, designated laymen who felt "called" by the Holy Spirit would then preach or "prophesy" about the Scripture text. Prophesying or lay-preaching as practiced by the Separatists loosely followed the style of worship that had been practiced by English exiles and others in Switzerland during the Reformation—although prophesying in the Swiss churches was generally done by ministers and seminary students. Prophesying was condemned by the Church of England because Church officials believed it could expose worshippers to uninformed opinion and false doctrine. Separatist leaders such as Robinson countered that it was the responsibility of the local congregation, not a church hierarchy, to preserve the truth of Scripture within the local church.

A brief eyewitness account of a Separatist worship service at the time of Robinson's ministry at Scrooby was preserved in a letter written to a relative by English Separatists Hugh and Ann Bromhead:

<hr />

I will give you a brief view of the causes of our separation and of our purposes in practice. First, we seek above all things the peace and protection of the Most High, and the kingdom of our

Located in Lincolnshire, in the East Midlands, the town of Gainsborough was a regional river port—and home to a growing congregation of Separatists.

THE ROMANTIC STORY OF THE MAYFLOWER PILGRIMS

In Gainsborough, a Separatist congregation of about sixty members met in the Gainsborough Manor Hall, where they were led by Pastor John Smyth, who had been dismissed from the Church of England for his Separatist views.

THE ROMANTIC STORY OF THE MAYFLOWER PILGRIMS

Lord Jesus Christ. Secondly, we seek and fully purpose to worship God aright, according as He hath commanded in His most holy word. Thirdly, we seek the fellowship of His faithful and obedient servants, and together with them to enter covenant with the Lord, and by the direction of His Holy Spirit to proceed to a godly, free, and right choice of minister and other officers, by Him ordained to the service of His church. Fourthly, we seek to establish and obey the ordinances and laws of our Saviour, Christ, left by his last will and testament to the governing and guiding of His church. Fifthly, we purpose by the assistance of the Holy Ghost,…to leave our lives, if such be the good will of our heavenly Father. And sixthly, now that our forsaking and utterly abandoning these disordered assemblies as they generally stand in England may not seem strange or offensive to any that will judge or be judged by the word of God.…

The order of the worship and government of our Church is, 1: We begin with a prayer; after, read some one or two chapters of the Bible, give the sense thereof, and confer upon the same: 2: that done, we lay aside our books, and after a solemn prayer made by the first speaker, he propoundeth some text

"I will give you a brief view of the causes of our separation"

In the village of Scrooby, located near Gainsborough, a sister congregation of Separatists were led by Pastor Richard Clifton, who had also been defrocked for his Separatist theology.

A POPULAR HISTORY
OF THE UNITED
STATES

"We seek the fellowship of his faithful and obedient servants"

out of the Scripture, and prophesieth out of the same by the space of one hour or three quarters of an hour. After him standeth up a second speaker, and prophesieth out of the said text, the like time and place, sometimes more, sometimes less. After him the third, the fourth, the fifth, etc., as the time will give leave.

Then the first speaker concludeth with prayer as he began with prayer, with an exhortation to contribution to the poor, which collection being made, is also concluded with prayer. This morning exercise begins at eight of the clock and continueth unto twelve of the clock. The like course and exercise is observed in the afternoon from two of the clock unto five or six of the clock. Last of all, the execution of the government of the Church is handled....

Yours in the Lord, at all times to use,
Hugh and Anne Bromhead[4]

They "Were Hunted and Persecuted on Every Side"

The Separatists of Scrooby and Gainsborough Seek Escape

To Pastor Robinson and the Scrooby Separatists, forty-year-old William Brewster was a godsend. In 1607, Brewster was the royal bailiff and postmaster at Scrooby, and the local congregation of Separatists worshipped in his home. It was a sprawling, two-story brick-and-timber manor house with almost forty rooms and a chapel. It had been built more than a century earlier as the palatial residence of the Anglican archbishop of York. King Henry VIII had visited once in the previous century, and had even owned it for awhile. Now, it remained government property, managed by bailiff Brewster, who opened it to Robinson's Separatist congregation.

Brewster had been raised in Scrooby, where his father was bailiff and postmaster before him. The royal appointment allowed Brewster's father to raise his family in the rambling manor house, and also provided ample income—which allowed young William to enroll at Cambridge University while he was still in his teens. Bright, affable, and resourceful, Brewster was a natural student who would prove to be a lifelong booklover, but for unknown reasons he did not remain at Cambridge long enough to graduate.

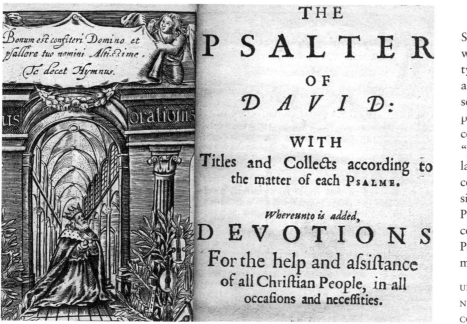

Separatist worship services typically featured a Bible-based sermon by the pastor, commentary or "prophesying" by lay leaders, and congregational singing from the Psalter, which consisted of Psalms set to music.

UNIVERSITY OF NEBRASKA COMMUNICATIONS

"He required him to take an oath…which he obstinately and utterly refused"

Instead, he exercised his family connections to become a trusted aide to one of Queen Elizabeth's secretaries of state, who valued him for his abilities, discretion, and integrity. As the assistant to a prominent government official, Brewster was exposed to the inner workings of government, along with the skills of diplomacy and the experience of travel outside England. In 1589, after more than half a decade in high places, he returned home to Scrooby to assist his ailing father. When his father died a year later, Brewster was appointed district postmaster in his place. He married a local woman, and began raising his family.

He raised them as Separatists. Although Brewster had spent little time at Cambridge, it was there, like so many other Separatist leaders, that he had been introduced to Puritan theology, which eventually led him to the Separatist movement. At Scrooby, Brewster embraced the growing congregation of Separatists from the surrounding areas, opened his huge home as their meeting place and worship center, and served as a lay leader under pastors Clyfton and Robinson. Eventually, Brewster would become a ruling elder in the congregation as well as its promoter and protector—a "dear friend, and brother" in Pastor Robinson's words. With Brewster's help, the Separatist congregation at Scrooby attracted increasing numbers of converts—as well as the attention of a new and determined enemy.

His name was Tobias Matthew, and he was the Church of England's new archbishop of York. Appointed in 1606, Archbishop Matthew oversaw the Church in England's northern diocese, which included Scrooby and the surrounding areas. He was an Oxford alumnus—a former dean and vice-chancellor of the university—and his influence within the English government was second only to the archbishop of Canterbury's. A favorite of King James, he had preached the closing sermon at the 1604 Hampton Court Conference, and although now in his sixties, he was a relentless pursuer of all those who resisted King James or dissented from the Church of England. In the wake of the Gunpowder Plot, his primary targets were English Catholics—who were required to renounce the authority of the pope and take an oath of allegiance to the king—but in 1607, he began targeting the Separatists of the East Midlands.

Matthew's zeal to go after the Separatists may have been increased by a personal scandal—his son and namesake had just converted to Catholicism. Occurring so soon after the Gunpowder Plot, his son's newfound Catholicism was a political and ecclesiastical embarrassment for the new archbishop of York, and he may have been desperate to demonstrate his fidelity to Church and King. Using warrants from the Church's Court of High Commission, he arrested scores of Catholics, and—even though their numbers were far fewer—he also rounded up Separatists. In a joint campaign with Archbishop of Canterbury Richard Bancroft, Matthew employed the Church's High Commission to prosecute the dissenters. Separatists in the East Midlands—mainly members of the congregations at Scrooby and Gainsborough—were arrested and fined, including bailiff and postmaster William Brewster, who was charged with being "a Brownist or disobedient in matters of religion." Others feared that they would be next to undergo arrest.

William Brewster, the bailiff and postmaster in the village of Scrooby, played a critical role as a lay leader in Pastor John Robinson's Separatist congregation.

LIBRARY OF CONGRESS

One Scrooby Separatist, Gervase Nevyle, boldly confronted his accusers in court, displaying the spirit of the persecuted apostles in the New Testament book of Acts, when they told their persecutors, "We ought to obey God rather than men." Nevyle refused to take the oath that was required to give testimony before the High Commission, claiming the court

William Brewster allowed Scrooby's Separatist congregation to worship in his sprawling manor house, which at one time had been the official residence of the Anglican archbishop of York.

THE ROMANTIC STORY OF THE MAYFLOWER PILGRIMS

was illegal under English law. He also denounced the archbishop's authority as an unbiblical, "antichristian hierarchie." His outspoken resistance landed him in prison, but it also produced a court document that preserved a record of what Scrooby Separatists and others faced from Archbishop Matthew and the ecclesiastical court.

Nov. 10, 1607

Office of the Court v. Gervase Nevyle of Scrooby

Information hath been given and presentment made that the said Gervase Nevyle is one of the sect of Barrowists or Brownists, holding and maintaining erroneous opinions and doctrine repugnant to the Holy Scriptures and Word of God, for which his disobedience and schismatical obstinacy an attachment was awarded to William Blanchard messenger, etc. to apprehend him: by virtue whereof being by him brought before His Grace and said Associates and charged with his errors and dangerous opinions and disobedience, his Grace in the name of himself having charged him therewith, as also with certain contemptuous speeches and frequenting of conventicles and company of others of his profession, he required him to take an oath to make answer (so far as he ought and was bound by law) to certain interrogatories or questions by them conceived and set down in writing to be propounded and ministered unto him, and others of his brethren of the separation and sect aforesaid, which he obstinately and utterly refused, denying to give his Grace answer, and protesting very presumptuously and insolently in the presence of God against his authority and (as he termed it) his Antichristian Hierarchy; but yet yielded to answer to the rest of the said Commissioners (excepting his Grace only), although it was by them shown unto him that his Grace was chief of the Ecclesiastical Commission by virtue whereof he was convented and they all did then and there sit.

And then, after divers godly exhortations and speeches to him, they did propound and read the said interrogatories unto him and presently set down his answers unto the same in their presences under his hand.

In 1606, Anglican leader Tobias Matthew was appointed as archbishop of York, which made him the ranking Church of England official in northern England. He promptly launched a campaign against the region's Separatists.

WIKIMEDIA COMMONS

And forsomuch as thereby, as also by his unreverent, contemptuous, and scandalous speeches, it appeared that he is a very dangerous schismatical Separatist Brownist and irreligious subject, holding and maintaining divers erroneous opinions, the said lord Archbishop with his colleagues have by their strait warrant committed him, the said Gervase, to the custody of William Blanchard, by him to be therewith delivered to the hands, ward and safe custody of the keeper or his deputy keeper of his Highness's Castle of York, not permitting him to have any liberty or conference with any, without special license from three at least of the said Commissioners, whereof one to be of the Quorum.[5]

"It appeared
that he
is a very
dangerous
schismatical
Separatist"

"They Resolved to Get Over into Holland"

Persecuted Separatists Seek Self-Exile from England

I t was the growing threat from Archbishop Matthew—part of the nationwide crackdown on Separatists by King James—that spurred Separatists in the East Midlands to seek sanctuary in Holland. Although their attempts to escape England aboard the Dutch ship *Francis* and other vessels were blocked by English authorities, hundreds of Separatists in Scrooby, Gainsborough, and elsewhere were determined to escape England. Led by their pastors—Robinson, Clyfton, and Smyth—and by lay leaders such as William Brewster and Thomas Helwys, Separatists from the East Midlands took the risks, endured imprisonment, gave up their homes and belongings, and repeatedly tried to flee to Holland. In 1607 and 1608, many eventually made it.

An English dissenter makes his case before an English court. The crackdown on Separatists following the Gunpowder Plot resulted in numerous arrests for worshipping outside of the Church of England.

LIBRARY OF CONGRESS

Among them was William Brewster, who resigned his lucrative position as postmaster, went into hiding with his family, then managed to board passage to Holland. Their repeated attempts to flee England were difficult and dangerous, and yet—in the words of future Pilgrim leader William Bradford—"by God's assistance they prevailed and got the victory." As an eighteen-year-old member of the Scrooby congregation, Bradford was one of them. He would later pen an account of how the desperate exiles "resolved to get over into Holland."

When as by the travail and diligence of some godly and zealous preachers, and God's blessing on their labors, as in other places of the land, so in the North parts, many became enlightened by the Word of God and had their ignorance and sins discovered unto them, and began by His grace to reform their lives and make conscience of their ways; the work of God was no sooner manifest in them but presently they were both scoffed and scorned by the profane multitude; and the ministers urged with the yoke of subscription, or else must be silenced. And the poor people were so vexed…as truly their affliction was not small. Which, notwithstanding, they bore sundry years with much patience.…

But, after these things, they could not long continue in any peaceable manner, but were hunted and persecuted on every side, so as their former afflictions were but as molehills to mountains in comparison to these which now came upon them. For some were taken and clapped up in prisons, others had their houses beset and watched night and day, and hardly escaped their hands; and the most were fain to fly and leave their houses and habitations, and the means of their livelihood. Yet these, and many other sharper things which afterward befell them, were no other than they looked for, and

"Some were taken and clapped up in prisons, others had their houses beset and watched night and day"

Untold numbers of Separatist men and women from Scrooby, Gainsborough, and elsewhere in the East Midlands found themselves arrested for their faith.

ILLUSTRATED HISTORY OF ENGLAND

Under Tobias Matthew, the archbishop of York, English authorities raided Separatist congregations in the East Midlands, arresting and jailing worshippers.

NATIONAL AND DOMESTIC HISTORY OF ENGLAND

therefore were the better prepared to bear them by the assistance of God's grace and spirit.

Yet seeing themselves thus molested, and that there was no hope of their continuance there, by a joint consent they resolved to go into the Low Countries, where they heard was freedom of religion for all men, as also how sundry from London and other parts of the land, that had been exiled and persecuted for the same cause, were gone thither, and lived at Amsterdam, and in other places of the land. So after they had continued together about a year, and kept their meetings every Sabbath in one place or another, exercising the worship of God amongst themselves, notwithstanding all the diligence and malice of their adversaries, they seeing they could no longer continue in that condition, they resolved to get over into Holland. . . .

"By a joint consent they resolved to go into the Low Countries, where they heard was freedom of religion"

70

For some, the sea voyage from England to Holland was even more life-threatening than the persecution they faced at home, as Bradford reported:

> *Afterwards they endured a fearful storm at sea, and it was fourteen days or more before they reached port, in seven of which they saw neither sun, moon, nor stars, being driven near the coast of Norway. The sailors themselves often despaired, and once with shrieks and cries gave over all, as if the ship had foundered and they were sinking without hope of recovery.*
>
> *But when man's hope and help wholly failed, there appeared the Lord's power and mercy to save them; for the ship rose again, and gave the crew courage to manage her. If modesty permitted, I might declare with what fervent prayers the voyagers cried to the Lord in their great distress—even remaining fairly collected when the water ran into their mouths and ears; and when the sailors called out, "We sink, we sink," they cried (if not with miraculous, yet with sublime faith). "Yet Lord, Thou canst save; yet Lord, Thou canst save!"*
>
> *Upon which, the ship not only righted herself, but shortly afterwards the violence of the storm began to abate, and the Lord filled their afflicted minds with such comfort as but few can understand, and in the end brought them to their desired haven, where the people came*

"Hunted and persecuted on all sides"—in the words of William Bradford—Separatists from Scrooby and Gainsborough sold their homes and belongings and fled England in search of religious freedom.

ILLUSTRATED HISTORY OF ENGLAND

In the early seventeenth century, Dutch ships brought Protestant refugees from various nations into Holland, making it a melting pot of Protestant denominations. By 1609, scores of Separatists from Scrooby and Gainsborough were among them.

RIJKSMUSEUM OF AMSTERDAM

"They endured a fearful storm at sea, and it was fourteen days or more before they reached port"

flocking, astonished at their deliverance, the storm having been so long and violent…. In the end, notwithstanding the storms of opposition, they all got over, some from one place, some from another, and met together with no small rejoicing.[6]

CHAPTER FOUR

"Butter-Mouths," "Lubbers," and "Manifold Temptations"

For an eighteen-year-old, William Bradford had experienced a lot of life, and much of it had been hard. He was born in the village of Austerfield, about four miles north of Scrooby, in 1590. His father William, whose name he bore, owned a prosperous farm and other real estate, and his mother, formerly Alice Hanson, was a shopkeeper's daughter. He was the youngest of three Bradford children—the only son. In the culture of his day, he could have grown up in a comfortable home with the expectation of one day inheriting family property and living as a man of means. Instead, his father unexpectedly sickened and died while William was still a toddler. When he was four, his mother remarried, and for unknown reasons William was sent to live with his grandfather. Two years later, his grandfather died, and the youngster was brought back home, but within a year his mother also died. Left an orphan at age seven, the boy was sent by his stepfather

A conjectural portrait of Pilgrim leader William Bradford as he might have appeared in later life.

UNITED STATES HISTORY

Future Pilgrim leader William Bradford was born in this house in the English village of Austerfield, which was located about four miles from Scrooby.

THE ROMANTIC STORY OF THE MAYFLOWER PILGRIMS

Bradford was a sickly child who was often unable to tend to the farm's sheep flock, so his uncles arranged for him to learn how to read and write—skills that would shape his future life.

DAVID M. RUBENSTEIN LIBRARY, DUKE UNIVERSITY

to live with two uncles on a nearby farm, and they put him to work watching their sheep.

Bradford was a sickly child, unable to work the flocks at times, so in order to make him useful around the farm, his uncles arranged for him to learn how to read and write. He is believed to have been tutored by a pastor at the small Anglican church in Austerfield. Wherever he received his schooling, Bradford excelled at it. He was a natural student—bright, inquisitive, analytical, and disciplined—and developed a scholar's heart, a writer's craft, and a lifelong love of books. By age twelve he had become a serious student of the Bible, and a few years later he began attending worship services at Pastor Clyfton's church in Babworth.

There, the fatherly Pastor Clyfton took interest in the orphan boy, and when Clyfton established the Separatist congregation at nearby Scrooby, Bradford joined the congregation. He was reportedly mentored by William Brewster, and by age seventeen he was a committed Separatist. Doubtlessly aware of the risks to their nephew and themselves, Bradford's uncles tried to dissuade him from embracing Separatism. Their efforts did not deter him, nor did the ridicule he received from his peers. Bradford believed that he was

As a teenager, William Bradford was befriended by the Separatist pastor and congregation in nearby Scrooby. There—to the dismay of his uncles—he became a devout Separatist.

ILLUSTRATED NOTES ON ENGLISH CHURCH HISTORY

being obedient to the Word of God, and he would not abandon his faith. He had endured much in his young life from what he called "the grave mistress Experience," and he was willing to endure more for his faith. "I am not only willing to part with everything that is dear to me in this world for this cause," he wrote his uncles, "but I am also thankful that God has given me an heart to do, and will accept me to suffer for Him."

When the Scrooby and Gainsborough Separatists escaped to Holland, Bradford was with them, apparently as one of those who "endured a fearful storm at sea." The pastors—Scrooby's Clyfton and Robinson and Gainsborough's Smyth—remained in England until later in 1608, so they could lead the final and "weakest" of their congregations into exile. In Holland, the Separatists were finally able to meet and worship as they felt led without fear, but the transition from England was not easy. In the words of Scripture, they were "strangers and pilgrims" in a foreign land.[1]

At some point, William Bradford slipped aboard a departing ship with other Separatists and left England for Holland. "I am…willing to part with all that is dear to me," he wrote.

ILLUSTRATED HISTORY OF ENGLAND

The Scrooby and Gainsborough Separatists initially settled in Amsterdam, which was a bustling, cosmopolitan city of fifty thousand.

RIJKSMUSEUM OF AMSTERDAM

"Armed with Faith and Patience"

*The Scrooby and Gainsborough Separatists
Begin a New Life in Holland*

They settled first in Amsterdam, a sprawling, cosmopolitan city of more than fifty thousand people then on the verge of becoming an international financial center, boosted by Dutch shipping interests and a booming economy. A decade earlier, other English Separatists had established a church in Amsterdam. Known as the Ancient Brethren, their congregation numbered about three hundred by 1608, and they were worshipping in a newly constructed church building. The Ancient Brethren welcomed the newly exiled congregations from Scrooby and Gainsborough, and the three congregations worshipped together—at least for awhile.

Once in Holland, Pastor Smyth of the Gainsborough congregation surprised the other Separatists by announcing that he had come to accept doctrines that differed from Separatist theology. He had come to believe, he explained, that infant baptism had no solid Scriptural grounds, and that believer baptism alone was biblical. Furthermore, he concluded, any baptism performed under the authority of the Church of England was unbiblical, and therefore most of his congregation needed to be baptized again. He had also come to believe that the Bible should be read in worship services only in its original languages—Hebrew and Greek—and translated on the spot into English by the preacher.

Eventually, Smyth would join the Anabaptist movement and become instrumental in the founding of America's Baptist denominations, but theological debate was not why Pastor Robinson and the Scrooby congregation had come to Holland. The solution to the unexpected dilemma, Robinson and others concluded, was to relocate elsewhere. Pastor Clyfton did not want to leave Amsterdam and eventually would become a teacher with the Ancient Brethren, so the Scrooby congregation turned

Anabaptist exiles joyfully conduct a baptism in Holland. Soon after relocating to Amsterdam, Pastor Smyth, leader of the Gainsborough Separatists, announced that he had adopted Anabaptist theology.

RIJKSMUSEUM OF AMSTERDAM

to Pastor Robinson. He agreed to lead those who wished to follow him to the Dutch city of Leiden, which was located about thirty miles southwest of Amsterdam. By 1608, exiled Puritans and Presbyterians had established English congregations in a half-dozen Dutch cities, including Amsterdam, The Hague, Rotterdam, and Leiden. The Dutch government allowed Protestant exiles to establish churches in Holland and even sometimes provided financial support and meeting space.

Robinson and his Separatist congregation asked for nothing from the Dutch government—except permission to move to Leiden and establish their church there. Relocating to Leiden would not only enable Robinson and his followers to avoid being ensnarled in Pastor Smyth's baptism controversy, but the city offered employment opportunities for the newcomers. In February of 1609, they petitioned a Dutch court to allow "one-hundred persons born in England" to move to Leiden by the

In 1609, Pastor Robinson led the Scrooby exiles from Amsterdam to Leiden, Holland's second-largest city, which lay about twenty-five miles to the south.

ILLUSTRATED HISTORY OF ENGLAND

first of May, promising that they would not be "a burden in the least to anyone." English authorities in Holland, who had reportedly kept the Separatist exiles under surveillance, protested to the Dutch government on behalf of King James I. The Dutch court granted permission anyway, noting that Dutch law "did not refuse any honest persons free and unrestrained ingress, provided they behaved themselves honestly and submitted to all the laws."

So, in the spring of 1609, Pastor Robinson led most of the former Scrooby congregation to Leiden. Chronicler William Bradford, who made the move with Pastor Robinson, later recalled the congregation's early days in Holland.

***

Being now come into the Low Countries, they saw many goodly and fortified cities, strongly walled and guarded with troops of armed men. Also they heard a strange and uncouth language, and beheld the different manners and customs of the people, with their strange fashions and attires; all so far differing from that of their plain country villages (wherein they were bred, and had so long lived) as it seemed they were come into a new world. But these were not the things they much looked on, or long took up their thoughts; for they had other work in hand, and another kind of war to wage and maintain. For though they saw fair and beautiful cities, flowing with abundance of all sorts of wealth and riches, yet it was not long before they saw the grim and grisly face of poverty coming upon them like an armed man, with whom they must buckle and encounter, and from whom they could not flee; but they were armed with faith and patience....

"They heard a strange and uncouth language, and beheld the different manners and customs of the people"

Now when Mr. Robinson, Mr. Brewster, and other principal members were come over, (for they were of the last, and stayed to help the weakest over before them,) such things were thought on as were necessary for their settling and best ordering of the church affairs. And when they had lived at Amsterdam about a year, Mr. Robinson, their pastor, and some others of best discerning, seeing how Mr. John Smith and his company was already fallen in to contention with the church that was there before them, and no means they could use would do any good to cure the same, and also that the flames of contention were like to break out in that ancient church itself (as afterwards lamentably came to pass); which things they prudently foreseeing, thought it was best to remove, before they were any way engaged with the same; though they well knew it would be much to the prejudice of their outward estates, both at present and in likelihood in the future; as indeed it proved to be.

For these and some other reasons they removed to Leiden, a fair and beautiful city, and of a sweet situation, but made more famous by the university wherewith it is adorned, in which of late had been so many learned men. But wanting that traffic by sea which Amsterdam enjoys, it was not so beneficial for their outward means of living and estates. But being now here, they fell to such trades and employments as they best could; valuing peace and their spiritual comfort above any other riches whatsoever. And at length they came to raise a competent and comfortable living, but with hard and continual labor.

Being thus settled (after many difficulties) they continued many years in a comfortable condition, enjoying much sweet and delightful society and spiritual comfort together

Two seventeenth-century Dutch weavers take a break from the loom to exchange a story. Many of the Separatists took jobs in Holland's booming textile industry, despite the long hours, tedious work, and low pay.

RIJKSMUSEUM OF AMSTERDAM

in the ways of God, under the able ministry and prudent government of Mr. John Robinson and Mr. William Brewster, who was an assistant unto him in the place of an Elder, unto which he was now called and chosen by the church. So as they grew in knowledge and other gifts and graces of the spirit of God, and lived together in peace, and love, and holiness; and many came unto them from diverse parts of England, so as they grew a great congregation.

And if at any time any differences arose, or offences broke out (as it cannot be, but some time there will, even amongst the best of men) they were ever so met with, and nipped in the head betimes, or otherwise so well composed, as still love, peace, and communion was continued; or else the church purged of those that were incurable and incorrigible, when, after much patience used, no other means would serve, which seldom came to pass. Yea such was the mutual love, and reciprocal respect that this worthy man had to his flock, and his flock to him, that it might be said of them as it once was of that famous Emperor Marcus Aurelius, and the people of Rome, that it was hard to judge whether he delighted more in having such a people, or they in having such a pastor.

His love was great towards them, and his care was always bent for their best good, both for soul and body; for besides his singular abilities in divine things (wherein he excelled), he was also very able to give directions in civil affaires, and to foresee dangers and inconveniences; by which means he was very helpful to their outward estates, and so was every way as a common father unto them. And none did more offend him than those that were close and cleaving to themselves, and retired from the common good; as also such as would be stiff and rigged in matters of outward order, and inveigh against the evils of others, and yet be remiss in themselves, and not so careful to express a virtuous conversation. They in like manner had ever a reverent regard unto him, and had him in precious estimation, as his worth and wisdom did deserve....[2]

"Diligent They Were in Their Callings"

The Separatists Earn the Respect of Their Dutch Neighbors

For Pastor Robinson, William Brewster, and the other Separatists, the years that followed their move to Leiden were a mixture of good times and hard times. Other English Separatists also

---

> "Being thus settled . . . they continued many years in a comfortable condition, enjoying much . . . spiritual comfort together in the ways of God"

escaped England and joined them, swelling their congregation to more than two hundred members. The congregation collectively purchased a large house for Robinson and his family near the *Pieterskerk*—St. Peter's Church—which was a former Catholic cathedral converted to a Dutch Reformed church. Robinson's home was also the congregation's worship center or meeting house. Members of the congregation bought or rented approximately twenty cottages around the meeting house, establishing a Separatist compound of sorts in the neighborhood.

Leiden lay on the Old Rhine River about twenty-five miles south of Amsterdam and twelve miles south of The Hague. At the time, it was the second largest city in Holland, and was in the midst of a growth boom, thanks to a thriving textile industry that steadily drew workers to the city and boosted its population to half the size of Amsterdam. It was also recognized as a rising center for the arts and publishing, and was home to Leiden University, which was quickly gaining acclaim as a center of European research and education. Leiden's architecture, numerous canals, and picturesque gardens also enhanced the city's reputation, leading a contemporary French travel writer to describe Leiden as one of the "grandest, cleanest and most agreeable cities of the world."

With a cityscape dominated by *Pieterskerk*—St. Peter's Church—the city of Leiden was renowned for its architecture, network of canals, and picturesque gardens.

WIKIMEDIA COMMONS

Like much of Holland, Leiden teemed with refugees who had fled from repression in other countries. The Reformation had been embraced by much of the Dutch population, and Holland was a melting pot of Protestant exiles—German Reformed, English Reformed, Puritans, Scots Presbyterians, French Huguenots, Walloons, Lutherans, Anabaptists, Mennonites, and others. Although it

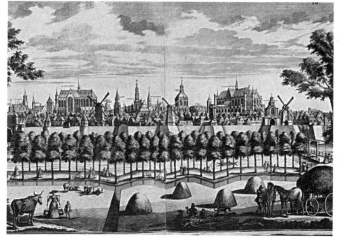

was the predominant faith, the Dutch Reformed Church was not the official government denomination, as was the Anglican Church in England. Like England, however, Catholicism was outlawed in Holland. In the late sixteenth century, the Dutch Revolt—a revolution led by Holland's Protestants—overthrew generations of rule by Catholic Spain in what would become known as the Eighty Years' War. In retaliation, Spanish troops slaughtered thousands of Dutch Protestants, almost wiping out entire populations in several Dutch cities. The city of Leiden barely survived a brutal siege by Spanish forces, which reduced the city's population to starvation. Now Holland was enjoying the peace resulting from a twelve-year truce with Spain, but memories of the bloody occupation were still fresh. While Catholic worship in private homes was tolerated by authorities in Holland, Catholicism was officially banned.

As depicted on this seventeenth-century illustrated map, the Old Rhine River flows around the walled city of Leiden and also slices through it via a canal system. Pastor Robinson and much of his congregation lived in homes near the *Pieterskerk*.

WIKIMEDIA COMMONS

As for the Scrooby Separatists, they now enjoyed the freedom of religion they had sought for so long and under such hardship back home in

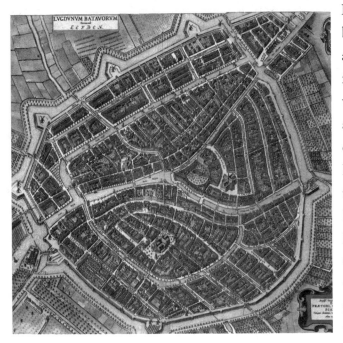

England. No longer did they fear being rounded up at worship or seized at home and taken to jail. They were free to live their faith in public, to worship without harassment, to talk aloud about what they believed with one another or others. Under Pastor Robinson's leadership, the congregation had grown substantially, and had become known for its "true piety, humble zeal and fervent love toward God and his Ways." The integrity and winsome ways demonstrated by the members of the congregation also won them favor among their Dutch neighbors. "First, though many of them were poor," William Bradford would recall, "there were none so poor but that if they were known to be of that congregation, the Dutch (either bakers or others) would trust them to any reasonable extent when they lacked money to buy what they needed. They found

Leiden University—with its steadily expanding library—was an up and coming center of learning in Holland. Pastor Robinson attended theology classes there and participated in the university's theological debates.

WIKIMEDIA COMMONS

by experience how careful they were to keep their word, and saw how diligent they were in their callings, that they would even compete for their custom, and employ them in preference to others."

In Leiden, Pastor Robinson ministered to the personal needs of his congregation, preached three sermons a week, wrote prolifically, attended theology classes at the university, and was invited to join in the university's theological debates. He and his wife Bridget would eventually have at least six children. William Brewster became a ruling elder in the church. For Brewster, coming to Holland was a financial hardship. He had walked away from his bailiff's income at Scrooby, and was untrained to work as a tradesman or laborer. Initially, he provided for his wife and five children by working as a tutor, teaching English to affluent Dutch and German students at the nearby university. Eventually, however, he found his calling as a book publisher. Under the imprint Puritan Press, he published books on Puritan theology and Bible commentaries—largely written by English authors—and exported them for sale in England, where many of them had been banned and were largely unavailable.

William Bradford got a job working in Leiden's textile industry, but upon his twenty-first birthday he received a long-awaited inheritance from

"The Dutch... would trust them to any reasonable extent when they lacked money"

85

As depicted by an artist, a seventeenth-century Separatist wedding was usually a simple affair. While in Holland, twenty-three-year-old William Bradford married sixteen-year-old Dorothy May.

LIBRARY OF CONGRESS

his parents. Unaccustomed to handling money, he soon lost most of it in various attempted investments and necessary living expenses. Humbly, he came to view his loss of fortune as an act of grace through which the Lord preserved his virtue. He managed to purchase a home in a modest Leiden suburb—flanked by the homes of a tanner and a cloth-maker—and made his way as a fustian weaver, fashioning heavy cotton material into a corduroy-like fabric that was popular in Europe in the day. He also became increasingly valuable to his congregation as his faith grew to reflect the biblical position stated by the Apostle Paul: "For I esteemed not to know anything among you, save Jesus Christ, and him crucified." Known for a biblically grounded faith that was consistent and unwavering, he habitually extended respect and charity to believers who disagreed with him, acknowledging—in his words—that "it is too great arrogancy for any man or church to think that he or they have so sounded the word of God to the bottom."

He also married while in Holland. On December 10, 1613, the twenty-three-year-old Bradford married sixteen-year-old Dorothy May in Amsterdam. Little is known of his young bride, who apparently belonged to an exiled English family from the village of Wisbech, which was located about forty miles north of Cambridge. The public proclamation of their intended vows was recorded according to Dutch and English customs, and was preserved in Leiden's court archives.

❖━━━━❖

Then appeared also as before William Bradford from Auster-field, fustian weaver, aged 23 years old, dwelling in Leyden, where the banns have been published, declaring that he has

> "They were betrothed to one another with true covenants"

no parents, on the one part, and Dorothy May, 16 years old, from Wisbeach in England, at present living on the New Dyke, assisted by Henry May, on the other part, and declared that they were betrothed to one other with true covenants, requesting their three Sunday proclamations in order after the same to solemnize the aforesaid covenant and in all respects to execute it, so far as there shall be no lawful hindrances otherwise. And to this end they declared it as truth that they were free persons and were not akin to each other by blood—That nothing existed whereby a Christian marriage might be hindered, and their banns are admitted.[3]

> "Then appeared... William Bradford from Austerfield, fustian weaver, aged 23 years"

"Butter-Mouths," "Great Lubbers," and "Manifold Temptations"

Strange Customs and Culture Shock in Holland

Although grateful for the religious liberty they enjoyed in Holland, the Leiden Separatists found the Dutch lifestyle to be a culture shock. The shock consisted of more than the differences between rural village life and urban living. Nor was it merely the challenge of having to learn a new language, master a new occupation, and adapt to the unfamiliar customs of the "butter-mouths"—the derisive term that some English travelers applied to the dairy-loving Dutch. Robinson, Brewster, Bradford, and the other Separatists appear to have successfully coped with all of those hurdles. What challenged and troubled them the most was what they viewed as the general Dutch attitude

Seventeenth-century Dutch aldermen discuss the issues of the day. Tolerant Dutch officials granted Pastor Robinson's Separatist congregation "free and unrestrained" movement in Holland.

RIJKSMUSEUM OF AMSTERDAM

toward morality—and especially its potential impact on their children.

Despite the widespread influence of the Dutch Reformed Church and the array of exiled Protestant communities in Holland, the Separatists found life in The Netherlands to be far more secular-minded than what they had known in England. While the relaxed, liberal attitude typical of Dutch culture allowed for greater religious tolerance than was found in England, the Separatists eventually concluded that it also produced a general lack of personal discipline and a casual attitude toward Bible-based morality. Despite its many attractions, William Bradford observed, Dutch culture also produced "great licentiousness" and "manifold temptations." Early seventeenth-century English travel writer Fynes Moryson, who was not a Separatist, concurred with Bradford's observation. In his classic work *An Itinerary*, Moryson advised English travelers to Holland to expect to find a casual attitude toward the Lord's Day, and he cited an example:

"Here is little respect had to sanctify the Sabbath"

Here is little respect had to sanctify the Sabbath; the young girls walked all Sabbath afternoon with cups in their hands; they were about five or six years of age; others, about twelve or thirteen, guided them and sung, screaming and squeaking and straining their voices. Such as they met gave them money, which they put into the cups, was intended to buy a them a wasail cup or a carouse. This continued all [day]....

Dutch men of the early seventeenth century, Moryson opined, were typically given to "excessive drinking," and Dutch women, he generalized, were often bold and brazen:

Dutch neighbors cheerfully cavort on the Lord's Day. Pastor Robinson, William Bradford, and other English Separatists were troubled by what they viewed as a frivolous attitude toward the Sabbath in Holland.

RIJKSMUSEUM OF AMSTERDAM

The women (as I have heard some Hollanders confess) not easily finding a husband, in respect of this disparity of the sexes in number, commonly live unmarried till they be thirty years old, and as commonly take husbands of twenty years of age, which must make the women more powerful. Nothing is more frequent than for little girls to insult their brothers much bigger then they, reproving their doings, and calling them great lubbers. I talked with some companions [who] told me it was a common thing for wives to drive their husbands and their friends out the door with scolding.... I may boldly say that the women of these parts, are above all others, truly taxed with this unnatural domineering over their husbands.

"Nothing is more frequent than for little girls to insult their brothers... calling them great lubbers"

The travel writer's critical and generalized observation of Dutch womanhood stood in contrast to the ideal of early seventeenth-century middle-class English women, whose lifestyle was stereotyped in a popular self-improvement book on English home life. The book was published at the time the Scrooby Separatists were in Leiden.

✦─•─✦

Next unto her sanctity and holiness of life, it is meet that our English housewife be a woman of great modesty and temperance, as well inwardly as outwardly; inwardly, as in her behaviour and carriage towards her husband, wherein she shall shun all violence of rage, passion and humour, coveting less to direct than to be directed, appearing ever unto him pleasant, amiable and delightful; and, tho' occasional mishaps, or the mis-government of his will may induce her to contrary thoughts, yet virtuously to suppress them, and with a mild sufferance rather to call him home from his error, than with the strength of anger to abate the least spark of his evil, calling into her mind, that evil and uncomely language is deformed, though uttered even to servants; but most monstrous and ugly, when it appears before the presence of a husband.

Outwardly... in her apparel... she shall proportion according to the competency of her husband's estate and calling.... Let therefore the housewife's garments be comely and strong, made as well to preserve the health, as to adorn the person, altogether without toyish garnishes, or the gloss of light colours, and as far from the vanity of new

A Dutch artist caricatured the relaxed moral values displayed by many people in Holland—a cultural tendency that contrasted sharply with the biblical worldview held by the Separatists.

RIJKSMUSEUM OF AMSTERDAM

Seventeenth-century Dutch citizens enjoy a balmy day along one of Holland's fabled waterways. Although Holland offered many attractions for the exiled English Separatists, it was still a foreign culture for them.

WIKIMEDIA COMMONS IMAGES

and fantastic fashions, as near to the comely imitation of modest matrons.

Let her diet be wholesome and cleanly, prepared at due hours, and cooked with care and diligence, let it be rather to satisfy nature, than her affections, and apter to kill hunger than revive new appetites; let it proceed more from the provision of her own yard, than the furniture of the markets; and let it be rather esteemed for the familiar acquaintance she has with it, than for the strangeness and rarity it brings from other countries....

To conclude, our English housewife must be of chaste thoughts, stout courage, patient, untired, watchful, diligent, witty, pleasant, constant in friendship, full of good neighbor-hood, wise in discourse, but not frequent therein, sharp and quick of speech, but not bitter or talkative, secret

With an ale jug placed conveniently nearby, a Dutch woman lights up with an attentive companion. As the years passed, the exiled Separatists began to fear that their children's faith would weaken amid the liberal Dutch culture.

RIJKSMUSEUM OF AMSTERDAM

in her affairs, comfortable in her counsels, and generally skillful in the worthy knowledge which do belong to her vocation.[4]

"How Hard the Country Was Where We Lived"

Life in Holland Begins to Take a Toll

If such an idealistic lifestyle was demanding for middle-class women in England, it was surely daunting for the wives and mothers among the Separatists in Leiden. Many of them—perhaps most—were forced by circumstance to put aside traditional homemaking skills and even important child-raising tasks in order to earn a wage in the commercial workplace. Holland's textile boom had attracted workers from throughout Western

Europe, leaving few high-paying jobs for the newcomers, most of whom were farmers and villagers unskilled in the urban trades. To survive on scanty pay, entire families—

An English family dines on simple fare in this seventeenth-century woodcut. For many of the English exiles, keeping the family fed, clothed, and housed in Holland required fathers, mothers, and even the children to join the local workforce.

WIKIMEDIA COMMONS

children included—went to work with long hours and monotonous tasks. They became weavers, drapers, twine-makers, ribbon-weavers, hat-makers, and wool-carders. Others found jobs outside the textile industry, working as bakers, coopers, chandlers, leather-workers, cobblers, dock workers, glover-makers, wood-sawyers, and pipe-makers.

Despite difficulties and hardship, the members of Robinson's congregation were frugal and responsible, and most managed to earn an adequate living, given that few appeared on Leiden's delinquent tax records. They generally accepted their new and demanding routines to be a fair trade for the freedom of faith they had so desperately sought. As the years passed, however, their hardscrabble lifestyle took a toll. They also began to fear that their children would be discouraged by continued hardship and that the worldly Dutch culture would lure them from their faith. Years later, one of them would recall "how hard the country was where we lived, how many spent their estate in it…how unable we were to give such good education to our children as we received." In a private account of the Pilgrim odyssey, William Bradford would later describe what the Separatists saw as the dark side of living in Holland.

※—————————————※

*After they had lived here for some eleven or twelve years—
the period of the famous truce between the Low Countries*

"Our English housewife must be of chaste thoughts, stout courage, patient, untired, watchful, diligent, witty, pleasant… and generally skillful"

Life in Holland was especially challenging for many of the Separatist mothers, who had to work long hours outside of the home while also raising children, cooking meals, and maintaining the household.

RIJKSMUSEUM OF AMSTERDAM

and Spain—several of them having died, and many others being now old, the grave mistress, Experience, having taught them much, their prudent governors began to apprehend present dangers and to scan the future and think of timely remedy....

First, they saw by experience that the hardships of the country were such that comparatively few others would join them, and fewer still would bide it out and remain with them. Many who came and many more who desired to come, could not endure the continual labor and hard fare and other inconveniences which they themselves were satisfied with. But though these weaker brethren loved the members of the congregation, personally approved their cause, and honored their sufferings, they left them, weeping, as it were ... for, though many desired to enjoy the ordinances of God in their purity, and the liberty of the gospel, yet, alas, they preferred to submit to bondage, with danger to their conscience, rather than endure these privations.

Some even preferred prisons in England to this liberty in Holland, with such hardships. But it was thought that if there could be found a better and easier place of living, it would attract many and remove this discouragement. Their pastor would often say, that if many of those who both wrote and preached against them were living where they might have liberty and comfortable conditions, they would then practice the same religion as they themselves did.

Secondly, they saw that though the people generally bore these difficulties very cheerfully, and with resolute courage, being in the best strength of their years; yet old age began to steal on many of them, and their great and continual labors, with other crosses and sorrows, hastened it before their time; so that it was not only probable, but certain, that in a few more years they would be in danger of scattering by the necessities pressing upon them. Therefore, according to the divine proverb that a wise man sees the plague when it cometh, and hides himself (Proverbs 22:3); they, like skillful and hardened soldiers, were wary of being surrounded by their enemies, so that they could neither fight nor flee, and thought it wiser to dislodge betimes to some place of better advantage and less danger, if any such could be found.

Thirdly, as necessity was a task-master over them, so they themselves were forced to be, not only over their servants, but in a sort over their dearest children; which not a little wounded the hearts of many a loving father and mother, and

A seventeenth-century Dutch baker removes a loaf from the oven. In Holland, family members of the English Separatists worked as bakers, chandlers, wood-cutters, weavers, wool-carders, ribbon-makers, cobblers, leather-workers, laborers, and in other occupations.

RIJKSMUSEUM OF AMSTERDAM

"[They] began to apprehend present dangers and to scan the future" *produced many sad and sorrowful effects. Many of their children, who were of the best disposition and who had learned to bear the yoke in their youth and were willing to bear part of their parents' burden, were often so oppressed with their labors, that though their minds were free and willing, their bodies bowed under the weight and became decrepit in early youth—the vigor of nature being consumed in the very bud, as it were.*

But still more lamentable, and of all sorrows most heavy to be borne, was that many of the children, influenced by these conditions, and the great licentiousness of the young people of the country, and the many temptations of the city,

were led by evil example into dangerous courses, getting the reins off their necks and leaving their parents. Some became soldiers, others embarked upon voyages by sea and others upon worse courses tending to dissoluteness and the danger of their souls, to the great grief of the parents and the dishonor of God. So they saw their posterity would be in danger to degenerate and become corrupt.[5]

Should they leave Holland? That's the question some of the Separatists in Holland

Over time, the English Separatists in Holland began to assimilate into the surrounding Dutch culture. Parents became increasingly concerned that their children would become more Dutch than English.

RIJKSMUSEUM OF AMSTERDAM

began seriously asking themselves by the year 1617. For many of them, life in Holland continued to be difficult. Some feared their children might spend their childhood in child labor. Or lose their English identity. Or even lose their faith to what they saw as Holland's worldly ways. That year a theological dispute among professors at the University of Leiden escalated into street riots, and rising tension related to the dispute threatened to make Holland's religious melting pot boil out of control.

Seeing their children forced to take difficult jobs at an early age deeply concerned many Separatists in Holland. Eventually, many began to believe that they could find better lives for their families outside Holland.

RIJKSMUSEUM OF AMSTERDAM

In 1617, a theological dispute among faculty members at the University of Leiden escalated into street riots, adding a new, troubling dimension to life in Leiden for the Separatists.

RIJKSMUSEUM OF AMSTERDAM

"Their bodies... became decrepit in early youth"

Meanwhile, as the peace treaty between Holland and Spain neared an end, rumors of renewed warfare began to circulate. The Separatists knew that if Catholic Spain invaded and reoccupied Holland, they and their families could be killed the same way that tens of thousands of other Protestants had been executed by Catholic rulers in Spain, France, and Portugal a century before. So Pastor Robinson and church leaders began to seriously consider making another move. But if they left Holland, where could they go?[6]

The Separatists were well aware that tens of thousands of Protestants had been massacred by Catholic troops during fighting in Holland years earlier. As the peace treaty between Holland and Spain neared expiration, many of the Separatists began to fear that Spain would again invade Holland.

WIKIMEDIA COMMONS

CHAPTER FIVE

"They Knew
They Were Pilgrims"

Why not go to America?

That's the question that Pastor Robinson and members of the Separatist church at Leiden had begun seriously asking in 1617. By then, the reasons for considering a move from Holland were well-established—the low-paying jobs and difficult lifestyle, the concerns about their children succumbing to worldly ways or losing their English identity, worries about rising religious tensions in Holland, fears of possible invasion and persecution by Spain, along with the foundational Separatist desire to share the Gospel. But where would they go this time? By 1619, a consensus emerged: Why not go to America?[1]

There were other options. The Leiden Separatists still enjoyed the favor of their Dutch neighbors. "These English have lived amongst us now these twelve years," Leiden authorities noted, "and yet we have never had any suit or accusation come against them...." At one point Dutch contacts offered the opportunity of relocating to the colony of New Netherland, which Dutch investors were attempting to establish in the area of

99

Faced with a hardscrabble lifestyle, challenges to their values, and the threat of a possible Spanish invasion, Pastor Robinson's Separatist congregation began to consider leaving Holland. But where could they go?

STORIES OF THE PILGRIMS

modern-day New York City. After some initial interest, Robinson and the other church leaders abandoned the idea, along with a proposal to help settle a Dutch colony in South America. They also considered moving elsewhere in Holland, but there they would still be raising their families in Dutch culture, and as foreigners, they believed, they would never be fully accepted in Holland.

America seemed the wisest choice. Why not go to the new English colony in Virginia? It had been established at Jamestown in 1607, and would prove to be the first successful English colony in North America. Its early days had been desperate, as its ill-prepared colonists struggled in the American wilderness, nearly starving to death and reportedly even resorting to cannibalism at one point. By 1619, however, the Virginia colony had twelve years of survival behind it, and had somewhat stabi-

lized. Even so, Robinson and the congregation's leaders rejected that destination too, fearing that there they would again come under the iron rule of the Church of England.

But what if they were granted their own colony far away from Jamestown, perhaps in northern Virginia? And what if they were allowed self-government and full freedom to worship according to their consciences? With this vision in mind, a member of the congregation would report, "the Lord was solemnly sought in the congregation by fasting and prayer to direct us...." Church members afterward felt led to cobble together the funds to send Robert Cushman and John Carver, two of their trusted deacons, on a mission to London. There they would discuss the proposal with the principals of the Virginia Company, the joint

In wilderness America, English colonists had established a surviving colony at Jamestown in Virginia despite deadly hardship. Holland's Separatists considered relocating there.

THE LEADING FACTS OF AMERICAN HISTORY

stock corporation that had established Jamestown, and which held a royal charter to establish colonies in America. Although known largely for its Jamestown Colony, the Virginia Company actually had been granted territory that stretched from the Cape Fear River in modern North Carolina to Long Island Sound in what would become New York. In London, Cushman and Carver received a favorable response. One of the Virginia Company's chief principals, Sir Edwin Sandys, was a devout Christian who was sympathetic to the Separatists—plus the company sorely needed colonists for its New World ventures. Even so, the proposed Separatist colony would be required to have the approval of King James I, who was no friend of Separatists.

Pastor Robinson and church leaders drafted a carefully worded letter to Virginia Company officials, which was designed to reassure them that the congregation was worthy of support despite the controversy associated with the Separatist movement. It was a masterpiece of diplomacy. In it, they acknowledged King James as the "Supreme Governor in his Dominion" and that he had the right to govern "civilly according to the laws of the land." However, on the principal and controversial Separatist doctrine that the king did not have biblical authority to oversee their congregation or anyone's personal faith, they remained silent.

To seek God's direction about their future, Pastor Robinson and his Leiden congregation held a solemn assembly. Afterward, the congregation voted to examine the option of establishing a colony in America.

RIJKSMUSEUM OF AMSTERDAM

In another letter to Edwin Sandys and other officials of the Virginia Company, Pastor Robinson and Elder Brewster stated the reasons why the Leiden Separatists believed they could succeed in the New World.

"We verily believe and trust the Lord is with us"

Right Worshipful,

Our humble duties, with grateful acknowledgment of your singular love, especially shown in your earnest endeavor for our good in this weighty business about Virginia. We have set down our request in writing, subscribed as you wished by the majority of the congregation and have sent it to the Council of the Virginia Company by our agent, John Carver, a deacon of our Church, whom a gentleman of our congregation accompanies.

We need not urge you to any more tender care of us, since, under God, above all persons and things in the world, we rely upon you, expecting the care of your love, the counsel of your wisdom, and the countenance of your authority. Notwith-standing, for your encouragement in the work we will mention these inducements to our enterprise:

1. We verily believe and trust the Lord is with us, unto Whom and Whose service we have given ourselves in many trials; and that He will graciously prosper our endeavors according to the simplicity of our hearts therein.

2. We are well weaned from the delicate milk of our mother country, and inured to the difficulties of a strange and hard land, which yet in a great part we have by patience overcome.

3. The people are, for the body of them, industrious and frugal, we think we may safely say, as any company of people in the world.

4. We are knit together in a body in a most strict and sacred bond and covenant of the Lord, of the violation whereof we make great conscience, and by virtue whereof we do hold ourselves straightly tied to all care of each other's good, and of the whole by everyone, and so mutually.

5. Lastly, it is not with us as with other men whom small things can discourage, or small discontentments cause to wish themselves home again. We know our entertainment in England and Holland; we shall much prejudice both our arts and means by removal; if we should be driven to return, we should not hope to recover our present helps and comforts, neither indeed look ever for ourselves to attain unto the like in any other place during our lives, which are now drawing towards their periods.

These motives we have been bold to put to you, and, as you think well, to any other of our friends of the Council. We

Pastor Robinson and other church leaders contacted officials of the Virginia Company, which had backed establishment of the Jamestown settlement. One of the company's founders, Sir Edwin Sandys, was sympathetic to the Separatists and their plight.

WIKIMEDIA COMMONS

"It is not with
us as with
other men
whom small
things can
discourage"

*will not be further troublesome, but with our humble duties
to your Worship, and to any other of our well-willers of the
Council, we take our leaves, committing you to the guidance
of the Almighty. Yours much bounden in all duty,*

  John Robinson
  William Brewster
  Leyden, Dec. 15th, 1617[2]

"We Resolved to Hire a Ship"

The Leiden Separatists Decide to Go to America

Pastor Robinson and his congregation faced a daunting task: they had to receive royal permission to establish a colony in America, obtain an official patent from the Virginia Company, acquire funding for the expedition and settlement, and receive assurances from the king and the Church that they would be allowed religious freedom in America. All of that had to transpire before they could even set sail. Initially, all seemed to go well. Influenced no doubt by the sympathetic Edwin Sandys, the principals of the Virginia Company appeared enthusiastic, and even King James initially seemed agreeable to the idea of a Separatist colony in North America. He was petitioned by an influential member of the Virginia Company, who assured his royal highness that the colony would provide revenue from offshore fishing. "So God have my soul, 'tis an honest trade," the king reportedly proclaimed, "'twas the apostles' own calling!"

Then the grand proposal began to unravel. Officials in the Church of England were unenthusiastic, and the king stopped short of openly granting the Separatists freedom of religion in America. The best he would promise was that he would "not molest them, if they carried themselves peaceably." The king's limited support for the proposed colony unsettled the officers of the Virginia Company, who were also unexpectedly distracted by internal issues. In the spring of 1619, they finally granted a patent for a colony "in the most northern parts of Virginia" at the mouth of the Hudson River near modern New York City—but the would-be colonists still needed to raise their funding. Meanwhile, news reached them of a deadly disaster that had befallen another

King James agreed not to block the Separatists from establishing a colony in America—especially when he was assured they could produce a profit from fishing. "So God have my soul, 'tis an honest trade," he reportedly announced, "'twas the apostles' own calling!"

DOMESTIC HISTORY OF ENGLAND

group of Separatists while they were sailing for Virginia. Their overcrowded ship was blown off course and lost its way, the ship's drinking water ran out, and the "bloody flux"—severe dysentery—killed twothirds of the 180 passengers. Faced with such discouragement, many of the Leiden Separatists gave up on relocating. It appeared to be the death of the vision.

Robinson, Brewster, and others remained determined, however, and their determination increased when a sixty-three-year-old church member was inadvertently injured in religion-fueled street fighting. Then, in 1620, an English businessman appeared in Leiden, introduced himself to church leaders, and offered to raise the capital needed to underwrite the colony. His name was Thomas Weston. He was a fortythree-year-old London hardware merchant-turned-exporter who had somehow learned of the Separatists' plans—and came to make them

Robert Cushman, sent back to England by the Leiden congregation, roamed crowded English docks, looking for a ship and crew to transport his fellow Separatists to America.

WIKIMEDIA COMMONS

"We resolved to hire a ship"

an extraordinary offer. He was a principal in a London investment group, he explained, and his firm—the Merchant Adventurers—could also provide a patent for a colony near the mouth of the Hudson River. He and his backers would pay for the necessary trans-Atlantic ship, its crew, provisions for the voyage, and whatever was necessary until the colonists were established. In return, they would work four days a week for the company, producing profits by offshore fishing and fur trapping, and be allowed to work two days for themselves—with no work on the Sabbath. At the end of seven years, their land and houses would become their private property.

They enthusiastically accepted Weston's offer, and signed a contract. Some, including William Bradford, promptly sold their homes and began making preparations for the voyage to America. Next, they planned to hire two ships—one in Holland, one in England—to transport them to America. Then they discovered that Thomas Weston could not back up his bold talk. Apparently he had hoped to obtain a profitable fishing monopoly for the colony. When unable to do so, he insisted on changing the terms, requiring the colonists to work six days a week for the company, which—at the end of seven years— would also keep half their homes and property. Robinson and the other church leaders declared the new requirements to be "fitter for thieves and bondservants rather than honest men," and instructed their deacon-turned-business-agent, Robert Cushman, who was still in London, to refuse the new terms.

Cushman was a middle-aged English grocer who had come to Holland with his wife and son in 1609, and had joined Pastor Robinson's church. As with other Separatists, life in Holland had not been easy for him. His wife had died, and—although he had been a man of some means in England—he had been forced to work as a wool-comber in Holland. He had become a lay leader in the church, had remarried, and had agreed to serve as the Leiden congregation's business agent back in London—a difficult job complicated by long-distance communications. Instead of rejecting Weston's revised offer, for instance, Cushman had pledged the congregation to accept it, fearing that the proposed colonization would otherwise collapse.

Back in Leiden, church leaders were dismayed by the news and were also frustrated to learn that Weston had failed to hire a ship and crew in England as promised. Again, for some, it was the death of the vision. In Leiden and Amsterdam, some of those planning to go to America changed their minds, leaving those who remained committed short of both numbers and money. They forged ahead anyway, searching for a ship and crew they could hire in Holland to help transport them to America. To replace the Separatists who had backed out of the voyage, Weston and the Merchant Adventurers recruited other passengers in England. Most of the new recruits were motivated by the opportunities of a new life in a new land, rather than a desire for greater religious freedom. Perhaps due to this difference, or simply because they were generally unknown to them, the Leiden Separatists came to refer to the new recruits as "Strangers."

With their typical courtesy, Pastor Robinson and the leaders of the Leiden congregation allowed the "Strangers" to select a representative in England to help Cushman and Carver make arrangements for the voyage. They selected a man named Christopher Martin, who appears to have shared some of the same theology as the Leiden church members, but not their temperament. He soon fell to bickering with Carver and Cushman. "And to speak the truth," Cushman frankly observed, "… we are readier to go to dispute than to set forward a voyage." Cushman, however, continued working with Weston and the Merchant Adventurers to hire a second ship and crew. As evident in the excerpted letter below, he was brimming with frustration. Not only did he have to help find the second ship and deal with the unpredictable Thomas Weston, but he was also painfully aware that church leaders back in Holland had lost confidence in him because he had pleged them to Weston's new terms. If, he wrote them, they really believed that he had bungled the negotiations—that they "set a fool about your business"—then he would quit.

<hr>

Salutations, etc.

I received your letter [and] the many discouragements I find here together with the demurs and retirings [from] there made me to say, "I would give up my accounts to John Carver, and at his coming acquaint him fully with all courses; and so leave it quite, with only the poor clothes on my back." But gathering up myself, by further consideration, I resolved

A Separatist mother and child pack for America. After serious prayer and discussion, the Leiden congregation decided that one group would go to America immediately, and another would go later.

STORIES OF THE PILGRIMS

yet to make one trial more: and to acquaint Master Weston with the fainted state of our business. And though he hath been much discontented at something amongst us of late, which hath made him often say that save for his promise he would not meddle at all with the business any more, and yet…advising together, we resolved to hire a ship; and…a fine ship it is.

…I hope our friends there, if they be quitted of the ship hire, will be induced to venture the more. All that I now require is that salt and nets may there be bought; and for all the rest, we will here provide it. Yet if that will not be, let

❦

"Give us
quiet,
peaceable,
and patient
minds in
all these
turmoils"

❦

them but stand for it a month or two, and we will take order to pay it all. Let Master Reynolds tarry there and bring the ship to Southampton. We have hired another Pilot here, one Master Clarke, who went last year to Virginia with a ship of [cattle]....

I hope such as are my sincere friends will not think but I can give some reason of my actions. But of your mistaking about the matter, and other things tending to this business: I shall next inform you more distinctly. Meanwhile entreat our friends not to be too busy in answering matters before they know them. If I do such things as I cannot give reasons for, it is like you have set a fool about your business; and so turn the reproof to yourselves and send another, and let me come again to my combs. But (setting aside my natural infirmities) I refuse not to have my cause judged, both of God and all indifferent men; and when we come together I shall give account of my actions here.

The Lord, who judges justly without respect of persons, see unto the equity of my cause, and give us quiet, peaceable, and patient minds in all these turmoils, and sanctify unto us all crosses whatsoever! And so I take my leave of you all, in all love and affection,

Your poor Brother,
Robert Cushman
June 11, 1620[3]

Robert Cushman did not quit his post as the Pilgrims' business agent in England, nor was he recalled, and his search for an English ship worthy of a voyage to America would eventually prove successful.

"They Knew They Were Pilgrims"

The Leiden Separatists Become Pilgrims to America

Edward Winslow listened to his fellow Separatists sing from the Psalter and was moved to tears. It was late July of 1620, and the Leiden congregation was worshipping together in Leiden for a final time: the next day more than fifty of them were leaving for faraway America. Edward Winslow would be among them. A twenty-five-year-old Separatist from Droitwich, south of Birmingham, Winslow had been born to a prosperous family, and had discovered Pastor Robinson's Leiden congregation while traveling in Holland. He had taken up a trade as a printer, perhaps in William Brewster's publishing firm, and had also taken up an English wife, Elizabeth Baker Winslow, just two years earlier. He and Elizabeth were active members of the Leiden congregation, and now they were going to America together. Finally, the long-planned, much-discussed vision of establishing a Separatist colony in America was becoming reality.

To determine how to proceed amid all the problems, Pastor Robinson had called for a solemn assembly, in which the congregation had engaged in fasting and prayer to determine the Lord's will. They had thus determined to go forward with their plans—but only those who felt so led would go to America. Almost the entire congregation professed an intent to go, but funding an expedition that would accommodate all who wished to go was tremendously expensive. Some would have to go later. Pastor Robinson, it was decided, would head whichever group proved to be larger, and the remainder would be led by Elder Brewster.

When the numbers were finally tallied, fifty to sixty members of the congregation chose to go to America immediately. The rest, which

Twenty-five-year-old Edward Winslow, who would become a leader in the new colony in America, recorded an account of the Leiden congregation's heart-rending final worship service together in Holland. He wrote: "we refreshed ourselves, after tears, with the singing of psalms…."

PILGRIM HALL MUSEUM

included older members of the congregation, would follow later—presumably when the colony was established and secure. According to Edward Winslow, "the difference in number was not great," but the group that would come later outnumbered those who chose to leave immediately. That meant Pastor Robinson would not go. Robinson may also have worried that his presence as a Separatist minister might unnerve the Merchant Adventurers and undermine their support. So, after all the prayers, all the planning, and all the problems—he would remain behind. When the colony was secure, the plan was for him to lead the other group to America. The capable Elder Brewster, meanwhile, would lead the first group on the voyage to America, and could act as lay pastor as well as group leader. At the moment, however, Brewster was keeping a low profile: his Leiden publishing firm had printed and distributed a work that was harshly critical of King James. English authorities wanted Brewster arrested, and in response Dutch officials were also searching for him. So as the Separatists bound for America were preparing for their departure, their leader had become a hunted man forced into hiding.

While Cushman and the Merchant Adventurers searched for a ship and crew in England, church leaders had found a ship in Holland—the *Speedwell*—and had hired a captain and crew for a year. At sixty tons and not quite fifty feet in length, the *Speedwell* was small but adequate for the voyage across the Atlantic. Smaller ships had made the voyage for decades, sailing to America to haul fish from its rich offshore waters. Church leaders intended to use the *Speedwell* as a backup to the larger ship that the Merchant Adventurers would provide, and it could also be used for the fishing trade once in America. Those who had chosen to go to America sold their homes or made other arrangements, disposed of their furniture and furnishings, and packed the belongings they planned to take to America. All that done, it was finally time to say goodbye.

It was no small decision to go. Those leaving for America knew that they might never again see those loved ones and friends they were leaving behind. They also knew at least some of the dangers they faced. Would they drown in a storm crossing the fierce Atlantic or die of the "bloody flux" like others before them? Would illness or accident claim them in the mysterious American wilderness? Would they be murdered by the natives—the Indians—who were known as "savages" in England? Would they be up to the hard labor of building new homes and lives in a strange and untamed new land? For most, who had fled England a decade earlier, this would be their second exodus: Would it finally resolve their quest for freedom of faith? The answers to such life-and-death questions, they left to the sovereignty of God. After all—in the words of William Bradford—"they knew they were pilgrims, and looked not much on those

While their investors were searching for a ship and crew in England, the leaders of the Leiden congregation conducted their own search in Holland—and they were successful.

RIJKSMUSEUM OF AMSTERDAM

things, but lifted up their eyes to heaven, their dearest country, and quieted their spirits."

Bradford's observation was an obvious reference to chapter eleven of the New Testament book of Hebrews, which cites a hall of heroes of the faithful, and notes that believers, who are promised a true home in heaven, are but temporary "pilgrims" on earth: *All these died in faith, and…confessed that they were strangers and pilgrims on the earth.* It was also a clear reference to chapter two of the New Testament book of I Peter, which emphasizes salvation in Christ and the responsibility of believers as "pilgrims" in this world:

"[They] lifted up their eyes to heaven, their dearest country, and quieted their spirits"

> *But ye are a chosen generation, a royal Priesthood, an holy nation, a peculiar people, that ye would show forth the virtues of him that hath called you out of the darkness into his marvelous light…. Dearly brethren, I beseech you as strangers and pilgrims, abstain from fleshly lusts, which fight against the soul, and have your conversation honest among the Gentiles, that they which speak evil of you as evil doers, may by your good works which they shall see, glorify God….*

Now, in July of 1620, these "Pilgrims" from England via Holland would board the *Speedwell* at the Dutch port of Delftshaven, which was located near Rotterdam at the mouth of the Meuse or Maas River. From there, they would sail to the English port of Southampton, where Deacons Cushman and Carver and the "Strangers" all awaited them aboard the larger ship leased in England.

The day before their departure, the congregation held another solemn assembly, led by Pastor Robinson. The sermon text came from the Old Testament book of Ezra, chapter eight, where Ezra preached to a large group of Jews gathered on a riverside in Babylon before leading them back to Jerusalem from exile.

> *And there at the river, by Ahava, I proclaimed a fast, that we might humble ourselves before our God, and seek of him a right way for us, and for our children, and for all our substance.*

The application was obvious: like the exiled Jews leaving Babylon for Jerusalem, the Pilgrims would be abandoning Europe for a freedom of faith in "New Jerusalem"—America. Unlike Ezra, however, Pastor Robinson would not be going with his people.

On the eve of their departure for Delftshaven, the Pilgrims were treated to a farewell feast by the rest of the congregation at Robinson's home in Leiden. There, in their Sabbath meeting place, they also united in an emotional farewell worship service. It was marked by praise, prayer, and tears, as recorded by Edward Winslow:

In July of 1620, the Pilgrims and others from the Leiden congregation traveled to the Dutch port of Delftshaven, depicted here in a seventeenth-century engraving. From there, they would depart for England and on to America.

WIKIMEDIA COMMONS

> *I persuade myself, never people upon earth lived more lovingly together and parted more sweetly than we, the church at Leyden, did; not rashly, in a distracted humor, but upon joint and serious deliberation, often seeking the mind of God by fasting and prayer; whose gracious presence we not only found*

"Never people
upon earth
lived more
lovingly
together and
parted more
sweetly"

with us, but his blessing upon us, from that time to this instant, to the indignation of our adversaries, the admiration of strangers, and the exceeding consolation of ourselves, to see such effects of our prayers and tears before our pilgrimage here be ended....

Whereupon...we further sought the Lord by a public and solemn Fast, for his gracious guidance. And hereupon we came to this resolution, that it was best for one part of the church to go at first, and the other to stay, viz. the youngest and strongest part to go. Secondly, they that went should freely offer themselves. Thirdly, if the major part went, the pastor to go with them; if not, the elder only. Fourthly, if the Lord should frown upon our proceedings, then those that went to return, and the brethren that remained still there, to assist and be helpful to them; but if God should be pleased to favor them that went, then they also should endeavor to help over such as were poor and ancient and willing to come.

These things being agreed, the major part stayed, and the pastor with them, for the present; but all intended (except a very few, who had rather we would have stayed) to follow after. The minor part, with Mr. Brewster, their elder, resolved to enter upon this great work, (but take notice the difference of number was not great.) And when the ship was ready to carry us away, the brethren that stayed having again solemnly sought the Lord with us and for us, and we further engaging ourselves mutually as before, they, I say, that stayed at Leyden feasted us that were to go, at our pastor's house, being large; where we refreshed ourselves, after tears, with singing of psalms, making joyful melody in our hearts, as well as with the voice, there being many of the congregation very expert in music; and indeed it was the sweetest melody that ever mine ears heard....[4]

"Indeed it was the sweetest melody that ever mine ears heard"

"Store We Up...Patience against the Evil Day!"

The Pilgrims Depart with Words of Wisdom from Pastor Robinson

More tears marked events the next day, as the Pilgrims headed for the docks at Delftshaven where the *Speedwell* lay at anchor. They presumably traveled the twenty-five miles by canal, which consumed most of the day. They were accompanied by the congregation members who were staying behind, who again hosted a meal for them in Delftshaven. There too were friends and perhaps family from the church in Amsterdam. Among the departing Pilgrims was William Bradford, now age thirty, and his wife Dorothy. Departure was no doubt especially painful for both: they had chosen to leave their only child, three-year-old John, in the care of others—most likely Dorothy's parents in Amsterdam—until he could be brought to America when the colony was securely established. Mentored by Pastor Robinson and Elder Brewster, Bradford had become a key lay leader in the Leiden congregation, and played a major role in preparations for the expedition to America. "The night was spent with little sleep by the most," Bradford would later recall, "but with friendly entertainment and Christian discourse and other real expressions of true Christian love."

The next morning—Saturday, July 22, 1620—they assembled at the *Speedwell*, which was riding at anchor dockside. There, Pastor Robinson preached a final sermon, charging the Pilgrims with biblical advice "of great and weighty consequences," in the words of Edward Winslow. In America, he counseled them, they should focus on unity and not

William Brewster, the revered elder of the Leiden congregation, would lead the Pilgrims to America, church leaders decided. Pastor Robinson planned to come later with more members of the congregation.

ARCHITECT OF THE U.S. CAPITOL

division, including unity with other Christian believers outside of the Separatist ranks, such as the Puritans. He also urged them to let the Bible be their guide in all things—"to take heed what we received for truth; and well examine and compare and weigh it with other Scriptures of truth before we received it." Then, kneeling, he led the group in prayer. Many realized they might not see one another again in this world, and "tears did gush from every eye," according to Bradford. The *Speedwell* was moored dockside outside a Reformed church—the *Herformde Kerk*—and even Dutch onlookers watching the gathered congregation were moved to tears.

The tide was shifting from incoming to outgoing, the Pilgrims were advised, and it was time to go. The *Speedwell*'s sails were hoisted and were immediately filled by a strong breeze. Lines were loosed, and the ship and its passengers slowly moved away from the Delftshaven dock and headed seaward for the North Sea and England. For many, including Pastor Robinson, the *Speedwell*'s departure would indeed be a final farewell. Various events would prevent Robinson from joining the Pilgrims in America as planned. Five years later, a deadly plague would ravage Leiden, killing thousands of its residents. Among the dead would be many members of the Leiden congregation—and their beloved pastor, John Robinson.

As the Pilgrims sailed into the open seas toward England was a letter of farewell written to them by their their pastor. It would be read aloud at dockside in Southampton, likely by William Brewster. In it, Pastor Robinson again encouraged them to be tolerant of each other— not to "give, no, nor easily take offense"—and to demonstrate "wisdom and charity" to all. When the time came to establish a form of government—"a Body Politic," he called it—he urged them to "let your wisdom and godliness appear, not only in choosing persons as do entirely love, and will diligently promote the common good, but also in yielding to them all due honor and obedience...." Remember, he beseeched them, to always choose "the glorious ordinance of the Lord" and a "virtuous mind" over the ways of the world. Pilgrim leader John Robinson would never see America, but his vision and his words would deeply inspire and mold America's Pilgrims. Here, reprinted in full, is his farewell letter:

Loving and Christian Friends,

I do heartily, and in the Lord, salute you all: as being they with whom I am present in my best affection, and most earnest longings after you, though I be constrained, for a while, to be bodily absent from you. I say, constrained: God knowing how willingly much rather than otherwise, I would have borne my part with you in this first brunt, were I not, by strong necessity, held back for the present. Make account of me in the meanwhile, as of a man divided in myself, with great pain, and as, natural bonds set aside, having my better part with you. And though I doubt not but, in your godly wisdoms, you both foresee, and resolve upon, that which concerns your present state and condition, both severally and jointly; yet have I thought but my duty, to add some further spur of provocation unto them who run already, if not because you need it, yet because I owe it in love and duty. And first, as we are daily to renew our repentance with our God, special, for our sins known, and general, for our

At the docks in Delftshaven, Pastor Robinson preached a final sermon to the departing Pilgrims. Their tearful departure for America inspired this dramatic nineteenth-century painting.

LIBRARY OF CONGRESS

unknown trespasses: so doth the Lord call us, in a singular manner, upon occasions of such difficulty and danger as lie upon you, to a both more narrow search, and careful reformation, of our ways in his sight, lest he (calling to remembrance our sins forgotten by us, or unrepented of) take advantage against us; and, in judgment, leave us for the same to be swallowed up in one danger or other. Whereas, on the contrary, sin being taken away by earnest repentance, and pardon thereof from the Lord sealed up unto a man's conscience by his Spirit, great shall be his security and peace in all dangers, sweet his comforts in all distresses, with happy deliverance from all evil, whether in life or in death.

Now, next after this heavenly peace with God and our own consciences, we are carefully to provide for peace with all men, what in us lies, especially with our associates: and, for that end, watchfulness must be had, that we neither at all in ourselves do give, no, nor easily take offence being given by others. Woe be unto the World for offences! For though it be necessary (considering the malice of Satan, and man's corruption) that offences come; yet woe unto the man, or woman either, by whom the offence cometh! said Christ (Matt, xviii. 7). And if offences, in the unseasonable use of things in themselves indifferent, be more to be feared than death itself, as the Apostle teaches (I Corinthians ix. 15) how much more in things simply evil, in which neither honor of God, nor love of man, is thought worthy to be regarded. Neither yet is it sufficient that we keep ourselves, by the grace of God, from giving offence; except withal, we be armed against the taking of them, when they are given by others. For how imperfect and lame is the work of grace in that person who wants charity to cover a multitude of offences, as the Scriptures speak. Neither are you to be exhorted to this grace, only upon the common grounds of Christianity, which are, That persons ready to take offence, either want charity to cover offences, or wisdom duly to weigh human frailty; or lastly, are gross, though close, hypocrites, as Christ our Lord teaches (Matthew vii. 1, 2, 8). As indeed, in mine own experience, few or none have been found, which sooner give offence, than such as easily take it; neither have they ever

> "Watchfulness must be had, that we neither at all in ourselves do give, no, nor easily take offence being given by others"

proved sound and profitable members in societies, which have nourished in themselves that touchy humor.

But besides these, there are [various] special motives provoking you, above others, to great care and conscience this way. As, first, you are, many of you, strangers as to the persons so to the infirmities one of another, and so stand in need of more watchfulness this way, lest when such things fall out in men and women as you suspected not, you be inordinately affected with them, which doth require at your hands much wisdom and charity for the covering and preventing of incident offences that way. And, lastly, your intended course of Civil Community will minister continual occasion of offence, and will be as fuel for that fire, except you diligently quench it with brotherly forbearance. And if taking offence causelessly, or easily, at men's doings be so carefully to be avoided, how much more heed is to be taken that we take not offence at God himself, which yet we certainly do, so oft as we do murmur at his Providence in our crosses, or bear impatiently such afflictions as wherewith he pleases to visit us. Store we up therefore patience against the evil day! without which, we take offence at the Lord himself in his holy and just works.

A fourth thing there is carefully to be provided for, to wit, That with common employments, you join common affections truly bent upon the general good, avoiding (as a deadly plague of your both common and special comfort) all [repression] of mind for proper advantage, and all singularly affected any manner of way. Let every man repress in himself, and the whole body, in each person (as so many

> "Store we up therefore patience against the evil day!"

rebels against the common good) all private respects of men's selves not sorting with the general convenience! And as men are careful not to have a new house shaken with any violence before it be well settled, and the parts firmly knit, so be you, I beseech you, brethren, much more careful that the House of God, which you are, and are to be, be not shaken with unnecessary novelties, or other oppositions, at the first settling thereof.

Lastly, whereas you are to become a Body Politic, using amongst yourselves Civil Government, and are not furnished with any persons of special eminency above the rest to be chosen by you into Office of Government, let your wisdom

When his sermon ended, Pastor Robinson led the Pilgrims in prayer as their newly leased ship, the *Speedwell*, prepared to lift anchor.

ARCHITECT OF THE U.S. CAPITOL

123

"My daily
incessant
prayers unto
the Lord
[are that]
He…would
so guide and
guard you"

and godliness appear, not only in choosing such persons as do entirely love, and will diligently promote, the common good; but also in yielding unto them all due honor and obedience in their lawful administrations. Not beholding in them the ordinariness of their persons, but God's ordinance for your good, nor being like unto the foolish multitude, who more honor the gay coat than either the virtuous mind of the man, or glorious ordinance of the Lord. But you know better things, and that the Image of the Lord's power and authority, which the Magistrate bears, is honorable in how mean persons whatsoever. And this duty you both may the more willingly, and ought the more conscionably to perform, because you are, at least for the present, to have only them for your ordinary Governors which yourselves shall make choice of for that work.

Sundry other things of importance I could put you in mind of, and of those before mentioned in more words, but I will not so far wrong your godly minds, as to think you heedless of these things, there being also divers among you so well able to admonish both themselves and others, of what concerns them. These few things, therefore, and the same in few words, I do earnestly commend unto your care and conscience, joining therewith my daily incessant prayers unto the Lord, that He (who hath made the heavens and the earth, the sea and all rivers of water, and whose Providence is over all his works, especially over all his dear children for good) would so guide and guard you in your ways (as inwardly by his Spirit, so outwardly by the hand of his power) as that both you, and we also for and with you, may *have after matter of praising his name, all the days of your, and our, lives.*

Fare you well in him in whom you trust, and in whom I rest!

An unfeigned well-willer of your happy success in this hopeful voyage,

J.R.[5]

CHAPTER SIX

"They Put to Sea Again with a Prosperous Wind"

The *Mayflower* lay anchored at the English port of Southampton. It was the ship that Thomas Weston and the Merchant Adventurers had hired to help transport the Pilgrims to America. When the Leiden Separatists sailed into port aboard the *Speedwell* and caught a first look at the vessel, there was little to impress them other than its size—at 180 tons, the *Mayflower* was much larger than the *Speedwell*. The tonnage of vessels in the day was based upon the number of wine barrels or "tuns" a ship could carry, meaning the *Mayflower* was theoretically able to transport 180 large barrels in its hold, making her about three times the size of the *Speedwell*. Even so, she was likely outsized by other ships in port at Southampton.

When new, the *Mayflower* had been one of the largest merchantmen in England, but now she was fifteen years old and commercial ships had become larger. She bore three masts, and measured about one hundred feet in length from bow to stern and about twenty-five feet across from starboard to port. On the deck, a high forecastle sheltered crew and cargo forward of the ship, with a similar aftcastle in the stern. Although not a military vessel, she was fitted with gun ports like many English merchant ships, and may have carried as many as ten artillery pieces of different calibers. Despite her age, the *Mayflower* was solidly seaworthy, and was well prepared to make a trans-Atlantic voyage to America. So was her commander.[1]

"Beseeching the Lord to Give a Blessing to Our Endeavour"

The Pilgrims Are Introduced to the Mayflower

Christopher Jones was his name, and not only was he the *Mayflower*'s captain or master, he was also one of the ship's owners. About fifty years of age, Jones was a seasoned ship commander—but he had never been to America. He had sailed the *Mayflower* to many other places, however, mainly to and from France,

Awaiting the Pilgrims at the English port of Southampton was a fifteen-year-old 180-ton merchantman. The ship's name: the *Mayflower*.

SHORT HISTORY OF THE UNITED STATES

swapping cargoes of English woolens for imported French wines. He had also taken the ship to Spain, Germany, faraway Norway, and perhaps even on a whaling voyage to the icy waters off Greenland. His master's mate and pilot, a middle-aged seaman named John Clarke, had several voyages to America behind him. His other pilot, sailor Robert Coppin, had also been to America. Back in May, Jones and the

Mayflower had just returned from France with a cargo of wine from Bordeaux when Thomas Weston hired the ship and crew for the Merchant Adventurers to help transport the Pilgrims to America. If Master Jones had reservations about transporting controversial Separatists to distant America aboard the *Mayflower,* he left no record of it. England's economy was rapidly sinking into a severe depression in 1620, and it was no time to turn down business. He had years of deep water sailing behind him, and he was adequately prepared for the voyage to America.

In London, the *Mayflower* had taken on the passengers recruited by the Merchant Adventurers, along with friends and relatives of the Leiden Separatists. Among them were church leaders Robert Cushman and John

The medieval walls of Southampton loom over the port's harbor. It was in Southampton, on the southern coast of England, that the Leiden Separatists first saw the *Mayflower.*

SOUTHAMPTON
MARITIME
ARCHAEOLOGY TRUST

Carver, both of whom had been in England acquiring provisions and dealing with the Adventurers, and now were reunited with their friends from Leiden at the Southampton dock. Located at the junction of the Test and Itchen Rivers on England's southern coast, Southampton was an old city, even by English standards, and was a moderately busy port in 1620. The Separatists from the two ships and some friends from Southampton enjoyed a brief reunion beneath Southampton's Medieval city walls, which towered above the city's docks. William Brewster was there too, although he would keep a low profile until out of England; he was still a hunted man because of the book he had printed that had so offended King James. Brewster had either traveled incognito from Holland or had been in hiding in England. The joy of being reunited with friends and family from England apparently was short-lived, however, since a confrontation quickly erupted between the Leiden leaders and Thomas Weston.

As the official representative of the Merchant Adventurers, Weston had come down from London and immediately launched into a discussion of the new and more demanding terms his investors required of the Pilgrims. Weston likely did not know that to avoid delaying the expedition, Robert Cushman had consented to the new demands without the approval of the Leiden congregation or its leaders. Echoing Pastor Robinson's opinion, the Leideners' spokesmen—presumably Brewster and William Bradford—explained to Weston that the Pilgrims could not agree to the new terms. In response, Weston angrily refused to issue any more funds—including what was needed to leave Southampton. He abruptly ended the discussion by storming off the dock, huffing that the Pilgrims would now have to "stand on their own legs."

Adding to the Pilgrims' frustration and bewilderment, they also had to deal with another disagreeable agent representing the Merchant Adventurers—Christopher Martin, the Adventurers' purchasing agent, who was coming along on the voyage. Already, Martin had rankled

"Those which came over first, in the year 1620 ... were by the blessing of God the first beginners and ... the foundation of all the Plantations and Colonies in New England"

Cushman and Carver as the three had jointly purchased supplies for the voyage. "If I speak to him," Cushman complained, "he flies in my face as mutinous...." Now, as designated by the Merchant Adventurers, Martin was stalking the decks of the *Mayflower* with the title of "governor" of the voyage. He had brought his wife, stepson, and servant with him, and quickly provoked both passengers and crew with his haughty,

The *Mayflower* was a triple-masted vessel measuring about one hundred feet from bow to stern, and had carried cargoes of woolens and wines to ports as far away as Spain and Norway. Despite her age, she was fit for a trans-Atlantic voyage.

WIKIMEDIA COMMONS

quarrelsome manner. He treated everyone with "scorn and contempt," Cushman reported, "as if they were not good enough to wipe his shoes." To raise the funds necessary to leave Southampton without Weston's payoff, the Pilgrims sold a large store of Dutch butter brought from Leiden aboard the *Speedwell*.

At some point before departure, Pastor Robinson's farewell letter was read to the Pilgrims, probably by Brewster or Bradford. Their beloved pastor's advice to "give, no, nor easily take offense" now undoubtedly seemed especially relevant to many. Consequently, two days before sailing, the Pilgrim leaders wrote a conciliatory letter to the Merchant Adventurers, further explaining their opposition to the new terms and concluding with a gesture of friendship. "Thus saluting all of you in love," they wrote, "and beseeching the Lord to give a blessing to our endeavour, and keep all our hearts in the bonds of peace and love, we take leave and rest...." Despite the rancorous atmosphere that marked the launch of the voyage from England, the *Mayflower* and the

By 1620, English merchant vessels often carried a complement of artillery for protection against pirates and other raiders. The *Mayflower*'s artillery would prove useful for the Pilgrims in wilderness America.

WIKIMEDIA COMMONS

"Thus saluting all of you in love, and beseeching the Lord to give a blessing to our endeavour, and keep all our hearts in the bonds of peace and love, we take leave and rest"

Speedwell set sails and left Southampton for America on August 5, 1620. William Bradford would later record a list of the passengers who would actually make the voyage to America:

The names of those which came over first, in the year 1620, and were by the blessing of God the first beginners and (in a sort) the foundation of all the Plantations and Colonies in New England; (and their families).

Mr. John Carver; Katherine his wife; Desire Minter & 2 menservants, John Howland, Roger Wilder; William Latham, a boy, & a maidservant & a child that was put to him called Jasper More.

Mr. William Brewster; Mary, his wife, with 2 sons, whose names were Love & Wrestling; and a boy was put to him called Richard More; and another of his brothers. The rest of his children were left behind & came over afterwards.

Mr. Edward Winslow; Elizabeth his wife; and 2 menservants, called George Soule and Elias Story; also a little girl was put to him called Ellen, the sister of Richard More.

William Bradford and Dorothy his wife, having but one child, a son left behind, who came afterward.

Mr. Isaac Allerton and Mary, his wife; with 3 children, Bartholomew, Remember & Mary. And a servant boy, John Hooke.

Mr. Samuel Fuller, and a servant called William Button. His wife was behind & a child which came afterwards.

John Crackston, and his son, John Crackston.

Captain Myles Standish, and Rose, his wife. Mr. Christopher Martin, and his wife and 2 servants, Solomon Prower and John Langmore.

Mr. William Mullins, and his wife and 2 children, Joseph and Priscilla, and a servant, Robert Carter.

Mr. William White, and Susanna his wife, and one son called Resolved, and one born a-shipboard called Peregrine; and 2 servants named William Holbeck and Edward Thompson.

Mr. Stephen Hopkins & Elizabeth his wife, and 2 children called Giles and Constanta, a daughter, both by a former wife. And two more by this wife called Damaris & Oceanus; the last was born at sea. And 2 servants called Edward Doty and Edward Lester.

Mr. Richard Warren; but his wife and children were left behind and came afterwards.

A Separatist family in prayer at home. Their faith-based worldview failed to impress the representative placed aboard the *Mayflower* by the voyage's investors—who reportedly treated the Separatists "as if they were not good enough to wipe his shoes."

LIBRARY OF CONGRESS

John Billington, and Ellen his wife, and 2 sons, John and Francis.

Edward Tilley, and Ann his wife, and 2 children that were their cousins, Henry Sampson and Humility Cooper.

John Tilley, and his wife; and Elizabeth their daughter.

Francis Cooke, and his son John; But his wife & other children came afterwards.

Thomas Rogers, and Joseph his son. His other children came afterwards.

Thomas Tinker, and his wife and a son.

John Rigsdale, and Alice his wife.

James Chilton, and his wife, and Mary their daughter. They had another daughter that was married, came afterward.

Edward Fuller, and his wife, and Samuel their son.

John Turner, and 2 sons. He had a daughter came some years after to Salem, where she is now living.

Francis Eato, and Sarah his wife, and Samuel their son, a young child.

Moses Fletcher, John Goodman, Thomas Williams, Digory Priest, Edmund Margesson, Peter Browne, Richard Britteridge, Richard Clarke, Richard Gardiner, Gilbert Winslow.

John Alden was hired for a cooper at South-Hampton where the ship victualed; and being a hopeful young man was much desired but left to his own liking to go or stay when he came here; but he stayed and married here.

John Allerton and Thomas English were both hired, the latter to go master of a shallop here, and the other was reputed as one of the company, but was to go back (being a seaman) for the help of others behind. But they both died here, before the ship returned.

There were also other 2 seamen hired to stay a year here in the country, William Trevor, and one Ely. But when their time was out, they both returned.

These, being about a hundred souls, came over in this first ship and began this work; which God of His goodness hath hitherto blessed; let His holy name have the praise.[2]

"These, being about a hundred souls, came over in this first ship and began this work"

"Who Shall Be Meat First for the Fishes"

The Voyage to America Stalls Offshore England

Robert Cushman was ready to quit and go back home. It was August 17, 1620—almost two weeks since the *Speedwell* and the *Mayflower* had left Southampton—and both ships and their passengers were still in England. Negotiating with Weston and the Merchant Adventurers had been exasperating for Cushman, who had been unable to please either the colony's backers or his fellow Separatists in Leiden. Purchasing supplies for the voyage had been equally frustrating, thanks to the arrogant and belligerent Christopher Martin, who—happily for Cushman—was sailing with his family aboard the *Mayflower*, while Cushman was berthed aboard the *Speedwell*. Cushman's days aboard the *Speedwell*, however, proved even more frustrating than dealing with Martin and Weston: the *Speedwell* was in danger of sinking.

Soon after passing the chalky white cliffs of the Isle of Wight—off England's southern coast—the *Speedwell* sprang serious leaks in her hull. The vessel was as "open and leaky as a sieve," Cushman observed, and

On August 5, 1620, the *Mayflower* and the *Speedwell* set sail from Southampton, bound for America.

AMERICAN BOOK COMPANY

the amount of water spewing into the ship reminded him of a leaking dike in Holland. If the ship "had stayed at sea but three or four hours more," Cushman believed, "she would have sunk right down." The *Speedwell* and the *Mayflower* had turned into the mouth of the Dart River and sailed upstream to the port of Dartmouth, just over a hundred nautical miles from Southampton, and there they put in to make repairs to the *Speedwell*. The contention and delays left Cushman distraught.

As a deacon and the church's business agent in London, he took his responsibilities seriously. He too planned to make the voyage to America, accompanied by his second wife and his son. However, he now believed that the stress of organizing the expedition—compounded by delay due to the *Speedwell*'s leaks—had ruined his health. "What to call it I know not," he confided to a friend, "but it is a bundle of lead, as it were, crushing my heart more and more.... I am as but dead, but the will of God be done."

Shipwrights at Dartmouth repaired the *Speedwell*, but unfavorable winds kept both ships in port day after day. Aboard the *Mayflower*, some of the passengers wanted to abandon the voyage, but Christopher Martin—the "governor"—would not let anyone leave the ship. Finally, the wind shifted and the ships were able to leave port. They sailed downriver from Dartmouth between the high ridges that flanked the Dart River estuary, and, on their starboard side, passed beneath the looming towers and protruding cannon of Dartmouth Castle, which had protected the entrance to Dartmouth for more than two hundred years. Finally, the two ships cleared the estuary, and entered open sea. They passed Lizard Point, a peninsula in Cornwall that was the southernmost point of the English mainland, and turned westward for America.

Then, well into the Atlantic, some three hundred miles past Lizard Point, the *Speedwell* again sprung leaks, and these were even worse. Furious pumping by the crew did no good, and the *Speedwell*'s master signaled to the *Mayflower* that his ship again needed to return to port— that she "must bear up or sink." Reducing speed appeared to slow the

Soon after passing the high cliffs of the Isle of Wight, the *Speedwell* sprang several leaks in her hull, causing the ship and the *Mayflower* to turn back.

WIKIMEDIA
COMMONS

leaks, so the *Speedwell* was able to limp back to England, accompanied by the *Mayflower*. This time they put into the port of Plymouth, which lay about thirty-five nautical miles west of Dartmouth. There, it was decided that the *Speedwell* was too unreliable for the trans-Atlantic voyage. Later, William Bradford would hear rumors that on the eve of the voyage the *Speedwell*'s master had purposely over-masted the ship—intentionally mounting new masts that were so large that they forced the ship to leak at cruising speed, causing the voyage to be abandoned. If true, the ploy was a manageable risk: the ship could safely return to port at reduced speed, and the leaking allowed the master to abandon the voyage and his obligation to remain in America for a year. There was no conclusive evidence of such a plot, but Bradford believed the leaks were intentionally caused "by the cunning and deceit of the master and company."

The *Speedwell* and the *Mayflower* put into the port of Dartmouth, which was located at the mouth of the Dart River. There, the *Speedwell* underwent repairs.

BRITISH LIBRARY

At Plymouth, the Pilgrims decided to cram as many passengers as possible onto the *Mayflower* and go on to America with the single ship. The *Mayflower* could not hold all the passengers, but some no longer wished to continue: the contention, leaks, and delays had discouraged them. Seeing their numbers reduced even more, William Bradford was reminded of the biblical story of Gideon, who was granted great success after God thinned the ranks of his followers. "And thus," Bradford concluded, "like Gideon's army, this small number was divided, as if the Lord by this work of His providence thought these few too many for the great work He had to do."

One who chose to remain behind was Robert Cushman. By now, the expedition should have been halfway across the Atlantic, he believed, and he considered it nothing short of arrogant to continue in the face of such setbacks. It was a voyage "full of crosses," in his words, and he was certain that if he remained with the expedition, he would become "meat first for the fishes." In the future, Cushman would again assist the Pilgrims in mighty ways—but not this way: he and his wife and son would stay in England. In a letter to a friend while the expedition was docked in Dartmouth, he had shared his frustrations:

Dartmouth, August 17

LOVING FRIEND, my most kind remembrance to you and your wife, with loving E.M. etc., whom in this world I never look to see again. For besides the eminent dangers of this voyage, which are no less than deadly, an infirmity of body hath seized me, which will not in all likelihood leave me till death. What to call it I know not, but it is a bundle of lead, as it were, crushing my heart more and more these fourteen days; as that although I do the actions of a living man, yet I am but as dead, but the will of God be done. Our pinnace will not cease leaking, else I think we had been half-way to Virginia. Our voyage hither hath been as full of crosses as ourselves have been of crookedness. We put in here to trim her; and I think, as others also, if we had stayed at sea but three or four hours more, she would have sunk right down. And though she was twice trimmed at Hampton, yet now she is as open and leaky as a sieve; and there was a board a man might have pulled off with his fingers, two foot long, where the water came in as at a mole hole.

"Our pinnace will not cease leaking.... she is as open and leaky as a sieve"

"Our victuals will be half eaten up, I think, before we go from the coast of England"

A wrecked ship is pounded by waves on the shore of the English Channel. The Pilgrims and the crews of their two ships understood the dangers of the open seas—and took the *Speedwell* back into port when she continued leaking.

WIKIMEDIA COMMONS

We lay at Hampton seven days in fair weather, waiting for her, and now we lie here waiting for her in as fair a wind as can blow, and so have done these four days, and are like to lie four more, and by that time the wind will happily turn as it did at Hampton. Our victuals will be half eaten up, I think, before we go from the coast of England, and if our voyage last long, we shall not have a month's victuals when we come in the country. Near £700 hath been bestowed at Hampton, upon what I know not; Mr. Martin said he neither can nor will give any account of it, and if he be called upon for accounts, he cried out of unthankfulness for his pains and care, that we are suspicious of him, and flings away, and will end nothing. Also he so insulteth over our poor people, with such scorn and contempt, as if they were not good enough to wipe his shoes. It would break your heart to see his dealings, and the mourning of our people; they complain to me, and alas! I can do nothing for them. If I speak to him, he flies in

my face as mutinous, and says no complaints shall be heard or received but by himself, and says they are forward and waspish, discontented people, and I do ill to hear them.

There are others that would lose all they have put in, or make satisfaction for what they have had, that they might depart; but he will not hear them, nor suffer them to go ashore, lest they should run away. The sailors are so offended at his ignorant boldness in meddling and controlling in things he knows not what belongs to, as that some threaten to mischief him; others say they will leave the ship and go their way. But at the best this cometh of it, that he makes himself a scorn and laughing stock unto them. As for Mr. Weston, except grace do greatly sway him, he will hate us ten times more than ever he loved us, for not confirming the conditions. But now, since some pinches have taken them, they begin to revile the truth and say Mr. Robinson was in the fault who charged them never to consent to those conditions, nor choose me into office; but indeed appointed them to choose them they did choose. But he and they will rue too late, they may now see, and all be ashamed when it is too late, that they were so ignorant; yea and so inordinate in their courses. I am sure as they were resolved not to seal those conditions, I was not so resolute at Hampton to have left the whole business, except they would seal them, and better the voyage to have been broken off then than to have brought such misery to ourselves, dishonor to God and detriment to our living friends, as now it is like to do. Four or five of the chief of them which came from Leyden, came resolved never to go on those conditions.

And Mr. Martin, he said he never received no money on those conditions; he was not beholden to the merchants for a

At Plymouth, it was decided that the *Speedwell* was not seaworthy, and that the *Mayflower* would continue the voyage with as many passengers as possible. Some families, however, gave up the quest and chose to remain in England.

STORIES OF THE PILGRIMS

pin, they were bloodsuckers, and I know not what. Simple man, he indeed never made any conditions with the merchants, nor ever spoke with them. But did all that money fly at Hampton, or was it his own? Who will go and lay out money so rashly and lavishly as he did, and never know how he comes by it or on what conditions? Secondly, I told him of the alteration long ago and he was content, but now he domineers and said I had betrayed them into the hands of slaves; he is not beholden to them, he can set out two ships himself to a voyage. When, good man? He hath but £50 in and if he should give up his accounts he would not have a penny left him, as I am persuaded, etc.

Friend, if ever we make a plantation, God works a miracle, especially considering how scant we shall be of victuals, and most of all ununited amongst ourselves and devoid of good tutors and regiment. Violence will break all. Where is the meek and humble spirit of Moses? And of Nehemiah, who re-edified the walls of Jerusalem, and the state of Israel? Is *not the sound of Rehoboam's brags daily here amongst us? Have not the philosophers and all the wise men observed that, even in settled commonwealths, violent governors bring either themselves or people or both to ruin? How much more in the raising of commonwealths, when the mortar is yet scarce tempered that should bind the walls!*

If I should write to you of all things which promiscuously forerun our ruin, I should over-charge my weak head and grieve your tender heart. Only this, I pray you prepare for evil tidings of us every day. But pray for us instantly, it may be the Lord will be yet entreated one way or other to make for us. I see not in reason how we shall escape even the gaspings of hunger-starved persons; but God can do much, and His will be done. It is better for me to die than now for me to bear it, which I do daily and expect it hourly, having received the sentence of death both within me and without me. Poor William Ring and myself do strive who shall be meat first for the fishes; but we look for a glorious resurrection, knowing Christ Jesus after the flesh no more, but looking unto the joy that is before us, we will endure all these things and account them light in comparison of that joy we hope for. Remember me in all love to our friends as if I named them, whose prayers I desire earnestly and wish again to see, but not till I can with more comfort look them in the face. The Lord give us that true comfort which none can take from us.

I had a desire to make a brief relation of our estate to some friend. I doubt not but your wisdom will teach you seasonably to utter things as hereafter you shall be called to it. That which I have written is true, and many things more which I have forborn. I write it as upon my life, and last

"Like Gideon's army, this small number was divided"

confession in England. What is of use to be spoken presently, you may speak of it; and what is fit to conceal, conceal. Pass by my weak manner, for my head is weak, and my body feeble. The Lord make me strong in Him, and keep both you and yours.

Your loving friend,
Robert Cushman
August 17, 1620[3]

❖——————❖

"They Put to Sea again with a Prosperous Wind"

Despite False Starts, the Pilgrims Go to Sea

On Wednesday, September 6, 1620, the *Mayflower* weighed anchor at dockside in Plymouth, and sailed into sprawling Plymouth Sound with a blustery wind filling her sails. The *Speedwell* and twenty would-be Pilgrims were heading back to London, and the *Mayflower* was heading on to America. The port of Plymouth was located on the edge of Plymouth Sound, at the junction of the Tamar and Plym Rivers. The *Mayflower* sailed across the wide-open sound, passing the fortifications on St. Nicholas's Island, the towering bluffs of Staddon Point, and the high, craggy bluffs of the Rame Peninsula. A generation before the *Mayflower*'s passage, the famous English privateers Francis Drake and John Hawkins had gone forth on the same waters to raid the riches of Spain. So had the ships of Sir Walter Raleigh, bound for his ill-fated attempt to colonize Virginia. Over these waters too, in 1588, had come the news of England's nation-changing defeat of the fearsome Spanish Armada—an event celebrated annually in the Pilgrims' day by the ringing of Plymouth's church bells. Here too, in 1403, a deadly flotilla of French ships from Bretagne brought a horde of raiders who had ransacked Plymouth and afterwards burned it to the ground.

On September 6, 1620, the *Mayflower* set sail from Plymouth, England, bound for faraway America with more than one hundred passengers aboard.

HISTORY OF THE UNITED STATES

Now, propelled by "a fine small gale," the *Mayflower* cut a sharp white wake through the deep waters of Plymouth Sound, again reentered the open sea, and headed westward. Two weeks had been lost in Plymouth, but the Pilgrim leaders may have salvaged something of value from the delay. Plymouth had long been England's principal departure point for the New World, and offered a rare opportunity for the Pilgrims to gain important insights. Among the sailors and officers striding about Plymouth's docks were numerous seafarers who had been to America, harvesting great hauls of codfish from its offshore waters, exploring its bays and inlets, or transporting colonists to Virginia. It was probably there in Plymouth that the Pilgrim leaders met the famous Captain John Smith, who had saved the mismanaged Jamestown colonists from disaster and death, and who had mapped and named portions of the American coast. Smith would later write of an encounter with the Pilgrim leaders, and Plymouth was a likely place for the meeting.

Captain John Smith was by then one of England's foremost celebrities. He had produced a well-circulated map of the New World, and had recently fascinated English readers with a published memoir of his adventures in the New World. Entitled *A Description of New England: Observations and Discoveries in the North of America*, it was a dramatic, rambling, and self-promotional work, but was replete with detailed insights about the American wilderness. Their meeting with Smith afforded the Pilgrim leaders an invaluable opportunity to gain

It may have been while docked for repairs in Plymouth that Pilgrim leaders met with English explorer John Smith, who had explored America's northern coast. Smith later claimed that the Pilgrims had unwisely turned down his offer to accompany them to the New World.

WIKIMEDIA COMMONS

advice from England's foremost expert on the New World—and it also resulted in a surprising offer. Apparently eager for another odyssey, the forty-year-old adventurer volunteered to join the Pilgrims on their voyage to America—at least that was the story Smith later reported. To his surprise, the Pilgrim leaders turned him down—no doubt for reasons that seemed prudent to them. They already had a military commander aboard—Captain Myles Standish—and after selling their butter and other wares to clear Southampton, they surely had no money to hire the famous explorer—although they did buy a copy of his book. They also may have been wary of Smith's forceful, commanding personality, and mindful that in his book's dedication he had declared himself to be a "true and faithful servant" of the English monarchy, and thus was no friend to Separatists and other dissenters from the Church of England.

About that, the Pilgrims were correct. In another memoir published nine years later, Smith dismissed them as "Brownists" and derided them for what he called their "humorous ignorance." Obviously ruffled by their rejection of his services, he grumped that the Pilgrims "had to endure a wonderful deal of misery" because they concluded "that my books and maps were much better cheap to teach them, than myself." Armed with what they believed to be adequate preparation and the "special work of God's providence," the Pilgrims again sailed westward into the deep waters of the Atlantic. "These troubles being blown over," William Bradford wrote, "and now more compact together in one ship, they put to sea again with a prosperous wind...." As the *Mayflower* passed Lizard's Point once more, did the Pilgrims go topside and watch England's receding coast disappear over the horizon? And, as they found themselves surrounded with nothing but the expanse of ocean, did they ponder Captain Smith's description of Virginia and "the North of America" as recorded in *A Description of New England*?

Virginia is no isle, as many do imagine, but part of the continent adjoining to Florida, whose bounds may be stretched to the magnitude thereof without offense to any Notes of Christian inhabitant. For, from the degrees of 30 to 45, his majesty hath granted his letters patent, the coast extending southwest and northeast about fifteen hundred miles, but to follow it aboard the shore may well be two thousand at the least, of which twenty miles is the most gives entrance into the Bay of Chesapeake, where is the London plantation, within which is a country (as you may perceive by the description in a book and map printed in my name of that little I there discovered), may well suffice three hundred thousand people to inhabit....

"And now more compact together in one ship, they put to sea again with a prosperous wind"

A few years before the Pilgrims sailed for America, John Smith had published a map of New England based on his exploration. The Pilgrims apparently carried Smith's book and map with them to America, but their decision not to employ Smith caused him to deride them for what he called "humorous ignorance."

WIKIMEDIA COMMONS

The route of the Pilgrims' voyage from Holland to England and into the Atlantic—with their repeated false starts—placed them in three ports in southern England before their final departure.

MAP BY
AMBER COLLERAN

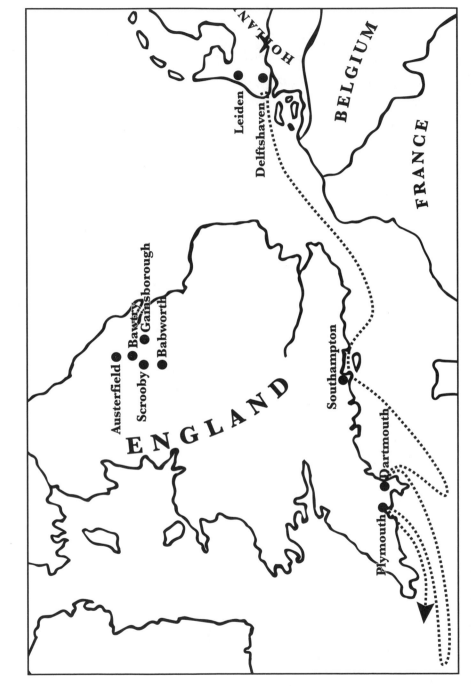

Thus, you may see, of this two thousand miles more than half is yet unknown to any purpose, no, not so much as the borders of the sea are yet certainly discovered. As for the goodness and true substances of the land, we are for most part yet altogether ignorant of them, unless it be those parts about the Bay of Chesapeake and Sagadahoc, but only here and there we touched or have seen a little the edges of those large dominions which do stretch themselves into the main, God doth know how many thousand miles....

That part we call New England is betwixt the degrees of 41 and 45, but that part this discourse speaks of stretches from Penobscot to Cape Cod, some seventy-five leagues by a right line distant each from other, description of within which bounds I have seen at least forty several habitations upon the sea coast, and sounded about twenty-five excellent good harbors, in many whereof there is anchorage for five hundred sail of ships, in some of them for five thousand; and more than two hundred isles overgrown with good timber of divers sorts of wood, which do make so many harbors as requires a longer time than I had to be well discovered....

Betwixt Sagadahoc and Sowocatuc there are but two or three sandy bays, but betwixt that and Cape Cod very many; especially the coast of the Massachusetts is so indifferently mixed with high clayey or sandy cliffs in one place, and then tracts of large, long ledges of divers sorts, and quarries of stone in other places so strangely divided with tinctured veins of divers colors, as freestone for building, slate for tiling, smooth stone to make furnaces and forges for glass or iron,

"Not so much as the borders of the sea are yet certainly discovered"

"Could I have
but means
to transport
a colony, I
would rather
live here than
anywhere"

and iron ore sufficient conveniently to melt in them; but the most part so resembles the coast of Devonshire, I think most of the cliffs would make such limestone…. And of all the four parts of the world that I have yet seen not inhabited, could I have but means to transport a colony, I would rather live here than anywhere….

This is only as God made it when he created the world. Therefore I conclude, if the heart and entrails of those regions were sought, if their land were cultivated, planted, and manured by men of industry, judgment, and experience, what hope is there, or what need they doubt, having those advantages of the sea, but it might equalize any of those famous kingdoms, in all commodities, pleasures, and conditions; seeing even the very edges do naturally afford us such plenty, as no ship need return away empty, and only use but the season of the sea, fish will return an honest gain, besides all other advantages, her treasures having yet never been opened, nor her originals wasted, consumed, nor abused….[4]

"Biscuit," "Thwart Saws," and "Black Oakum"

The Pilgrims Pack the Mayflower *for a One-Way Voyage*

Not only did the crowded *Mayflower* have to transport crew and passengers across the stormy northern Atlantic, it was also loaded with rations for the voyage, the Pilgrims' carefully selected personal possessions, and a cargo of tools, equipment, and supplies deemed necessary for setting up life in the wilderness and for engaging in a fur and fishing trade. If the *Mayflower* carried a cargo manifest, it was lost over the passage of time, but a list of tools, equipment, and supplies bound for a colony in Newfoundland a few years later did survive, and it likely lists much of what accompanied the Pilgrims to America. The Pilgrims probably equipped themselves with rations ranging from biscuits (which had a long shelf-life)—to beer (a staple of

A woodcutter at work on a tree. The Pilgrims had to bring tools aboard the *Mayflower* to make a new life in the wilderness of America.

WIKIMEDIA COMMONS

the English dict due to the lack of safe drinking water), along with butter, peas, cheese, and aqua-vitae (a survival drink made of distilled wine or brandy). The tools needed to hack out a new life in the American wilderness likely would have included hammers, nails, axes, mattocks, and thwart-saws (the period name for a cross-cut saw). Based on the cargo list for the Newfoundland colony, the equipment stowed aboard the *Mayflower* by the Pilgrims probably included kettles, frying pans, pots, platters, ladles, bread-baskets, and flaskets (a long, shallow clothesbasket). Nautical equipment brought along to be used in the Pilgrims' fishing trade may have included orlop nails (used in repairing a ship's lower deck), canvas necessary for repairs, seine nets, fishing hooks and lines, sow lead (a wedge of lead for making weights), and black oakum (ship's calking made from linen).

Excerpted below is the list from the early seventeenth-century Newfoundland expedition:

Dutch children tote jugs of milk in the wintertime. A variety of containers used in everyday life had to be transported with the passengers aboard the *Mayflower*.

STORIES OF THE PILGRIMS

10,000 *weight of biscuit*

2 *Hogsheads of English beef*

Fat hogs, salted with salt, and casks

2 *Firkins of butter*

1 *Bushel of mustard*

15 *Wood to dress meat withal*

2 *Small kettles*

34 *Platters, ladles, and cans*

26 *Taps, borers, and funnels*

100 *Weight of candles*

Mats and dunnage

Particulars for the persons aboard

Keep 8 fishing boats at sea with 3 men to boat

Canvas to make boat-fails and small ropes

4000 *Nails*

500 *Weight of pitch*

Other small necessaries

200 *Weight of black oakum*

26 *Tuns of beer and cider*

2 *Hogsheads of Irish beef*

30 *Bushels of peas*

200 *Weight of cheese*

1 *Hogshead of vinegar*

1 *Great copper kettle*

2 *Frying-pans*

A pair of bellows for the cook

Locks for the bread-rooms

130 *Quarters of salt*

Salt shovels

500 *feet of elm boards 1-inch thick*

10 *Rod ropes*

2000 *Nails for the 8 boats*

2000 *orlop nails*

Twine for Kipnets and gagging hooks

A barrel of tar

100 *Thrums for pitch maps*

16 Bowls, buckets, and
   pumps
12 Dozen fishing hooks
Squid line
Iron works for the
   boats' rudders
10 good nets
200 weight of sow-lead
100 Dry-fats to
   keep them in
Flaskets and
   bread-baskets

Canvas for boat-fails and
   small ropes
24 Dozen of fishing hooks
Pots and liver maunds
10 Kipnet irons

2 Seines, a great and a less
Couple of ropes for the seines
Twine for store

Hair cloth

An English mother bakes bread in the kitchen of her cottage. Possessions taken to the New World in the 1600s typically included pots, pans, platters, ladles, and bread-baskets.

BRITISH LIBRARY

A cutaway image of a period galley reveals the amount of cargo stored in the ship's hold. Passenger cargo had to be stowed carefully aboard the *Mayflower*, which carried a full capacity of passengers.

WIKIMEDIA COMMONS

3 Tuns of vinegar
  cask for water
2 Barrels of oatmeal
2 Good axes
3 Yards of woolen cloth
  for cuffs
A Grindstone or two

1 Hogshead of aqua-vitæ
4 hand saws
3 augers
3 fledges
2 pick-axes
4 hammers

1 Dozen deal boards

100 Weight of spikes
4 drawers, 2 drawing irons
8 Yards of good canvas

2000 of poor-john to spend
  in going
4 arm saws
4 thwart saws
2 crows of iron
4 shod shovels
4 mattocks
4 hand-hatchets

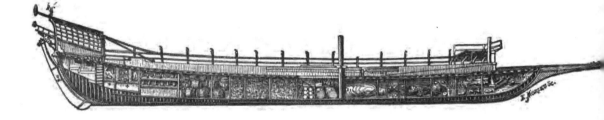

As the *Mayflower* sailed into open waters and headed westward, the Pilgrims were already in trouble. They were now two months behind schedule, and ahead of them lay two more months on the dangerous north Atlantic.[5]

CHAPTER SEVEN

"They…Encountered…
Many Fierce Storms"

Ferocious, stormy seas battered the *Mayflower* with giant waves, sending foaming seawater splashing over its decks, while sheets of wind-driven rain pelted the stricken ship relentlessly. Halfway between England and America, the *Mayflower* was caught in a deadly North Atlantic gale, which threatened to sink the ship and drown its passengers and crew. Although the voyage had begun with fair weather and "a prosperous wind," about a thousand miles into its three-thousand-mile voyage the ship was slammed by a series of furious, deadly storms. According to William Bradford, "the ship was [severely] shaken, and her upper works were made very leaky."

In a violent gale, even a 180-ton vessel like the *Mayflower* could be rendered helpless by the mighty North Atlantic. Mammoth, billowing waves could hurl a ship upward toward a foamy, watery peak and then send it plunging downward through a chasm of waves to what appeared to be certain destruction. At one point, caught in the violent vortex of gale-force winds and seas, the *Mayflower* appeared to be facing its end.

Waves rolled over the decks, seawater seeped through the vessel's hull, and then—to the horror of passengers and crew—the massive interior wooden beam supporting the *Mayflower*'s deck began to crack.[1]

❖———————❖

"Swallowed Up by the Sea"

The Fierce Atlantic Demonstrates Its Violent Nature

A thousand miles across the Atlantic, the *Mayflower* was pummeled by a series of furious storms that threatened to end the Pilgrim colony before it could begin.

AMERICAN BOOK COMPANY

A s the *Mayflower* was dangerously pounded by wind and waves, the Pilgrims aboard may have thought about the fate of General Humphrey Gilbert, whose ship—the *Hind*—and all aboard were lost in an Atlantic storm in 1583. Gilbert, half-brother of explorer Sir Walter Raleigh, had led a five-ship flotilla from England to North America, where he had attempted to establish a colony in Newfoundland. On his return voyage, he had rashly sailed his ship into an Atlantic gale. In seas like those that battered the *Mayflower*, Gilbert and his ship were lost with all aboard.

Details of the general's death at sea were common knowledge among the English people in 1620, and his story was undoubtedly familiar to the Pilgrims. As the *Mayflower* was buffeted by the fierce Atlantic, did they think about Gilbert and what befell him in the same ocean? His fate, which easily could have befallen the Pilgrims, was recorded by one of his officers:

❖———————❖

I will hasten to the end of this tragedy, which must be knit up in the person of our General.

And as it was God's ordinance upon him, even so the vehement persuasion and entreaty of his friends could nothing avail to divert him from a willful resolution of going through [the storm] in his frigate, which was overcharged upon their decks with fights, nettings, and small artillery, too cumbersome for so small a boat, that was to pass through the ocean sea at that season of the year, when by course we might expect much storm [and] foul weather, whereof indeed we had enough.

But when he was entreated by the captain, master and others…not to venture out in the frigate, this was his answer: "I will not forsake my little company going homeward, with whom I have passed so many storms and perils." And in very truth, he was urged on by hard reports given of him that he was afraid of the sea, albeit this was rather rashness…to prefer the wind of a vain report to the weight of his own life.

Seeing he would not bend to reason, he had provisions out of the Hind such as was wanting aboard his frigate. And so we committed him to God's protection, and set him aboard his ship, we being more than 300 leagues onward of our way home. By that time we had brought the Islands of Azores south of us, yet we then keeping much to the north, until we had got into the height and elevation of England, we met with very foul weather and terrible seas, breaking short and high…as we see hills and dales upon the land….

However it came to pass, men which all their lifetime had occupied the sea never saw more outrageous seas. We had

"Men which all their lifetime had occupied the sea never saw more outrageous seas"

Sir Humphrey Gilbert

TORONTO PUBLIC LIBRARY

157

Period illustration of Humphrey Gilbert's flagship, the *Golden Hind*, which sank in an Atlantic storm. As they endured their own stormy ordeal, did the Pilgrims think about Gilbert and his lost ship?

WIKIMEDIA COMMONS

"Suddenly her lights were out"

also upon our mainyard, an apparition of a little fire by night, which seamen do call Castor and Pollux. But we had only one, which they take an evil sign of more tempest: the same is usual in storms Monday the ninth of September, in the afternoon, [General Gilbert's] frigate was near cast away, oppressed by waves, yet at that time it recovered, giving forth signs of joy. The General, sitting [in the stern] with a book in his hand, cried out to us in the Hind, "We are as near to heaven by sea as by land," [which was] speech well becoming a soldier resolute in Jesus Christ, as I can testify he was.

The same Monday night, about twelve of the clock, or not long after, the frigate being ahead of us in the Golden Hind, suddenly her lights were out. Whereof, as it were in a moment, we lost the sight and our watch cried that the General was cast away, which was too true. For in that moment, the frigate was devoured and swallowed up by the sea.[2]

"This Disease Is Very Often Deadly"

The Pilgrims Face the Threat of Shipboard Killers

Unlike General Gilbert's ship, the *Mayflower* survived its close brush with disaster in the stormy Atlantic—thanks to savvy seamanship, Pilgrim ingenuity, and—in William Bradford's words—"the will of God." As the *Mayflower*'s main beam began to buckle, threatening to disable and perhaps even sink the ship, Captain Jones desperately conferred with key crew members and the Pilgrim leaders. Together, they conceived an ingenious plan to keep the main beam from buckling. The Pilgrims had stowed a peculiar device aboard the *Mayflower*—something Bradford would later describe as "a great iron screw." Historians would later ponder its purpose. Was it part of a printing press, brought to America to print Separatist literature or Bibles? Or was it a simple house jack, prudently hauled to the New World to help the Pilgrims build homes in the wilderness? Whatever its purpose, the "great iron screw" was wedged under the long interior beam where it was splitting and was secured by the ship's carpenter, preventing the beam from buckling.

At one point in the voyage, when high seas and strong winds made sailing impossible, Captain Jones decided to put the *Mayflower* "to hull"—furling the ship's sails, tying down everything on deck and then securing the ship's helm leeward or downwind. The nautical maneuver, skillfully executed by Jones, steadied the ship amid the violent, rolling seas. Although the ship had been "shrewdly shaken, and her upper works made very leaky," the tactic allowed the *Mayflower* to easily ride out the storm. "So they committed themselves to the will of God…," Bradford observed.

To steady the *Mayflower* in the Atlantic's high stormy seas, the *Mayflower*'s master put the ship "to hull"—an extreme maneuver designed to save a ship in a killer storm.

HALLWYL MUSEUM

Although spared widespread death on the voyage across the Atlantic, many of the Pilgrims suffered continuously with seasickness, and the many delays had depleted their food supply.

AMERICAN BOOK COMPANY

If they survived their long voyage across the stormy North Atlantic, the Pilgrims faced other deadly perils en route to America—including deadly shipboard illnesses. Dying aboard ship on a long sea voyage was more than just a possibility in the early seventeenth century; it was a common fate— and the Pilgrims knew it. Passengers on some New World expeditions had died in droves, and so had ships' crews. Smallpox and tuberculosis killed countless passengers on the high seas, but the most common death-dealing diseases aboard ship were scurvy and the bloody flux. Scurvy was a progressive disease caused by a severe deficiency of vitamin C. By 1620, seasoned ship commanders were learning to avoid the illness among crews by issuing lemons and oranges, but the illness was still a notorious killer. A few decades before the *Mayflower*'s voyage, another Atlantic traveler—Englishman Thomas Stevens—wrote his father a letter in which he recorded a graphic eyewitness account of how scurvy affected those aboard his ship:

After most humble commendations to crave your daily blessings, with the commendations unto my mother—

On the 4ᵗʰ of April, five ships departed, wherein, besides shipmen and soldiers there were a great number of children, which in the seas bear out better than men, and no marvel, many women also pass very well. Notwithstanding when it should please God, it pleased his mercy suddenly to fill our sails with wind.…

The 29th of July.… And by reason of the long navigation, and want of food and water, [our passengers and crew] fall into sundry diseases. Their gums wax great and swell, and they are fain to cut them away.

Their legs swell and all the body becomes sore and so benumbed that they cannot stir hand nor foot, and so they die of weakness. Others fall into fluxes and agues and die thereby. Yet, though we had more than one hundred and fifty sick, there died not past twenty-seven; which loss they esteemed not much in respect of other voyages.

Though some of ours were diseased in this sort, yet thanks be to God, I had my health all the way, contrary to the expectation of many.

Now this shall suffice for the time. If God send me my health, I shall have opportunity to write once again. Now…I wish you the most prosperous health.

Your loving son,
Thomas Stevens[3]

"Their legs swell and all the body becomes sore"

"They cannot stir hand nor foot, and so they die of weakness"

The bloody flux was severe dysentery caused by an inflammation of the intestines. It was marked by intense intestinal pain—"gripes" in the medical language of the day—along with bloody diarrhea and dehydration. Victims often grew increasingly weak, then died. The deadly malady was described in grim detail by a seventeenth-century English physician:

In this seventeenth-century engraving, a valiant caregiver tries in vain to save hopeless victims of the bloody flux. On a long ocean voyage, scurvy and the bloody flux could kill off passengers and entire crews.

RIJKSMUSEUM OF AMSTERDAM

"There are always great tortures ... and pain"

Sometimes it begins with shaking and shivering, and a heat of the whole body follows, as is usual in fevers, and soon after the gripes and stools. But oftentimes there is no appearance of a fetter before the gripes begin, and stools soon follow. There are always great tortures and a depression of the bowels, and pain when the sick goes to stool. The Stools are likewise frequent, with a very troublesome descent, as it were, of the guts; and they are all mucous.... These mucous stools are streaked with blood, but sometimes there is no blood at all mixed with them through the whole course of the disease. Yet notwithstanding, if the stools are frequent with gripes and a mucous filth, the disease may as properly be called a dysentery.

Moreover, the sick, if he is in the flower of his age or has been heated by cordials, has a fever and his tongue is covered thick with a kind of whitish mucilage, and if he is much heated it is black and dry. The strength is much dejected, the spirits are dissipated and all the signs of an ill-fated fever are present. And this disease does not only cause violent pains and sickness, but unless it is skillfully treated, it endangers the patient's life…for when a many of the spirits and a great deal of the vital heat have been exhausted by these frequent stools, he will be in danger of dying.

And if he should escape death at this time, yet many symptoms of a different kind attend the poor man. For instance, sometimes in the progress of the disease…. the greater vessels of the intestines are corroded, and so the patient is in danger

of death; and sometimes also by reason of the great burning…the intestines are gangrened. Moreover, a thirst at the end of this disease does very often affect the mouth and jaws, especially when the body has been a long time heated.…But though this disease is very often deadly in the adult, and especially to old people, yet 'tis very gentle in children,

"And if he should escape death at this time, yet many symptoms of a different kind attend the poor man"

Despite stormy seas and recurring seasickness, the Pilgrims managed to endure their long season at sea with the loss of a single life. They may have been spared the common shipboard diseases because of their discipline and careful hygiene.

RIJKSMUSEUM OF AMSTERDAM

*who sometimes have it some months without any injury, if it
be left to nature.*[4]

◆――――――――◆

"Many Were Afflicted with Seasickness"

The Pilgrims Endure a Hard Passage across the Atlantic

Camped day after day in dim, makeshift quarters between decks
aboard the *Mayflower*, the Pilgrims were ideal targets for the
bloody flux, scurvy, and other common shipboard killers.
Remarkably, they escaped the widespread death that so often spread
through passenger quarters on long voyages. Perhaps they maintained
better hygiene in their quarters than typical ships' passengers, and were
more disciplined about emptying their toilets into the sea. Or, as some
historians would later speculate, did the *Mayflower*'s long service as a
merchant vessel hauling French wines to England produce enough
alcohol-laced spillage to somehow make the ship's planking antiseptic?
Whatever the reasons, their voyage aboard the *Mayflower* was surpris-
ingly free of death. One passenger died at sea. His name was William
Butten, an apprentice, who was believed to have been about fifteen
years old.

The Pilgrims counted 102 passengers aboard the *Mayflower*,
including three pregnant women. They were composed of twenty-four
families, which included fifteen families from Holland and the rest
from England. Among their ranks were sixty-nine adults—fifty men
and nineteen women—along with fourteen teenage youths, and nineteen children aged twelve or younger. Counting the unborn children,
there were 105 passengers, including an infant born on the voyage who
was appropriately named "Oceanus." Most of the adults were under
age forty.

Although Christopher Martin was the *Mayflower*'s "governor" and represented the interests of the Merchant Adventurers, he and the other non-Separatists—the "Strangers"—were not the driving force among the Pilgrims, even though they may have been a numerical majority. The group's direction and motivation came from the fifteen families from Holland—the Leiden Separatists—along with the other Separatists who had joined the expedition in England. It was their vision and leadership that had launched this daring mission into the American wilderness, and they would continue to set its course even though their numbers were at least equaled by the "Strangers."

The occupations represented among the Pilgrims included merchants, textile workers, tailors, servants, seamen, homemakers, and at least one carpenter, printer, physician, blacksmith, tanner, cobbler, hatmaker, cooper, sawyer, and soldier. The soldier was Myles Standish, the Pilgrims' military commander, who had joined the voyage with his wife Rose. In his mid-thirties, red-headed, short in stature, and bold in personality, Standish had fought the Spanish in Holland as a lieutenant with English mercenary troops. When the twelve-year truce brought peace to Holland, Standish reportedly settled in Leiden, where he was befriended by Pastor Robinson's Separatist congregation, and agreed to make the voyage to America as the colony's military advisor.

Three of the passengers aboard the *Mayflower* were pregnant women. While sailing on the open sea, Elizabeth Hopkins, the wife of Stephen Hopkins, gave birth to a son. Appropriately, the couple named him Oceanus.

AMERICAN BOOK COMPANY

The printer was, of course, William Brewster, the church elder who would serve as the lay leader and substitute for Pastor Robinson. Brewster was accompanied by his wife Mary and their two sons, who bore the Puritan-style names of Love and Wrestling—the latter presumably named from the Genesis account of Jacob wrestling with an angel. Also aboard was Deacon John Carver, the church leader who had helped arrange the voyage with Robert Cushman in London, although he apparently had been spared the controversy that Cushman experienced. In his mid-forties, Carver made the voyage with his wife Katherine and five servants. The other church leader to whom the Pilgrims looked for guidance was William Bradford, who weathered the stormy voyage with his wife Dorothy, comforted perhaps by the knowledge that their young son was safely back home. Bradford would prove, among many roles, to be the foremost chronicler of the Pilgrim story, but another passenger—Edward Winslow—would also record much of the Pilgrim experience. About twenty-five years old at the time of the voyage, Winslow was the son of an English salt merchant, and worked in William Brewster's printing firm in Holland. There he had joined Pastor Robinson's church, where he married his wife Elizabeth, who accompanied him on the voyage.

Notable among the "Strangers" aboard the *Mayflower* was Stephen Hopkins, who had been shipwrecked in Bermuda en route to the colony of Virginia in 1609. In Bermuda, he had been caught up in an attempted

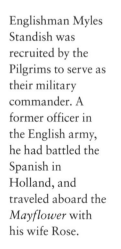

Englishman Myles Standish was recruited by the Pilgrims to serve as their military commander. A former officer in the English army, he had battled the Spanish in Holland, and traveled aboard the *Mayflower* with his wife Rose.

LIBRARY OF CONGRESS

mutiny and was sentenced to be hanged, then was reprieved and sent on to Jamestown for two years. His adventures reportedly inspired Shakespeare's play *The Tempest*, and now he was again sailing to America—this time with the largest family aboard. Accompanying Hopkins were his two daughters, his son, two servants and his wife Elizabeth—who gave birth to baby Oceanus en route. Also on the voyage was the quarrelsome John Billington along with his family, who had joined the group in England. Described by Bradford as a "knave," Billington would be hanged for murder a decade later. Aboard the *Mayflower*, he and his family—"one of the profanest families amongst them," in Bradford's opinion—were apparently a cantankerous lot. Another unusual family was composed of the four More children—Mary, Richard, Jasper, and Ellen—whose aristocratic father, Samuel More, had discovered that the four children were the result of a secret adulterous relationship conducted by his wife. To give the children a new and less scandalous start in life, he sent them to America aboard the *Mayflower* in the care of John Carver. To see that the children received adequate attention, Carver and his wife cared for one, and placed the others with the Brewsters and Winslows. Also aboard the *Mayflower* were two dogs the Pilgrims had brought along—a spaniel and a huge mastiff.

Although spared widespread death aboard the *Mayflower*, the Pilgrims undoubtedly suffered aboard ship. Seriously behind schedule, they were low on rations, and in the cramped, dark quarters between decks, many of them were severely stricken by bouts of seasickness. Adding to their misery, they were mercilessly taunted as people of faith by a mean-spirited member of the *Mayflower*'s crew. The sailor—"a proud and very profane young man" in Bradford's words—tormented the Separatists day after day, repeatedly mocking and cursing them, and declaring that he hoped to see them die and cast overboard. Instead, he was struck down by "a grievous disease" halfway across the Atlantic, and—to the sobering astonishment of the crew—it was his body that was "thrown overboard." A near-death drama did befall one of John Carver's servants, a young man named John Howland, who was swept overboard in a storm. Miraculously, he managed to grasp a loose line trailing the ship and was hauled ashore by crewmen using a boat hook.

Years later, William Bradford would pen a brief but memorable recollection of the *Mayflower*'s stormy passage to America.

These troubles being blown over, and now being all compact together in one ship, they put to sea again with a prosperous wind, which continued for divers days together, which was some encouragement to them; yet according to the usual manner, many were afflicted with seasickness. And I may not omit here a special work of God's providence. There was a proud and very profane young man, one of the seamen, of a lusty, able body, which made him the more haughty; he would always be condemning the poor people in their sickness, and cursing them daily with grievous execrations, and did not let to tell them that he hoped to help cast half of them overboard before they came to their journey's end, and to make merry with what they had; and if he were gently reproved by any one, he would curse and swear most bitterly. But it pleased God, before they came half [the] seas over, to smite the young man with a grievous disease, of which he died in a desperate manner, and so was himself the first that was thrown overboard. Thus his curses fell upon his own head, and it was an astonishment to all his fellows for they noted it to be the just hand of God upon him.

After they had enjoyed fair winds and weather for some time, they were encountered many times with cross winds and many fierce storms by which the ship was severely shaken, and her upper works made very leaky. One of the main beams amidships was bowed and cracked, which put them in some fear that the ship might not be able to perform the voyage. So some of the chief of the company, perceiving the mariners to fear the sufficiency of the ship, as appeared by their mutterings, they entered into serious consultation with the master and other officers of the ship to consider the danger and to return rather than to cast themselves into desperate and inevitable peril. And truly there was great distraction and difference of opinion among the mariners themselves….

But in examining all opinions, the master and others affirmed they knew the ship to be strong and firm [under the water-line], and for the buckling of the main beam, there was a great iron screw the passengers brought out of Holland, which would raise the beam into his place; the which being done, the carpenter and master affirmed that with a post put under it, set firm in the lower deck and otherwise bound, he would make it sufficient. And as for the decks and upper works, they would caulk them as well as they could, and though with the working of the ship they would not long keep staunch, yet there would otherwise be no great danger, if they did not overpress her with sails. So they committed themselves to the will of God and resolved to proceed.

In several of these storms the winds were so fierce and the seas so high, as they could not bear a knot of sail, but were forced to hull for divers days together. And in one of them, as they thus lay at hull in a mighty storm, a lusty young man called John Howland, coming upon some occasion above the gratings was, with a roll of the ship, thrown into the sea; but it pleased God that he caught hold of the topsail halyards which hung overboard and ran out at length. Yet he held his hold (though he was several fathoms under water) till he was

"He hoped to help cast half of them overboard"

169

"The winds were so fierce and the seas so high"

It was every sailor's fear in the seventeenth century—being washed overboard in a stormy sea. It happened aboard the *Mayflower*—but with an unlikely rescue.

RIJKSMUSEUM OF AMSTERDAM

hauled up by the same rope to the brim of the water, and then with a boat hook and other means got into the ship again and his life was saved. And though he was something ill with it, yet he lived many years after and became a profitable member both in church and commonwealth. In all this voyage there died but one of the passengers, which was William Butten, a youth, [and a] servant to Samuel Fuller....[5]

"Lions and Tigers as well as Unicorns"

The Pilgrims Ponder What Awaits Them in the Wilderness

What awaited them in the wilderness of America? Surely that question was repeated day after day among the Pilgrims, and it no doubt tormented some. In their quest for freedom of faith, they had turned away from all that was familiar to them and had abandoned the comforts as well as the challenges of

The Pilgrims chose to make the long, perilous voyage across the Atlantic despite the sensational accounts of deep-ocean travel that circulated in the early seventeenth century. One popular illustration of the day depicted Atlantic travelers assaulted by flying fish.

RIJKSMUSEUM OF AMSTERDAM

European civilization. Would their new lives in the wilderness be marked by joys and success? Or would they die of illness or starvation and, like so many others, be swallowed up by the New World? As Bradford would repeatedly observe, they trusted in the sovereignty of God, had "committed themselves to the will of God and resolved to proceed," and although at times fearful, they were undoubtedly curious about what they would discover in America when their difficult voyage finally ended. They had unquestionably been exposed to reports from decades of American explorations, including some that were dependable—and others that were not. As the Pilgrims prepared for their voyage to America, published reports of English explorer John Hawkins's adventures in America were circulating in England. According to the accounts of Hawkins's 1565 visit to an ill-fated French Huguenot colony in Florida, the American wilderness contained tigers, three-headed snakes, and unicorns:

"They committed themselves to the will of God"

171

Some European explorers to America returned with wildly fanciful reports of prancing unicorns, prowling tigers, and three-headed snakes. At the time of the *Mayflower*'s voyage, this Dutch artwork depicted an Indian chieftain ruling from an ornate chariot pulled by unicorns.

RIJKSMUSEUM OF AMSTERDAM

The Floridians have pieces of unicorn horns which they wear about their necks, whereof the Frenchmen obtained many pieces. Of those unicorns they have many: for that they do affirm it to be a beast with one horn, which coming to the river to drink, puts the same into the water before he drink. Of this unicorn horn there are of our company, that having gotten the same of the Frenchmen brought home thereof to show. It is therefore to be presupposed that there are more commodities as well as that, which for want of time, and people sufficient to inhabit the same, can not yet come to light: but I trust God will reveal the same before it be long, to the great profit of them that shall take it in hand.

Of beasts in this country besides deer, foxes, hares, pole-cats, conies, and leopards, I am not able certainly to say: but it is thought that there are lions and tigers as well as unicorns; lions especially. If it be true that is said, of the enmity between them and the unicorns; for there is no beast but hath his enemy, as the coney, the polecat, a sheep, the wolf, the elephant, the rhinoceros; and so of other beasts the like: insomuch, that whereas the one is, the other can not be missing.

Seeing I have made mention of the beasts of this country, it shall not be from my purpose to speak also of the venomous beasts, as crocodiles, whereof there is great abundance, adders of great bigness, whereof our men killed some of a yard and half long. Also I heard a miracle of one of these adders, upon one a falcon seizing, the said adder did clasp her tail about her; which the French captain seeing, came to the rescue of the falcon, and took her, slaying the adder. This falcon being wild, he did reclaim her, and kept her for the space of two months, at which time for very want of meat he was forced to cast her off. On these adders the Frenchmen did feed, to no little admiration of us, and affirmed the same to be a delicate meat. The captain of the

"It is thought that there are lions and tigers as well as unicorns"

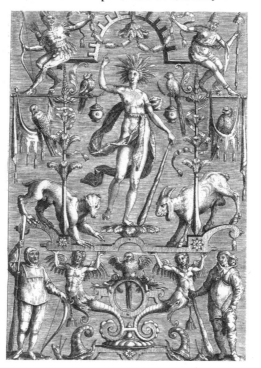

One popular work of art circulating in Europe in 1620 purported to depict the inhabitants that the Pilgrims would likely encounter in America: exotically costumed Indians, giant snails, huge birds, ferocious mammals—and mermaid-like humanoids.

RIJKSMUSEUM OF AMSTERDAM

173

Perhaps the Pilgrims' greatest fear was what might befall them at the hands of the New World's indigenous peoples—the American Indians. The Pilgrims' concerns were fueled by early seventeenth-century works of art such as this one, which depicted Native Americans as bloody-thirsty, cannibalistic head-hunters.

RIJKSMUSEUM OF AMSTERDAM

Frenchmen saw also a serpent with three heads and four feet, of the bigness of a great spaniel, which for want of a harquebus he did not attempt to slay. Of fish also they have in the river, pike, roche, salmon, trout, and divers other small fishes, and of great fish, some of the length of a man and longer, being of bigness accordingly, having a snout much like a sword of a yard long....[6]

"Readier to Fill Their Sides Full of Arrows"

Among the Pilgrims' Concerns—Fear of Native Americans

"The place they had thoughts on was...vast and unpeopled," William Bradford would later observe, recalling the original concerns the Pilgrims had expressed in Holland when considering relocating to America. Even then, the prospect of facing the American wilderness "caused many fears and doubts," he admitted. The most fearful among them presumably remained in Holland or England, but Bradford conceded that fear of the wilderness and the dangers it contained was "neither unreasonable nor unprobable." Even the drinking water in America was believed it be harmful. In reality, the freshwater streams in America were far healthier than the water sources in England. There, water quality was so questionable that the beverage commonly consumed by English families, including Puritans and Separatists, was beer or ale. The water in America was just one worry for the Pilgrims: they had also been led to fear indigenous foods—and even the air itself. "The change of air, diet and drinking of water would affect their bodies with sore sicknesses and grievous disease," it was commonly believed.

Perhaps most feared of all were the native peoples of America—the American Indians. As reported by William Bradford, Native Americans were believed to be "cruel, barbarous and most treacherous, being most furious in their rage and merciless where they overcome; not to be content only to kill and take away life, but delighting to torment men in the most bloody manner…." When they landed in America, Bradford believed, the first Indians they encountered would be "readier to fill their sides full of arrows" than to greet them peaceably.

Fear of America's Indian tribes was fueled by graphic and sometimes sensationalist reports from early explorers and colonists who had battled Native Americans in the New World. One of the most widely read accounts in England during the Pilgrims' day was *The Fourth Voyage Made to Virginia in the Yere 1587*. It featured excerpts from the journal of John White, who was governor of the first English colony in North America—the unsuccessful, short-lived Roanoke settlement on the coast of North Carolina. White recounted how his assistant, George Howe, and several other English colonists were killed by Indians:

"The captain… saw also a serpent with three heads and four feet"

Algonquin Indians perform a ceremonial dance in a late sixteenth-century artwork by Englishman John White. While his art depicted Native Americans much more accurately than most European artists, even White's accounts were enough to stoke the Pilgrims' fear of Indians.

BRITISH MUSEUM

We also understood from the men of Croatoan, that our man Master Howe was slain by the remnant of [Chief] Wingino's men dwelling then at Dasamonguepeuk, with whom Wanchese kept company, and also we understood by them of Croatoan, how that the 15 Englishmen left at Roanoke the year before by Sir Richard Grenville were suddenly set upon by 30 of the men of Secota, Aquascogoc, and Dasamonguepeuk in the manner following. They conveyed themselves secretly behind the trees near the houses where our men carelessly lived. And having perceived that of those fifteen they could see but eleven, only two of those Savages appeared to the 11 Englishmen calling to them by friendly signs, that but two of their chief men should come unarmed to speak with those two savages, who seemed also to be unarmed. Wherefore two of the leaders of our Englishmen went gladly to them. While one of those savages traitorously

embraced one of our men, the other with his sword of wood, which he had secretly hidden under his mantel, struck him on the head and slew him.

Presently the other eight and twenty savages showed themselves. The other Englishman, perceiving this, fled to his company, whom the savages pursued with their bows and arrows so fast that the Englishmen were forced to take the house, wherein all their victuals and weapons were. But the savages forthwith set the same on fire. Our men were forced to take up such weapons as came first to hand, and without order to run forth among the savages, with whom they skirmished above an hour. In this skirmish another of our men was shot in the mouth with an arrow. He died, and also one of the savages was shot into the side by one of our men…whereof he died. The place where they fought was of great advantage to the savages, by means of the thick trees, behind which the savages, through their nimbleness, defended themselves. They so offended our men with their arrows that our men, being some of them hurt, retired fighting to the waterside where their boat lay, with which they fled towards Hatorask….[7]

"The other
. . . struck
him on the
head and slew
him"

"The Difficulties Were Many, but Not Invincible"

The Pilgrims Overcome Their Fears to Face the Unknown

A s they endured their ordeal in the Atlantic, the Pilgrims understood that the life which awaited them in America included dangers and challenges aplenty, even if the most sensational accounts of the New World were exaggerated. "And surely," Bradford

Despite the grave dangers they faced, the Pilgrims courageously chose to cross the treacherous Atlantic in a quest for freedom. "Yea, though they should lose their lives in this action…," observed William Bradford, "their endeavors would be honorable."

HISTORY OF THE UNITED STATES

"Another of our men was shot in the mouth with an arrow"

would write, "it could not be thought but the very hearing of these things could not but move the very bowels of men to grate within them and make the weak to quake and tremble." They had chosen to go forward anyway, despite their fears. For they had come to believe—in Bradford's words—"that all great and honorable actions are accompanied by great difficulties and must be both enterprised and overcome with answerable courage." As the *Mayflower* neared the coast of America in November of 1620, its weary passengers faced the future with courage and faith. With extraordinary eloquence, William Bradford would later describe the Pilgrim heart:

It was granted the dangers were great, but not desperate. The difficulties were many, but not invincible.… It might be many of the things feared might never befall them; others by provident care and the use of good means might in a great measure be prevented; and all of them, through the help of God, by fortitude and patience, might either be borne or overcome. True it was that such attempts were not to be made and undertaken without good grounds and reason, not rashly or lightly as many have done for curiosity or hope of gain, etc.

But their condition was not ordinary, their ends were good and honorable, their calling lawful and urgent; and therefore they might expect the blessing of God in the proceeding. Yea, though they should lose their lives in this action, yet might they have comfort in the same and their endeavors would be honorable.[8]

"Their ends were good and honorable"

CHAPTER EIGHT

"They Fell upon Their Knees and Blessed the God of Heaven"

Behind them, the sun rose over the Atlantic horizon. Before them to the west, beneath a clear dawn sky, lay America. It was Thursday, November 9, 1620. After sixty-five days and 2,812 nautical miles at sea, the Pilgrims had reached their new home. Joyfully, they stared across the coastal waters and the distant, rolling surf at a pale line of high sand banks and, farther to the west, a bumpy line of forested

After sixty-five days at sea, the *Mayflower* finally came into sight of what the Pilgrims called "so goodly a land"—America.

LIBRARY OF CONGRESS

hills. Unlike the English coastline they had left behind, there were no whitewashed cottages, no lighthouses, no stone fortifications. Instead, as far as they could see to the north and south there was a tree line of virgin forest that rose just beyond the Atlantic beach. It was "wooded to the brink of the sea," they noted, and they were reassured to see what they considered to be "so goodly a land."[1]

✦•━━━•✦

"They Fell upon Their Knees and Blessed the God of Heaven"

The Pilgrims Reach America

Although overjoyed to have finally reached America, they all soon realized that they were *not* in Virginia. Their proposed destination was the mouth of the Hudson River on the northern border of the Virginia Colony—at the site of modern New York City. Instead of making landfall at the Hudson, they had arrived offshore what would become the state of Massachusetts—almost two hundred and fifty miles off course. Did Master Jones simply miss his mark? After all, this was his first voyage to America. Or did he intentionally make for the New England shore, planning to sail southward when he reached the mainland? No one aboard the *Mayflower* ever explained exactly what happened, and the reasons for the Pilgrims' landfall in New England would be debated for centuries to come. Although Master Jones had never taken a ship to America, his pilots had been to the New World before—which was presumably one reason why Master Jones had hired them—and Second Mate Robert Coppin had been to the *Mayflower*'s present landfall before. It was known to Europe's long-distance fishing fleets as Cape Cod, so named for the seemingly endless schools of codfish that were found in its offshore waters.

Realizing they had landed far north of their destination, the Pilgrims directed the *Mayflower* to sail southward—until they encountered treacherous seas. Then they turned back and hove to for the night off the coast of New England.

HISTORY OF THE UNITED STATES

Lying offshore the northern end of Cape Cod, Master Jones discussed options with the Pilgrim leaders—presumably with Governor Martin, John Carver, William Brewster, and William Bradford. They directed Jones to sail south for their intended destination on the northern fringe of the Virginia Colony—"to find some place about Hudson's River for their habitation," as Bradford put it. That was where they had been legally granted permission to establish a colony backed by the Merchant Adventurers. Accordingly, the *Mayflower* was steered southward, and they sailed toward the mouth of the Hudson River for half a day, keeping the coastland in sight on their starboard side. It was cold along the coast of New England in November, but it was a sunny, clear day and with good winds behind them, they smoothly sailed along at a favorable speed.

Then they hit shallow water—dangerous shoals and crashing waves. The wind dropped, and the *Mayflower* stood in danger of running aground or wrecking on the shoals—especially if forced to remain in treacherous waters at night. After two months crossing the storm-tossed

Atlantic, is this how their long-planned voyage to America would end—shipwrecked off the coast of the wilderness, alone, and with no one to rescue them? Onward they cruised through the rolling breakers and shallow waters, waiting any moment for disaster. Then the wind shifted and picked up—offering the *Mayflower* an avenue of escape back to the north. Master Jones took it, and turned the ship back in the direction in which they had come. A sense of relief surged through the *Mayflower*'s passengers and crew. By dusk, the *Mayflower* had cleared the shoals. Master Jones turned the ship into the wind and hove to for the night, suspending progress until dawn. Jones called for the Pilgrim leaders, and they made a historic decision: they would head north and establish their colony on the coast of New England.

On November 11, 1620, the *Mayflower* anchored in the sheltered waters of Cape Cod Bay. Upon finally reaching America, the Pilgrims "fell upon their knees and blessed the God of Heaven."

AMERICAN BOOK COMPANY

The next day they set sail on a northward course, this time passing the long, empty southern stretch of Cape Cod on their port side, as they headed back to where they had first sighted land. By dark on November 10, they had passed their original landfall and were nearing the northern end of Cape Cod, which—on a chart—curled back toward the mainland like a giant, beckoning finger. Master Jones again hove to for the night. At daylight the next day, November 11, 1620, the *Mayflower* entered Cape Cod Bay, and anchored in cold, calm waters off what is now Provincetown, Massachusetts. "Being thus arrived in a good harbor, and brought safe to land," William Bradford would recall, "they fell upon their knees and blessed the God of Heaven, who had brought them over the vast and furious ocean...."

Amid their joy and relief that their dangerous voyage was over, and best hopes of what awaited them ashore, they were also keenly aware of the stark reality immediately facing them: it was now time to enter the great unknown American wilderness and make it their home. Their situation reminded William Bradford of the biblical account of Moses viewing the Promised Land from atop Mount Pisgah—and also the story in the New Testament book of Acts which recounted how the Apostle Paul was shipwrecked in a strange new land:

Being thus passed the vast ocean, and a sea of troubles before in their preparation (as may be remembered by that which went before), they had now no friends to welcome them, or inns to entertain or refresh their weather-beaten bodies, no houses or much less towns to repair to, to seek for succor. It is recorded in scriptures, a mercy to the apostle and his shipwrecked company, that the barbarians showed them no small kindness in refreshing them, but these savage barbarians, when they met with them (as after will appear) were readier to fill their sides full of arrows than otherwise.

And for the season it was winter, and they that know the winters of that country know them to be sharp and violent, and subject to cruel and fierce storms, dangerous to travel to known places, much more to such an unknown coast. Besides, what could they see but a hideous and desolate wilderness, full of wild beasts and wild men? And what

"They had now no friends to welcome them"

185

On this nineteenth-century map of New England, Cape Cod extends from the coast of modern Massachusetts like a giant beckoning finger. The *Mayflower* eventually anchored in the sheltered waters of Cape Cod Bay.

SHORT HISTORY OF THE UNITED STATES

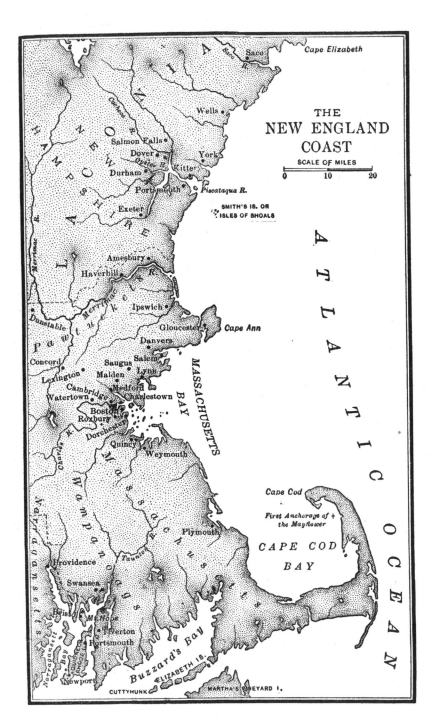

THE
NEW ENGLAND
COAST

SCALE OF MILES

0   10   20

multitudes there might be of them they knew not. Nether could they, as it were, go up to the top of Pisgah to view from this wilderness, a more goodly country, to feed their hopes; for whichever way they turned their eyes (save upward to the heavens) they could have little solace or content in respect of any outward objects. For summer being done, all things stand upon them with a weather-beaten face, and the whole country, full of woods and thickets, represented a wild and savage view.

If they looked behind them, there was the mighty ocean which they had passed, and was now as a main bar and gulf to separate them from all the civil parts of the world. If it be said they had a ship to succor them, it is true; but what heard they daily from the [master and crew was] that with speed they should look out a place with their shallop, where they would be at some near distance; for the season was such as he would not stir from there [with the ship and its crew until] a safe harbor was discovered by them where they would be, and he might go without danger; and that [the ship's rations must be] kept sufficient for themselves and their return. Yea, it was muttered by some, that if they got not a place in time, they would turn them and their goods ashore and leave them. Let it also be considered what weak hopes of supply and succor they left behind them, that might bear up their minds in this sad condition and trials they were under; and they could not but be very small. It is true, indeed, the affections and love of their brethren at Leyden were cordial towards them, but they had little power to help them.... What could now sustain them but the spirit of God and his grace?[2]

"What could now sustain them but the spirit of God and his grace?"

"We . . . Covenant and Combine Ourselves Together into a Civil Body Politic"

The Pilgrims Exercise Self-Government in America

As the *Mayflower* rode at anchor in Cape Cod Bay, a shipboard drama played out that would forever affect the Pilgrims, New England, and the culture, laws, and government of America. The Separatist leaders aboard the *Mayflower* had decided to establish their colony where they had made landfall—at Cape Cod. While the colony was financed by the Merchant Adventurers, its patent had been granted by the Virginia Company of London for a site some 250 miles to the south. Establishing the colony at Cape Cod meant it would be outside of the jurisdiction of the Virginia Company. So the Pilgrims would indeed have to "stand on their own legs," as Thomas Weston had threatened back in England. In New England, outside the jurisdiction of its patent, the Pilgrim colony would be independent, and would have much more liberty to become whatever its founders envisioned. The decision, however, was not welcomed by everyone aboard the *Mayflower*. As the ship headed back northward for Cape Cod, some of the Strangers reportedly began muttering about staging a mutiny.

Was the would-be uprising led by Stephen Hopkins, who had reportedly led an unsuccessful mutiny in Bermuda? Or was it encouraged by Christopher Martin, whose term as "governor" of the *Mayflower* was about to end, or was it instigated by the troublesome "knave" John Billington? No one knows. Neither William Bradford nor apparently anyone else aboard ever identified the potential mutineers—although Bradford did describe their outcry as "discontented and mutinous," and quoted some of the Strangers as vowing that when they came ashore "none had

While still aboard the *Mayflower*, the Pilgrims drafted and signed the Mayflower Compact, which would prove to be a cornerstone for law and government in America.

LIBRARY OF CONGRESS

power to command them." Despite the bold talk, the mutiny came to nothing, but it did reinforce the colony's need for government, especially as it would be established outside the authority of the colony's patent.

So, while still aboard the *Mayflower*, anchored in the waters of Cape Cod, the Pilgrims drafted a compact or constitution for their new colony. It would become known as the Mayflower Compact. It was unusually brief for a founding document, and was a mission statement as well, establishing a precedent for constitutional law in America based on two principles: faith and freedom. In its opening line, the document stated its source of authority: "In the Name of God, Amen." It also noted that King James, to whom the signers acknowledged their submission, held his royal position "by the Grace of God." In so stating, it reaffirmed the biblical doctrine that God, not government, is the author of basic human rights, or "unalienable rights," as the Declaration of Independence would later call them.

"Having undertaken for the Glory of God, and Advancement of the Christian Faith . . . a Voyage to plant the first Colony in the Northern Parts of Virginia"

It also reflected the Judeo-Christian tradition that government should be modeled on "covenant theology"—that a contract or "covenant" should exist between government and the governed in the way that God had established covenants with his people through the ages, according to the Bible. In keeping with this belief, the Compact's signers vowed to "Covenant and Combine ourselves together into a civil Body Politic" whose core values were intended to establish "just and equal Laws . . . for the general Good of the Colony." The main purpose of the Plymouth Colony and its government, the Compact unashamedly stated, was to promote "the Glory of God, and Advancement of the Christian Faith. . . ."

It thus also reflected the biblical worldview of the Reverend John Robinson—the Pilgrims' pastor. In his farewell message to the Pilgrims, he had predicted that some kind of civil government would be needed for the colony—"a Body Politic," he called it—and that it should govern in "the Image of the Lord's power and authority." When they reached America, Robinson had advised them, they should demonstrate "wisdom and godliness" by electing leaders who demonstrated a "virtuous mind" and honored "the glorious ordinance of the Lord." Lastly, he had cautioned, "let your wisdom and godliness appear, not only in choosing persons as do entirely love, and will diligently promote the common good, but also in yielding to them all due honor and obedience. . . ."

The Mayflower Compact would prove to be a cornerstone for American culture, law, and government, and was clearly founded on the Higher Law of the Bible rather than upon the whims of man. It stated in full:

----•----

In the Name of God, Amen. We, whose names are underwritten, the Loyal Subjects of our dread Sovereign Lord King

James, by the Grace of God, of Great Britain, France, and Ireland, King, Defender of the Faith, Etc.

Having undertaken for the Glory of God, and Advancement of the Christian Faith, and the Honour of our King and Country, a Voyage to plant the first Colony in the Northern Parts of Virginia; do by these Presents, solemnly and mutually, in the Presence of God and one another, Covenant and Combine ourselves together into a Civil Body Politic, for our better Ordering and Preservation, and Furtherance of the Ends aforesaid; and by Virtue hereof do enact, constitute, and frame, such just and equal Laws, Ordinances, Acts, Constitutions, and Offices, from time to time, as shall be thought most meet and convenient for the general Good of the Colony; unto which we promise all due Submission and Obedience.

In Witness whereof we have hereunto subscribed our names at Cape Cod the eleventh of November, in the Reign of our Sovereign Lord King James, of England, France, and Ireland, the eighteenth, and of Scotland the fifty-fourth. Anno Domini 1620.

"In the Presence of God and one another, [we] Covenant and Combine ourselves together into a Civil Body Politic"

It was an extraordinary act of democratic self-government: a tiny band of colonists in wilderness America had drafted and enacted a governing document for their colony. It was signed by forty-one men—from the well-to-do to laborers—who represented their families and others. Among the signers were the potential mutineers—Stephen Hopkins, John Billington, and Christopher Martin. The forty-one signers would now serve as the colony's General Court, and their next duty was another exercise in self-government: they elected a governor. It was not

To serve as governor of their new colony, the Pilgrims elected John Carver, their longtime and respected leader.

ARCHITECT OF THE U.S. CAPITOL

Christopher Martin, the bullying "governor" of the *Mayflower* who was appointed by the Merchant Adventurers. It was John Carver, the church deacon and devoted Separatist leader, who had served as an agent for the voyage with Robert Cushman in London. When Cushman abandoned the voyage, Carver remained, making the voyage with his wife and servants. Respected for his leadership in the Leiden church, Carver had a reputation as a "godly" man who was known for his humility, and was "well approved" by his fellow Separatists. Now, on November 11, 1620, he became the colony's first governor.[3]

"We Marched through Boughs and Bushes"

The Pilgrims Explore Their Wilderness Home

"The same day," one of them would recall, "so soon as we could, we set ashore…." Who was the first Pilgrim to set foot in America? No one knows. According to an anonymous 1622 publication entitled *Mourt's Relation*, it appears that the first Pilgrim to step on American earth was one of a small party who briefly left the *Mayflower* to gather firewood on Saturday, November 11. Was it Captain Myles Standish? Governor John Carver? William Bradford? The identity of the first ashore is lost to history—apparently no one thought it important to record names. *Mourt's Relation* would be published in London two years later to encourage emigration to the new colony. Eventually, primary authorship would be attributed to Edward Winslow, although William Bradford appears to have written important parts of it, and it also contains the writing of others. According to the booklet, the Pilgrims went ashore that first day because they were out of firewood, and because they also wanted to "see what the land was." After more than two months at sea, they surely yearned to

The same day that the *Mayflower* anchored off Cape Cod, the Pilgrims put ashore a small group of men to explore the area. After more than two months at sea, all were eager to set foot on dry land.

LIBRARY OF CONGRESS

put their feet on dry land. They came ashore on "a small neck of land" near modern Provincetown, and explored the coastal forest. A shovel's blade beneath the surface, they were pleased to find "excellent black earth," and they admiringly observed open woodlands of "oaks, pines, sassafras, juniper, birch, holly, vines, some ash, [and] walnut...." From the woods they toted armloads of cut juniper back to the ship, where they started fires that night and enjoyed a "very sweet and strong" aroma from the burning juniper. The next day was Sunday, which they spent in their customary worship and rest. On Monday, November 13, more of them went ashore, including many of the women, who sorely needed to wash clothes.

Everywhere around them were the wonders of the wilderness: they saw huge flocks of birds—"the greatest store of fowl that ever we saw." Offshore, whales repeatedly rose to the surface—so many that Master

After a day of Sunday worship and rest, more Pilgrims went ashore. On the beach, the men readied themselves for more exploration while the women engaged in a long-awaited Monday washday.

STORIES OF THE PILGRIMS

Jones speculated that a whaling ship could easily harvest "three or four thousand pounds worth of oil." Shellfish lay on the shoreline in great abundance, and some Pilgrims eagerly gathered and ate them—until they were struck by bouts of nausea. Meanwhile, the carpenters among them set to work repairing a thirty-five-foot-long boat—a shallop—which they had brought in sections from England. They intended to use it to explore the shore of the bay, but soon realized that repairing and reassembling it would take much longer than they expected. Instead, they decided, they would explore the area on foot.

The next day, Wednesday, November 15, a sixteen-man expedition commanded by Captain Myles Standish went ashore. The concept of the citizen-soldier was commonly accepted in England, and as Puritans, the Separatists undoubtedly viewed a militia as compatible with the biblical doctrine of self-defense. Some of the Pilgrims apparently were militia veterans. They had brought firearms, swords, and body armor with them, so Captain Standish's party carried itself with a martial bearing. They set off, single file, along the beach, and had barely marched a mile when they encountered a small party of Indians heading their way, accompanied by a dog. It was their first encounter with Native Americans—but it was short-lived: the Indians fled into the seaside forest. The Pilgrims followed their tracks, hoping to talk to them. However, they were unable to catch up with them by nightfall, so they posted guards and camped overnight in the woods.

The next morning they set out again, trying to follow the Indians' trail and make contact, but they ran into dense thickets and gave up. They had brought no water with them and by now were suffering from serious thirst. Then they stumbled onto a freshwater spring—their first drinking water in America. There, as recorded in *Mourt's Relation*, they "drunk our first New England water with as much delight as ever we drunk drink in all our lives." Refreshed, they moved out again, heading back toward the shore of the bay. They observed an abundance of wild game, and a lot of wild sassafras, which was highly prized back in England as medicine. At one point they found themselves in a patch of open land marked by "heaps of sand." They dug into one, uncovering a rotted bow and arrow, and realized they were in an Indian graveyard. Not wanting to offend the natives by disturbing their burial ground, they carefully replaced the objects, covered up the grave, and moved on. Further on, they found signs of earlier, temporary encampments by Europeans—and at one spot they discovered a cast iron kettle left behind by European fishermen, shipwreck survivors, or earlier English explorers. Of more importance to them at the time, they also discovered a large store of Indian corn buried under a mound of sand.

"When the Indians saw our men following them, they ran away"

Standing around the uncovered corn in the midst of the wilderness, they engaged in a serious ethical discussion about whether it was morally acceptable to take some of the corn with them back to the *Mayflower*. They had reached America far behind schedule and were now seriously short of food—and the dried corn could be used to seed a corn crop in the spring. But what first impression would they give to the native peoples if they took their corn? Finally, "after much consultation," they decided upon a compromise: they would take the corn, but they would pay for it whenever they encountered the Indian owners. So they "concluded to take the kettle and as much of the corn as we could carry away with us...."

The next day—November 17—after a cold, drizzly night around a fire in the woods, they moved on toward the bay. Along the way, they discovered a peculiarly bent sapling, which turned out to be a snare set by the Indians to trap game. Unintentionally, William Bradford stepped into it. It "gave a sudden jerk up," and Bradford was caught up in the snare. Instead of being alarmed or aggravated, the Pilgrims expressed their admiration for the clever trap "as a very pretty device." Back on the shore of the bay, they fired their guns to signal the *Mayflower*, which sent a boat to ferry them back to the ship. Within the pages of *Mourt's Relation*, Edward Winslow and William Bradford recorded the three-day expedition—the Pilgrims' first serious exploration of their New World home:

***

Wednesday, the 15th of November, they were set ashore; and when they had ordered themselves in the order of a single file and marched about the space of a mile by the sea, they sighted five or six people with a dog coming towards them, who were savages, who, when they saw them, ran into the

wood and whistled the dog after them, etc. First they supposed them to be Master Jones, the master, and some of his
men, for they were ashore and knew of their coming; but
after they knew them to be Indians, they marched after them
into the woods, lest other of the Indians should lie in ambush.
But when the Indians saw our men following them, they ran
away with might and main, and our men turned out of the
wood after them—for it was the way they intended to go—
but they could not come near them. They followed them that
night about ten miles by the trace of their footings, and saw
how they had come the same way they went, and at a turning
perceived how they ran up a hill to see whether they followed
them. At length night came upon them, and they were constrained to take up their lodging. So they set forth three

Captain Myles
Standish leads a
squad of armed
Pilgrims into the
wilderness. Soon
after the
Mayflower made
landfall, Standish
and a sixteen-man
party explored the
forest overlooking
Cape Cod Bay.

LIBRARY OF
CONGRESS

sentinels, and the rest, some kindled a fire, and others fetched wood, and there held our rendezvous that night.

In the morning, so soon as we could see the trace, we proceeded on our journey, and had the track until we had compassed the head of a long creek; and there they took into another wood, and we after them, supposing to find some of their dwellings. But we marched through boughs and bushes, and under hills and valleys, which tore our very armor in pieces, and yet could meet with none of them, nor their houses, nor find any fresh water, which we greatly desired and stood in need of; for we brought neither beer nor water with us, and our victuals were only biscuit and Holland cheese, and a little bottle of aqua-vitae, so as we were [severely thirsty]. About ten o'clock we came into a deep valley full of brush, [bayberry], and long grass, through which we found little paths or tracts; and there we saw a deer, and found springs of fresh water, of which we were heartily glad, and sat us down and drunk our first New England water with as much delight as ever we drunk drink in all our lives.

When we had refreshed ourselves we directed our course full south, that we might come to the shore, which within a short while after we did, and there made a fire, that they in the ship might see where we were (as we had direction), and so marched on towards this supposed river. And as we went in another valley, we found a fine clear pond of fresh water, being about a musket-shot broad, and twice as long; there grew also many small vines, and fowl and deer haunted there; there grew much sassafras. From thence we went on and found much plain ground, about fifty acres, fit for the plow, and some signs where the Indians had formerly planted their

"Because we deemed them graves, we ... left the rest untouched"

corn. After this some thought it best, for nearness of the river, to go down and travel on the sea sands, by which means some of our men were tired and lagged behind. So we stayed and gathered them up, and struck into the land again; where we found a little path to certain heaps of sand, one whereof was covered with old mats, and had a wooden thing like a mortar [turned upside down] on the top of it, and an earthen pot laid in a little hole at the end thereof. We, musing what it might be, digged and found a bow, and, as we thought, arrows, but they were rotten. We supposed there were many other things; but because we deemed them graves, we put in the bow again, and made it up as it was, and left the rest untouched, because we thought it would be odious unto them to ransack their sepulchers.

We went on further and found new stubble, of which they had gotten corn this year, and many walnut trees full of nuts, and great store of strawberries, and some vines. Passing thus a field or two, which were not great, we came to another, which had also been new gotten, and there we found where an house had been, and four or five old planks

As they explored the Cape Cod coastline, the Pilgrims encountered a variety of wild game. "We saw great flocks of wild geese and ducks," they reported.

WIKIMEDIA COMMONS

laid together. Also we found a great kettle, which had been some ship's kettle and brought out of Europe. There was also an heap of sand, made like the former, but it was newly done (we might see how they had paddled it with their hands), which we digged up, and in it we found a little old basket full of fair Indian corn; and digged further and found a fine great new basket full of very fair corn of this year with some 36 goodly ears of corn, some yellow, and some red, and others mixed with blue, which was a very goodly sight. The basket was round, and narrow at the top. It held about three or four bushels, which was as much as two of us could lift up from the ground, and was very handsomely and cunningly made. But whilst we were busy about these things, we set our men sentinel in a round ring, all but two or three which digged up the corn. We were in suspense what to do with it and the kettle, and at length after much consultation, we concluded to take the kettle and as much of the corn as we could carry away with us; and when our shallop came, if we could find any of the people and come to parley with them, we would give them the kettle again and satisfy them for their corn. So we took all the ears, and put a good deal of the loose corn in the kettle for two men to bring away on a staff. Besides, they that could put any into their pockets, filled the same. The rest we buried again; for we were so laden with armor that we could carry no more.

Not far from this place we found the remainder of an old fort or palisades, which, as we conceived, had been made by some Christians. This was also hard by that place which we thought had been a river; unto which we went, and found it so to be dividing itself into two arms by an high bank standing right by the cut or month, which came from the sea. That which was next unto us was the less; the other arm was more than twice as big, and not unlike to be an harbor for ships; but whether it be a fresh river, or only an indraught of the sea, we had no time to discover; for we had commandment to be out but two days. Here also we saw two canoes, the one on the one side, the other on the other side. We could not believe it was a canoe, till we came near it. So we returned, leaving the further discovery hereof to our shallop, and came that night back again to the fresh water pond; and there we made our rendezvous that night, making a great fire, and a barricade to windward of us, and kept good watch with three sentinels all night, every one standing when his turn came, while five or six inches of match was burning. It proved a very rainy night.

In the morning we took our kettle and sunk it in the pond, and trimmed our muskets, for few of them would go off because of the wet; and so coasted the wood again to come

In this nineteenth-century artist's conception, a New England Indian is outfitted in buckskin leggings, a bear-hide tunic, and a bear claw necklace. The first Native Americans that the Pilgrims sighted fled into the forest.

STORIES OF THE PILGRIMS

201

"We saw great flocks of wild geese and ducks"

home, in which we were shrewdly puzzled and lost our way. As we wandered we came to a tree, where a young [sapling] was bowed down over a bow, and some acorns strewed underneath. Stephen Hopkins said it had been to catch some deer. So as we were looking at it, William Bradford being in the rear, when he came looked also upon it, and as he went about it, it gave a sudden jerk up, and he was immediately caught by the leg. It was a very pretty device, made with a rope of their own making, and having a noose as artificially made as any roper in England can make, and as like ours as can be, which we brought away with us. In the end we got out of the wood, and were fallen about a mile too high above the creek, where we saw three bucks, but we had rather have had one of them. We also did spring three couple of partridges; and as we came along by the creek, we saw great flocks of wild geese and ducks, but they were very fearful of us. So we marched some while in the woods, some while on the sands, and other while in the water up to the knees, came

Native American hunters flush deer toward a forest snare in this early seventeenth-century illustration. Pilgrim William Bradford experienced a surprise encounter with such a snare.

LIBRARY OF CONGRESS

to fetch us. Master Jones and Master Carver being on the shore, with many of our people, came to meet us. And thus we came, both weary and welcome home....[4]

◆◇•————•◇◆

Where would they build their homes and establish their colony? Their three-day exploration had not provided an answer: they needed to venture out again. On November 27, the shallop was finally repaired and reassembled—and the Pilgrims set out on another exploratory expedition. This time, they gave the honor of commanding the expedition to Master Jones, and about one-third of the thirty-four members of the party were sailors from the *Mayflower.* Jones had agreed to make the *Mayflower* available for housing and help until the colonists had found a location for their fledgling colony. He could not feed the Pilgrims from the ship's rations, however, which had to be preserved for the return voyage. The Pilgrims had to find a location for their home—and they had to find it soon.

As they headed along the Cape Cod shoreline, a winter storm blew in, dropping the temperature to below zero with wind and snow. The Pilgrims now saw that New England winters could be far worse than England's. They put in at a bayside inlet at what would become known as Pilgrim Lake, and most splashed ashore through thigh-deep, icy cold water, leaving the boats with some of the sailors. They hiked inland for several miles through the blowing snow, then made camp. When they awakened the next day, a half-foot of snow blanketed the ground, and many of the men were coughing. They trudged back to the boats, and sailed southward along the shoreline to an anchorage at modern Pamet Harbor, which they dubbed Cold Harbor. From there, they hiked for several hours up and down wooded hills until Master Jones—whose sea legs were not accustomed to hiking through snow—called it quits. They made camp in a stand of pine trees, dressing and cooking "three fat geese and six ducks" that they shot.

The next day they returned to the place where they had unearthed the Indian corn, which they named Corn Hill. They took more corn, along with a store of dried beans they discovered. By now the ground was so frozen that they had to hack into it with their swords and cutlasses to retrieve the horde. This time, perhaps threatened by the severity of the weather, they apparently engaged in no prolonged debate about making off with someone else's grain. "And sure it was God's good providence that we found this corn," Winslow and Bradford later observed, "for else we know not how we should have done...."

Master Jones headed back to the boats and the *Mayflower*, presumably accompanied by his sailors, but Captain Standish and seventeen others remained ashore, camping again, and exploring more the next day. They wandered onto another graveyard, where they unearthed the skeletal remains of what appeared to be a blond-haired European, buried alongside the skeleton of a small child, along with a sailor's uniform, European tools, and Indian artifacts. They also examined some abandoned Indian dwellings, but encountered no Indians. With increasing numbers of their party cold and coughing, they returned to the *Mayflower*. Back aboard ship, as they reviewed their explorations, the Pilgrim leaders admitted that they had not encountered a suitable location for their colony. Next, they agreed, they would explore the western side of Cape Cod Bay.[5]

CHAPTER NINE

"The Best They Could Find"

"Indians! Indians!" The men in camp heard the alarm, but barely had time to react before a shower of arrows fell among them. For weeks, they had been searching for Indians—now they had found them and the Indians were attacking. Led by Captain Standish and Governor Carver, a ten-man expedition had left the *Mayflower* in the shallop on December 6, again searching for a good location for the colony. Among them were William Bradford, Edward Winslow, Stephen Hopkins, and *Mayflower* pilot Robert Coppin. It was Coppin, who had been to Cape Cod before, who had encouraged them to search for

Armed with a deadly long bow, an Indian archer stands ready to do battle. English artist John White made this watercolor portrait in the late sixteenth century.

LIBRARY OF CONGRESS

good ground on the other side of the bay. They were likely motivated by a rising sense of urgency: aboard ship, illness was spreading among the passengers and some appeared critically ill.[1]

"Their Arrows Came Flying amongst Us"

A First Encounter with Native Americans Turns Violent

"The water froze on our clothes, and made them … like coats of iron"

Two days before the latest expedition departed, one of the Pilgrims died. His name was Edward Thompson, and he was a servant to William and Susanna White. Ironically, a few days earlier, the White family had added new life to the *Mayflower*: Susanna White, one of the three pregnant women who had made the voyage, gave birth to a son. He was named Peregrine White—the first child born to the Pilgrims in America—and he would survive the grim shipboard conditions in which he was born to live a long life in America. Others among the Pilgrims, however, were not faring so well. They were now extremely low on food. Their reduced diet left them weakened and susceptible to illness, and the wet, bitterly cold New England weather was helping no one. The severe weather also complicated their search for a colony site: as the ten-man expedition rowed the shallop along the Cape Cod coastline on December 6, the salt spray froze on the men's clothing, making it "like coats of iron."

With their shallop—a light sailboat they had brought aboard the *Mayflower*—a ten-man exploration party set out to find the best location for the Pilgrim colony.

AMERICAN BOOK COMPANY

They put ashore near the modern Massachusetts town of Eastham, still on the east side of the bay. As they prepared to beach the shallop, they spotted a group of Indians farther down the shore, crowding around a large object on the edge of the bay. Instead of trying to make immediate contact, the party posted guards and encamped for the night. When they moved out the next day, the Indians were gone. On the beach, the Pilgrims found the remains of "a great fish like a grampus"—perhaps a beached killer whale—which the Indians had been butchering. They scouted around all day, but found neither the Indians nor a suitable location for the colony. At night, they built a makeshift fort of logs and brush, posted guards, and bedded down by a large fire. In the middle of the night they were abruptly awakened by "a hideous and great cry," which they attributed to wolves—but which later proved to be Indian war cries.

The next day they were attacked. Some of the Pilgrims had carelessly left their firearms on the shore where they had beached the shallop, and a band of Indians attempted to capture the weapons. To cover their raid on the firearms, the Indians unleashed a volley of arrows on the Pilgrims' campsite—which is how the explorers found themselves in a hail of arrows. Remarkably, no one was hit. The Pilgrims on the beach yelled a warning to the others—"Indians! Indians!"—and the men in camp opened up with their firearms. It was a brisk skirmish, but apparently no one on either side was killed. Outgunned, the Indians retreated into the forest, and the Pilgrims "gave God solemn thanks and praise for their deliverance." They dubbed the site of their skirmish "the First Encounter," and Winslow and Bradford recorded the combat in *Mourt's Relation*:

—◆◆————————◆◆—

Wednesday, the sixth of December, we set out, being very cold and hard weather. We were a long while after we launched from the ship, before we could get clear of a sandy

207

point, *which lay within less than a furlong of the same. In which time two were very sick, and Edward Tilley had like to have [fainted] with cold. The gunner also was sick unto death (but hope of trucking made him to go), and so remained all that day and the next night. At length we got clear of the sandy point, and got up our sails, and within an hour or two we got under the weather shore, and then had smoother water and better sailing. But it was very cold; for the water froze on our clothes, and made them many times like coats of iron.*

We sailed six or seven leagues by the shore, but saw neither river nor creek. At length we met with a tongue of land, being flat off from the shore, with a sandy point. We bore up to gain the point, and found there a fair income or road of a bay, being a league over at the narrowest, and some two or three in length; but we made right over to the land before us, and left the discovery of this income till the next day. As we drew near to the shore, we espied some ten or twelve Indians very busy about a black thing—what it was we could not tell—till afterwards they saw us, and ran to and fro, as if they

As they hiked through the forest surrounding Cape Cod Bay, the Pilgrim explorers were introduced to the severity of New England's winter weather— snow, freezing rain, and bitterly cold temperatures.

HISTORY OF THE UNITED STATES

had been carrying something away. We landed a league or two from them, and had much ado to put ashore anywhere, it lay so full of flat sands. When we came to shore, we made us a barricade and got firewood, and set out sentinels, and betook us to our lodging, such as it was. We saw the smoke of the fire which the savages made that night about four or five miles from us.

In the morning we divided our company, some eight in the shallop, and the rest on the shore went to discover this place. But we found it only to be a bay, without either river or creek coming into it. Yet we deemed it to be as good a harbor as Cape Cod; for they that sounded it found a ship might ride in five fathom water. We on the land found it to be a level soil, but none of the fruitfullest. We saw two [brooks] of fresh water, which were the first running streams that we saw in the country; but one might stride over them. We found also a great fish, called a grampus, dead on the sands. They in the shallop found two of them also in the bottom of the bay, dead in like sort. They were cast up at high water, and could not get off for the frost and ice. They were some five or six paces long, and about two inches thick of fat, and fleshed like a swine. They would have yielded a great deal of oil, if there had been time and means to have taken it. So we, finding nothing for our turn, both we and our shallop returned.

We then directed our course along the sea sands to the place where we first saw the Indians. When we were there, we saw it was also a grampus which they were cutting up.... We found here and there a piece scattered by the way, as it seemed, for haste. This place the most were minded we should

> *"About midnight we heard a great and hideous cry"*

call the Grampus Bay, because we found so many of them there. We followed the tract of the Indians' bare feet a good way on the sands. At length we saw where they struck into the woods by the side of a pond. As we went to view the place, one said he thought he saw an Indian house among the trees; so went up to see. And here we and the shallop lost sight one of another till night, it being now about nine or ten o'clock. So we lit on a path, but saw no house, and followed a great way into the woods. At length we found where corn had been set, but not that year. And on, we found a great burying place, one part whereof was encompassed with a large palisade, like a church-yard with young [saplings] four or five yards long, set as close one by another as they could, two or three foot in the ground. Within it was full of graves, some bigger and some less. Some were also paled about; and others had like an Indian house made over them, but not matted. Those graves were more sumptuous than those at Corn Hill; yet we dug none of them up, but only viewed them and went our way. Without the palisade were graves also, but not so costly. From this place we went and found more corn ground, but not of this year. As we ranged, we lit on four or five Indian houses, which had been lately dwelt in; but they were uncovered, and had no mats about them; else they were like those we found at Corn Hill, but had not been so lately dwelt in. There was nothing left but two or three pieces of old mats, a little sedge, also a little further we found two baskets full of parched acorns hid in the ground, which we supposed had been corn when we began to dig the same; we cast earth thereon again, and went our way. All this while we saw no people.

We went ranging up and down till the sun began to draw low, and then we hasted out of the woods, that we might come to our shallop, which, when we were out of the woods, we espied a great way off, and called them to come unto us; the which they did as soon as they could, for it was not yet high water. They were exceeding glad to see us, for they feared because they had not seen us in so long a time, thinking we would have kept by the shore side. So being both weary and faint—for we had eaten nothing all that day—we fell to make our rendezvous and get firewood, which always costs us a great deal of labor. By that time we had done and our shallop come to us, it was within night; and we fed upon such victuals as we had, and betook us to our rest, after we had set out our watch.

About midnight we heard a great and hideous cry, and our sentinel called, "Arm! Arm!" So we bestirred ourselves and shot off a couple of muskets, and the noise ceased. We concluded that it was a company of wolves or foxes, for one told us he had heard such a noise in Newfoundland.

About five o'clock in the morning we began to be stirring, and two or three which doubted whether their pieces would go off or no, made trial of them and shot them off, but thought nothing at all. After prayer we prepared ourselves for breakfast and for a journey, and it being now the twilight in the morning, it was thought meet to carry the things down to the shallop. Some said it was not best to carry the armor down. Others said, they would be readier.

Carrying early-style firearms, the Pilgrim explorers moved cautiously through the bayside woodlands, hoping for a peaceful first encounter with the region's Native American inhabitants. But it was not to be.

AMERICAN BOOK COMPANY

"Their arrows
came flying
amongst us"

*Two or three said they would not carry theirs till they went
themselves, but mistrusting nothing at all. As it fell out, the
water not being high enough, they laid the things down upon
the shore, and came up to breakfast. Anon, all upon a sudden, we heard a great and sudden cry, which we knew to be
the same voices, though they varied their notes. One of our
company, being abroad, came running in, and cried, "They
are men! Indians! Indians!" and [soon] their arrows came
flying amongst us. Our men ran out with all speed to recover
their arms, as by the good providence of God they did. In
the meantime Captain Miles Standish, having a [flintlock
firearm] ready, made a shot, and after him another. After
they two had shot, other two of us were ready; but he wished
us not to shoot till we could take aim, for we knew not what
need we should have; and there were four only of us which
had their arms there ready, and stood before the open side
of our barricade, which was first assaulted. They thought it
best to defend it, lest the enemy should take it and our stuff,
and so have the more vantage against us. Our care was no
less for the shallop, but we hoped all the rest would defend
it. We called unto them to know how it was with them, and
they answered "Well! Well!" every one, and, "Be of good
courage!" We heard three of their pieces go off, and the rest
called for a firebrand to light their matches. One took a log
out of the fire on his shoulder and went and carried it unto
them, which was thought did not a little discourage our
enemies. The cry of our enemies was dreadful, especially
when our men ran out to recover their arms. Their note was
after this manner, "Waath woach ha ha hach woach." Our*

men were no sooner come to their arms, but the enemy was ready to assault them.

There was a lusty man, and no whit less valiant, who was thought to be their captain, stood behind a tree within half a musket-shot of us, and there let his arrows fly at us. He was seen to shoot three arrows, which were all avoided, for he at whom the first arrow was aimed saw it, and stooped down, and it flew over him. The rest were avoided also. He stood three shots of a musket. At length one took, as he said, full aim at him, after which he gave an extraordinary cry, and away they went all. We followed them about a quarter of a mile; but we left six to keep our shallop, for we were careful of our business. Then we shouted all together two several times, and shot off a couple of muskets, and so returned. This

Indian warriors release a shower of arrows on their enemies in this late sixteenth-century illustration. While searching for a site to establish their colony, the Pilgrims experienced firsthand the prowess of Indian bowmen.

LIBRARY OF CONGRESS

we did that they might see we were not afraid of them, nor discouraged.

Thus it pleased God to vanquish our enemies and give us deliverance. By their noise we could not guess that they were less than thirty or forty, though some thought that they were many more. Yet, in the dark of the morning, we could not so well discern them among the trees, as they could see us by our fireside. We took up 18 of their arrows, which we have sent to England by Master Jones; some whereof were headed with brass, others with [deer] horn, and others with eagles' claws. Many more no doubt were shot, for these we found were almost covered with leaves; yet, by the especial providence of God, none of them either hit or hurt us, though many came close by us and on every side of us, and some coats which hung up in our barricade were shot through and through. So after we had given God thanks for our deliverance, we took our shallop and went on our journey....[2]

"[We] Saw Many Indians"

The Pilgrims Encounter Native American Culture

Although the Pilgrims would be the first Europeans to successfully colonize New England, they were not the first to explore it. Nor were they the first to make contact with its Native American inhabitants. Hundreds of years before Columbus landed in the New World in 1492, Viking adventurers such as Leif Ericson may have explored the New England coastline. A few years after Columbus's epic voyage, Italian navigator John Cabot sailed along the coast of New

England in the service of England's King Henry VII. In 1524, Giovanni de Verrazano, another Italian, explored the region on a long voyage up the American East Coast for France's King Francis I. French seaman Jacques Cartier cruised the region's waters ten years later, and French navigator Samuel Champlain, who would

be famous as the founder of Canada, also explored the New England coast and the Cape Cod region in 1604, noting that the Native Americans who inhabited Cape Cod Bay were skilled fishermen and farmers.

Between Cabot and Champlain, numerous English explorers sailed the waters off Cape Cod, probed its interior, and made contact with the Indians of the region. Among them were Bartholomew Gosnold in 1602, and Martin Pring in 1603—both of whom reported peaceful exchanges with Native Americans. On his 1614 voyage along the coast of what would become Massachusetts, Captain John Smith counted dozens of Indian villages, and noted numerous seaside fields of corn and flourishing gardens. Smith's personal contact with the region's Indians was mostly positive, and he condemned other English explorers for "treachery among the savages" that would complicate future relations with the Indians. Among those engaging in such "treachery" was Captain George Weymouth, who kidnapped Indians from the coast of Maine in 1605. More notorious, and much more damaging to future relations with New England's Indians, was Captain Thomas Hunt—"a worthless fellow" in the words of a contemporary—who commanded one of Smith's two ships on his 1614 expedition. After Smith had returned to England, Hunt ruthlessly captured a large number of Cape Cod area Indians and sold them to Spanish buyers as slaves.

In 1602, English explorer Bartholomew Gosnold attempted to establish the first English colony in New England. He failed, but did give Cape Cod its name. A popular account of his exploration may have aided the Pilgrims.

CALIFORNIA STATE UNIVERSITY LIBRARY

In response, some of the region's Indian tribes routinely attacked European strangers for years to come, wiping out almost the entire crew of a shipwrecked French ship in 1615. At about the same time, English sailors ambushed and killed a group of local Indians, which further embittered the area's tribes. In 1619, the year before the Pilgrims landed, English explorer Thomas Dermer and his crew were attacked and suffered serious casualties while exploring the area. Dermer blamed the attacks on Hunt and other European explorers who had needlessly provoked the Indians' hostility. "We had not now that fair quarter among the savages as before…," he wrote, "for now almost everywhere, where [the Indians] were of any strength, they sought to betray us." The English losses were minor, however, compared to the massive death that had swept through the region's Native American population in the early 1600s, following contact with European explorers. An unknown epidemic killed the region's native inhabitants by the thousands, reducing the local Indian population to a fraction of its former size and leaving

French explorer Samuel Champlain explored the Cape Cod region more than fifteen years before the Pilgrims arrived, and made note of the area's Native American population.

TORONTO PUBLIC LIBRARY

the region marked by barren clearings where Indian villages had once existed.

The Indians seen by the Pilgrims on their first venture ashore were from the small Pamet tribe, which had a reputation for being peaceable. Ironically, one of the reasons the Pilgrims decided to locate the colony across Cape Cod Bay from their original anchorage was because they feared they had offended the Pamet by taking their corn. Their decision to keep looking led them into the territory occupied by the more combative Nauset tribe, and the violent exchange of the "First Encounter."

Despite their debatable decision to raid the Indians' store of corn and other items, many historians would credit the Pilgrims with establishing a far better record of relations with Native Americans than that of most other European colonists in America. The English monarchy reportedly did not want to imitate the brutal methods by which the Spanish had conquered and occupied their New World claims. Even so, the territory claimed by England in the New World *was* inhabited by Native Americans. While they viewed land ownership dramatically differently than Europeans, the fact that they had battled one another for tribal territory over the ages demonstrated that Native Americans did recognize territory—a fact that many European colonists ignored. The English justified their claims in North America in large measure based on the ancient Roman doctrine of *vacuum domicilium*—that the continent was a wilderness inhabited by people of primitive cultures who were unable to develop or civilize it.

Under existing English law, the Pilgrims could legally lay claim to wilderness land in America based on the English Doctrine of Discovery by which King Henry VII commissioned famed explorer John Cabot to explore the New World in 1496. Henry VII had declared that "whatsoever islands, countries, regions or provinces of heathens and infidels, in whatsoever part of the world" discovered by English explorers thereafter

English King Henry VII commissioned navigator John Cabot to explore the New World, and in 1497 Cabot discovered North America. To lay claim to the continent, Henry VII proclaimed a "Doctrine of Discovery" that governed future explorations as well.

NATIONAL PORTRAIT GALLERY

belonged to the English monarchy and could therefore be colonized. The Doctrine of Discovery, like *vacuum domicilium*, was based on the argument that native populations could not possibly cultivate more than a fraction of available New World lands, and that unoccupied wilderness was therefore open to colonization. "In the interior of America," wrote English philosopher John Locke in his *Two Treatises on Government*, "there are individuals and families living in conditions not unlike the first peopling of the world.... That old rule of propriety—that everyone should have as much land as he could make use of—would still hold in the modern world without [inconveniencing] anyone."

Unlike many European colonists, who had no regard for Indian lands, the Pilgrims tried to do more than was required by the Doctrine of Discovery, claiming only what appeared to be unused land, and treating Indian-occupied property with comparative respect. Acting within those controversial parameters, the Pilgrims established a model for dealing with Native American people that would be unsurpassed by most European and American authorities in the three centuries to come. As twenty-first-century Pilgrim expert Jeremy D. Bangs would observe of Plymouth Colony: "There is no general pattern of ruthless defrauding of the Indians, despite the obvious expectation that in the end most of the territory would become the property of the English...."

Although its Native American population had been devastated by recent epidemics, the region of the future American state of Massachusetts—which included Plymouth Colony—was still inhabited by thousands of the Massachuset, the Pamet, the Nauset, the Mahican, the Pennacook, the Nipmuc, the Mashpee, and the Pocomtuc. A detailed description of the Native American culture that awaited the Pilgrims was recorded by John Brereton, a clergyman with Bartholomew Gosnold's 1602 expedition, which unsuccessfully attempted to establish the first English colony in New England. Gosnold landed briefly at Cape Cod, which he reportedly so named, then sailed southward to Buzzard's Bay and the islands on the southern coast of Massachusetts. Back home in England, Brereton published a popular account of the voyage, which fascinated readers with a colorful depiction of the Native Americans he had encountered. The tribe he described lived to the south of Cape Cod, but their dress and customs were undoubtedly similar to those of the Indian peoples encountered by the Pilgrims in 1620:

[We] saw many Indians, which are tall, big-boned men, all naked save they cover their private parts with a black-tewed skin, much like a blacksmith's apron, tied about their middle and between their legs in behind. They gave us of their fish, already boiled, which they carried in a basket made of twigs.... They also gave us their tobacco, which they [smoke] green, but dried into powder, very strong and pleasant, and much better than any I have tasted in England. The necks of their pipes are made of hard dried clay, both red and white, [and] the other part is a piece of hollow copper very finely closed and cemented together. We gave them certain trifles, such as knives, points and such like, which they much esteemed....

Now the next day…we sighted nine canoes or boats with fifty Indians in them, coming towards us from this part of the mainland, where we two days before had landed. We went out on the seaside to meet them; and coming somewhat near

"They also gave us their tobacco, which they [smoke] green"

them, they all sat down upon the stones, calling aloud to us (as we rightly guessed) to do the like, a little distance from them. Having sat a while in this order, Captain Gosnold willed me to go unto them, to see what countenance they would make; but as soon as I came up unto them, one of them…spoke unto their lord or captain, which sat in the midst of them, who presently rose up and took a large beaver skin from one that stood about him, and gave it unto me, which I requited for that time the best I could: but I pointed towards Captain Gosnold [and] made signs unto him that he was our captain, and desirous to be his friend, and enter league with him, which (as I perceived) he understood, and made signs of joy. Whereupon Captain Gosnold with the rest of his company, being twenty in all, came up unto them, and after many signs of congratulations (Captain Gosnold presenting their lord with certain trifles which they wondered at, and highly esteemed), we became very great friends. [We] sent for meat aboard our shallop, and gave them such meats as we had then already dressed, whereof they disliked nothing but our mustard, for which they made many a sour face. While we were thus being merry, one of them conveyed a target of ours into one of their canoes, [but] speaking angrily about him (as we perceived by his countenance), [their lord] caused it presently to be brought back again.

So the rest of the day we spent in trading with them for furs—beavers, lucerns, martins, wildcat skins, very large and deep fur, black foxes, [rabbit] skins the color of our hares but somewhat less, very large deerskins, seal skins and other beasts' skins unknown to us. They have also great store of copper, some very red and some of a paler color. [All] have chains, earrings or collars of this metal. They head some of their arrows with it, much like our broad arrow heads, very workmanlike. Their chains are many hollow pieces cemented together, each piece of the size of one of our reeds, a finger in length, ten or twelve of them together on a string, which they wear about their necks. Their collars they wear about their bodies like bandoliers…four hundred pieces in a collar, very fine and evenly set together. Besides these, they have large drinking cups, made like sculls, and other thin plates of copper made much like our boar spear blades, all which they so little esteem as they offered their fairest collars or chains for a knife or such like trifle.… I was desirous to understand where they had such store of this metal, and made signs to one of them (with whom I was very familiar). Taking a piece of copper in his hand, he made a hole with his finger in the ground, and pointed to the mainland from whence they came.

They strike fire in this manner: everyone carries about him in a purse of tewed leather, a mineral stone (which I take to be their copper), and with a flat emery stone tied fast to the end of a little stick, gently strikes upon the mineral stone. Within a stroke or two, a spark falls upon a piece of touch-wood (much like our sponge in England) and with the least

Explorer John Cabot

THE CABOTS AND THE DISCOVERY OF AMERICA

Decades before the Pilgrims landed at Cape Cod, various European explorers had kidnapped and otherwise mistreated local Indians, provoking their distrust of all newcomers. As a result, European expeditions to the region on the eve of the Pilgrims' arrival had been attacked by local tribes.

WIKIMEDIA COMMONS

"Their eyebrows and hair are black, which they wear long, tied up behind in knots"

spark makes a fire. We also had of their flax, with which they make many strings and cords, but it is not so bright of color as ours in England. I am persuaded they have great store [of it] growing upon the mainland, as also mines and many other rich commodities, which we, wanting both time and means, could not possibly discover....

These people are exceeding courteous, gentle of disposition and well conditioned, excelling all others that we have seen for shape of body and lovely favor. I think they excel all the people of America. Of stature [they] are much higher than we [and] of complexion or color much like a dark olive. Their eyebrows and hair are black, which they wear long, tied up behind in knots, whereon they prick the feathers of fowls in the fashion of a crown. Some of them are black thin-bearded. They make beards of the hair of beasts, and one of them offered a beard of their making to one of our sailors for his that grew on his face, which because it was of a red color, they judged to be none of his own. They are quick-eyed, and steadfast in their looks, fearless of others harming them, as intending none themselves. Some of the meaner sort are given to pilfering, which the very name of savage (not weighing their ignorance in good or evil) may easily excuse. Their garments are of deerskins, and some of them wear furs round and close about their necks. They pronounce our language with great facility. One day I spoke to one of them these words: "How now, sir, are you so saucy with my tobacco?" Without any further repetition, he suddenly spoke so plain and distinctly as if he had been a long scholar in the language. Many other such trials we had which are here needless to repeat....[3]

"These people are exceeding courteous, gentle of disposition and well conditioned"

"It Was the Best They Could Find"

The Pilgrims Pick a Site for Their Colony

Finally, they found it—the location for their colony. After battling the Indians, they had retreated to the shallop and again sailed westward, exploring Cape Cod Bay's southern shoreline. After several hours, the wind picked up and began to pelt them with snow and rain. The seas began to roll in large waves, and they realized they were in the midst of a heavy gale. "The seas were grown so great that we were much troubled and in great danger," Winslow and Bradford would later recall, "and the night grew on." In the darkness, tossed by rough seas and slammed with driving snow and rain, their shallop began to come apart. First a hinge holding the rudder in place popped off, then the boat's mast split into three sections. After surviving a potentially deadly Indian attack, would they now be killed by wind and waves? Ahead they saw an island in the darkness, but its shore was lined with rocks, and they appeared headed for a shipwreck—until the storm suddenly pushed their boat straight onto a stretch of sandy beach.

Safely beached, they built a bonfire to combat the cold, and there they spent the night. The next morning they realized they were on a forested island—Clark's Island, it would be called—and were safe from sea and Indians because "it pleased the Divine Providence." It was Saturday, December 9. The storm had passed, the sun appeared, and they remained on the island all day, drying weapons and equipment, and presumably repairing their shallop. They rested the next day, which was a Sunday, and the following day—Monday, December 11, 1620—they sailed westward from the island into a broad, sheltered harbor. There, they found their new home. On the shore before them lay a broad clearing that sloped upward from the harbor to a high hill. The site had been cleared of timber, presumably by the Indians, but there were no signs of Native Americans anywhere—just empty, abandoned cornfields.

Unknown to the Pilgrims at the time, the location was the former site of a sprawling village inhabited by the Patuxet Indians, who were allied with the larger Pokanoket tribe. It had been depicted on Frenchman Samuel Champlain's map as a bustling population center, but it had been ravaged by a deadly epidemic three years earlier, and was now forsaken and uninhabited. Encouraged by the favorable appearance of the site, they put ashore to explore the area, likely beaching their shallop

After battling Indians and a winter storm on Cape Cod Bay, a party of explorers from the *Mayflower* landed on the bay's western shore and warmed themselves with a bonfire. Their mission: to find a site for the Pilgrims' colony.

BRITISH LIBRARY

On December 11, 1620, Pilgrim leaders found a likely location for their colony—cleared, high ground with a freshwater brook overlooking a sheltered harbor. It would become the site of Plymouth Colony.

ECLECTIC HISTORY OF THE UNITED STATES

at or not far from a huge granite boulder that would become famous as the fabled "Plymouth Rock." If they stepped upon it, were near it, or noticed it, these first Pilgrims to come ashore on the site of Plymouth Colony did not record it—ever. Contrary to countless works of art, there were no women in the landing party that day, nor were there any Indians to greet them. The account of the Pilgrim forefathers landing on Plymouth Rock would not be recorded until more than a century later in 1741, when ninety-five-year-old John Faunce, the son of settlers who came to Plymouth Colony in 1623, insisted that his father had been told by some of the original Pilgrims that they had landed on the rock.

Ashore on the site—wherever they first landed—Carver, Standish, Bradford, Winslow, and the others walked the grounds of the sprawling clearing. It was cut by a small stream that ran along the base of the hill—Bradford called it "a very sweet brook"—and emptied into a salt marsh.

In this fanciful nineteenth-century lithograph, the Pilgrims explore the site of Plymouth Colony while the *Mayflower* rides at anchor nearby, and a Native American man observes their activity. In reality, a mere handful a Pilgrim leaders were the first to land on the site; they came in a small boat, saw no Indians, and the *Mayflower* lay some thirty miles away.

LIBRARY OF CONGRESS

Other, smaller brooks coursed through the area, which would provide an easily accessible source of drinking water, and the ground was good, composed of rich, black earth. Lying as it did on the west side of Cape Cod Bay, the site would be a long row from the offshore fishing grounds where the Pilgrims hoped to pay their way with hauls of codfish, but they sounded the harbor and found that it would accommodate ships as large as the *Mayflower*. They would have to make a long walk to cut firewood or fell timber, but having a cleared site would save countless man-hours of labor, help compensate for their late arrival in the midst of winter, and would offer protection from Indian attack. The crest of the hill was a perfect location for a defensive fortification that would have a clear field of fire for artillery over the entire site below and an unobscured view of the sprawling bay. The location was far superior to anything they had seen before, and they were cheered by the prospect of building their homes here—but it would have to be approved with a vote by all the passengers aboard the *Mayflower*.

In *Mourt's Relation*, Winslow and Bradford described the future site of Plymouth Plantation as it appeared to those first Pilgrims who explored it:

We marched also into the land, and found divers cornfields, and little running brooks, a place very good for situation.... there is a great deal of land cleared, and hath been planted with corn three or four years ago, and there is

Produced in 1869, almost 250 years after the Pilgrims selected the site for their colony, this dramatic image depicts Pilgrim men and women climbing ashore atop Plymouth Rock. At the actual initial landing, there were no women present, and while those who were first ashore likely landed near or at the rock, they left no record of it.

LIBRARY OF CONGRESS

a very sweet brook [that] runs under the hill side, and many delicate springs of as good water as can be drunk, and where we may harbor our shallops and boats exceeding well, and in this brook much good fish in their season; on the further side of the river also much corn-ground cleared. In one field is a great hill on which we point to make a platform and plant our ordnance, which will command all round about. From thence we may see into the bay, and into the sea, and we may see thence Cape Cod. Our greatest labor will be fetching of our wood, which is half a quarter of an English mile, but there is enough so far off.[4]

"There is a very sweet brook [that] runs under the hill side"

Likewise, William Bradford, writing in *Of Plymouth Plantation*, would also praise the location in a terse description.

"This news...did much to comfort them"

On Monday they sounded the harbor and found it fit for shipping, and marched into the land and found divers corn-fields and little running brooks, a place (as they supposed) fit for situation. At least it was the best they could find, and the season and their present necessity made them glad to accept of it. So they returned to their ship again with this news to the rest of their people, which did much to comfort them.[5]

CHAPTER TEN

"It Was the Lord Which Upheld Them"

When William Bradford returned to the *Mayflower*, he learned that his wife was dead. Several days earlier, twenty-three-year-old Dorothy May Bradford fell off the *Mayflower* into the icy waters of Cape Cod Bay and drowned. Bradford got the news the evening he climbed back aboard the *Mayflower* with the exploratory party. The couple had just observed their seventh wedding anniversary. How did she fall? Was she trying to board a ship's boat to go ashore to wash clothes again? Did she lean too far over the ship's railing? Or did she slip on the icy deck and tumble overboard? History has no answer. William Bradford recorded no details, and no other known record exists. Plymouth Colony historian Nathaniel Morton, who was Bradford's nephew, gave no details in his work, *New England's Memorial*. Neither did Puritan historian Cotton Mather, who simply reported more than seventy years later that Dorothy Bradford's drowning was an accident.[1]

Her decks covered in ice, the *Mayflower* rides at anchor in Cape Cod Bay. As William Bradford and other Pilgrim leaders explored the forested shores of Cape Cod, the rest of the *Mayflower*'s passengers awaited their return aboard ship.

LIBRARY OF CONGRESS

"Faint Not, Poor Soul, in God Still Trust"

William Bradford Grieves in Silence

"Fear not the things thou suffer must"

In all his writings, William Bradford kept silent about the death of "his dearest consort," as Mather described Dorothy Bradford. In an appendix to Bradford's *Of Plymouth Plantation*, among a list of deaths that occurred in the colony's early days, he penned a brief notation about himself and the tragedy—"his wife died soon after their arrival." Did he write nothing more because he considered his wife's death too personal? Was he simply too broken-hearted to record or recall the event? Or was there another reason? Centuries later, some would speculate that the ordeal of the Atlantic passage and the stark reality of the American wilderness overwhelmed young Dorothy, and that she committed suicide—jumping from the *Mayflower* into the near-freezing waters of Cape Cod Bay. No historical evidence confirms a suicide, but beginning in the late nineteenth century, the suggestion wormed its way into the Pilgrim story.

Back home in England, Bradford had a three-year-old son who would never get to grow up in his mother's loving care, and the plans Bradford had to build a home, a family, and a life in the wilderness

A nineteenth-century artist's conception of a young Pilgrim woman: did it resemble twenty-three-year-old Dorothy Bradford?

LIBRARY OF CONGRESS

with his "dearest consort" were not to be. How did he handle such grief and disappointment? Although he left no written record that expressed his feelings, he did eventually write these heart-felt words about trusting in the sovereignty of God:

> *Faint not, poor soul, in God still trust,*
> *Fear not the things thou suffer must,*
> *For, whom he loves, he doth chastise,*
> *And then all tears wipes from their eyes.*

It was a reference to a passage of Scripture in the New Testament that was familiar to Puritans and Separatists, and which would prove relevant to the trials and tribulations they would face in the wilds of the New World. It was one of the Bible passages from which William Bradford likely sought comfort as he grieved for his young wife:

My son, despise not the chastening of the Lord, neither faint when thou art rebuked of him.

For whom the Lord loveth, he chasteneth: and he scourgeth every son that he receiveth.

If ye endure chastening, God offered himself unto you as unto sons: for what son is it whom the father chasteneth not?

If therefore ye be without correction, whereof all are partakers, then are ye [illegitimate] and not sons.

Moreover we have had the fathers of our bodies which corrected us, and we gave them reverence: should we not much rather be in subjection unto the father of spirits, that we might live?

For they verily for a few days chastened us after their own pleasure, but he chastened us for our profit, that we might be partakers of his holiness.

Now no chastising for the present seemeth to be joyous, but grievous: but afterward, it bringeth the quiet fruit of righteousness, unto them which are thereby exercised.[2]

"For whom the Lord loveth, he chasteneth"

"Hard and Difficult Beginning"

The Pilgrims Struggle to Construct Their Homes

The sound of cast-iron axes chopping wood rang through the New England forest—the Pilgrims were felling trees to build homes. Although undoubtedly affected by Dorothy Bradford's drowning, the Pilgrims had gone forward with their plans—they had to start their colony. On Friday, December 15, 1620, the *Mayflower* had weighed anchor, and Master Jones had set sail across Cape Cod Bay to its western shoreline, which lay almost thirty miles away. On Saturday, the ship anchored in what would become Plymouth Harbor, and on Sunday, the Pilgrims observed the Lord's Day aboard ship. The next day, Monday, December 18, they put ashore another exploratory party. Its members found much to like about the site: cleared, high ground with fresh drinking water and easy access to the bay and the Atlantic beyond. Some of the colonists wanted another site, but on Wednesday, December 20—after prayer and consultation—a majority agreed to build the colony at the site of the cleared hillside discovered nine days earlier by Governor Carver's exploration party—on the abandoned Indian village site cut by the "very sweet brook."

Delayed by gale-force winds and driving rains, they were unable to go to work until Saturday, December 23. That day, a work force finally went ashore, hiked into the forest and went to work. Conditions were now becoming desperate: more people were falling ill in the confined quarters of the *Mayflower*, rations were running low, winter weather was fully upon them, and Master Jones was anxious to take his ship back to England. Their first chore was to build a "common house" for storage, protection, and temporary

A colonist fells trees in the New England forest. In late December of 1620, the Pilgrims went to work preparing the site for their settlement and building their homes.

AMERICAN BOOK COMPANY

The Pilgrims established their Plymouth settlement on high ground overlooking a sheltered harbor on the western shore of Cape Cod Bay.

MAP BY AMBER COLLERAN

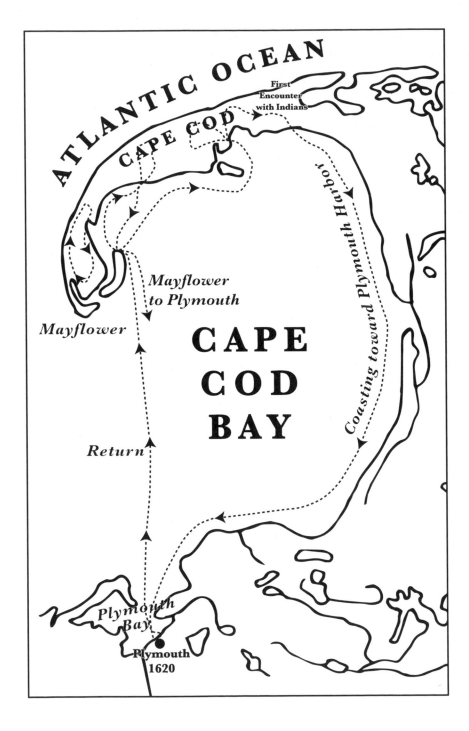

shelter as needed. By early January, it was complete—although it almost burned down soon afterward when a spark set the thatch roof afire. With the common house constructed, the Pilgrims turned to their homes.

With axes and saws, they felled trees, hauled the timber back to the site, split the logs, hewed rough planks, and began erecting their homes. Instead of the log cabins that would typify later eras of the American frontier, the Pilgrims initially built crude frame clapboard cottages equipped with plaster-like wattle-and-daub interior walls and dirt floors. They were topped with the thatched roofs familiar to the Separatists from England's East Midlands, although the New England version was apparently thatched with marsh reeds and cattail leaves. Most of them stayed on the *Mayflower* at night and worked during the day. They planned to put up at least nineteen houses on the broad clearing that had once been the Patuxet village. A rough town plan laid houses on both sides of a narrow street that extended up the hill with a single intersecting lane.

In the rush to erect housing, it was agreed that the single young men each would join a Pilgrim family, so that fewer houses would have to be built at first. Small plots of land were marked off, and lots were drawn to see who would build on each of them—except for Governor Carver and Captain Standish. A governor's home, it was determined, would be raised on a larger corner lot, and Captain Standish would build his house near the crest of the hill. There, the Pilgrims built a crude artillery emplacement, fortified with a battery of artillery composed of cannon from the *Mayflower*. The cannon tubes and artillery carriages were eventually wrestled ashore and hauled up the hill, where they were mounted on a wooden platform—all under the supervision of Captain Standish. The artillery thus had a clear field of fire over the lands surrounding the fledgling village as well as the shoreline and harbor.

Slowly, the row of thatch-roofed cottages rose—following the understanding "that every man should build his own house." From the beginning, it appears, the Pilgrims referred to their colony as Plymouth or New Plymouth—the name placed on it years earlier by Captain John Smith after exploring the region. The Pilgrim departure from Plymouth, England, no doubt reinforced the name, and it stuck—spelled at times as "Plimouth." Carved out of the American wilderness, Plymouth was hardly reminiscent of England's bustling southern port of the same name—and was actually the site of a massive graveyard. As they cleared the land for habitation, the Pilgrims began uncovering skeletal remains—a lot of them. It was grisly evidence of the killer epidemic that had wiped out the Patuxet villagers who had inhabited the site just a few years earlier. The grim discovery would prove ominous, for in time the site would also become a burial ground for many of the Pilgrims.

A simple planked cottage topped by a thatched roof was common in early seventeenth-century England. The Pilgrims built their homes in a similar fashion, although the first houses at Plymouth Colony were much smaller and more like cottages.

WIKIMEDIA COMMONS

Initially, however, the chief focus of the new inhabitants of Plymouth Colony was building homes and establishing the colony. Enduring the fierce New England winter weather, they steadily, resolutely worked to raise their wilderness homes, even as they battled illness, and watched warily for possible Indian attacks. They found that they could indeed catch fish, and successfully hunt for New World wildlife—including seal and eagle meat. They continued, unsuccessfully, to try to make peaceful contact with the area's Native Americans, and from time to time explored the surrounding forest. One trek into the wood led two Pilgrims to spend the night lost in the wilds, shivering from freezing temperatures and the unnerving screaming of cougars or wildcats, which they called "lions." It was a "hard and difficult beginning...," in the words of William Bradford. Those initial arduous and challenging weeks of raising Plymouth Colony were recorded diary-style in *Mourt's Relation*:

***

Saturday, [December] 23rd. So many of us as could, went on shore, felled and carried timber, to provide themselves stuff for building.

Sunday, the 24th. Our people on shore heard a cry of some savages (as they thought) which caused an alarm, and to stand on their guard, expecting an assault, but all was quiet.

Monday, the 25th.... We went on shore, some to fell timber, some to saw, some to rive, and some to carry, so no man rested all that day. But towards night some, as they were at work, heard a noise of some Indians, which caused us all to go to our muskets, but we heard no further. So we came aboard again, and left some twenty to keep the court of guard. That night we had a sore storm of wind and rain.

Monday, the 25.... Being Christmas day, we began to drink water aboard, but at night the master caused us to have some beer, and so on board we had divers times now and then some beer, but on shore none at all.

Tuesday, the 26th. It was foul weather, that we could not go ashore.

Wednesday, the 27th. We went to work again.

Thursday, the 28th of December. So many as could went to work on the hill where we purposed to build our platform for our ordnance, which doth command all the plain and the

Stumps still rise from the street in this late nineteenth-century artist's conception of an early Colonial Era settlement. Plymouth Colony's first structures also lined a street leading up a hill, but they were built of planks, not logs, and a wooden fortification topped the hill.

AMERICAN BOOK COMPANY

bay, and from whence we may see far into the sea, and might be easier [fortified], having two rows of houses and a fair street.

So in the afternoon we went to measure out the grounds, and first we took notice of how many families there were, willing all single men that had no wives to join with some family, as they thought fit, that so we might build fewer houses, which was done, and we reduced them to nineteen families. To greater families we allotted larger plots, to every person half a pole in breadth, and three in length, and so lots were cast where every man should lie, which was done, and staked out. We thought this proportion was large enough at the first for houses and gardens, to [fence] them round, considering the weakness of our people, many of them growing ill with cold, for our former discoveries in frost and storms, and the wading at Cape Cod had brought much weakness amongst us, which increased so every day more and more, and after was the cause of many of their deaths.

Friday and Saturday. We fitted ourselves for our labor, but our people on shore were much troubled and discouraged with rain and wet, that day being very stormy and cold. We saw great smokes of fire made by the Indians, about six or seven miles from us, as we conjectured.

Monday, the 1st of January. We went early to work. We were much hindered in lying so far off from the land and having to go as the tide served, that we lost much time, for our ship drew so much water that she lay a mile and almost a half off, though a ship of seventy or eighty tons at high water may come to the shore.

Wednesday, the 3rd of January. Some of our people being abroad to get and gather thatch, they saw great fires of the Indians, and were at their cornfields, yet saw none of the savages, nor had seen any of them since we came to this bay.

Thursday, the 4th of January. Captain Miles Standish, with four or five more, went to see if they could meet with any of the savages in that place where the fires were made. They went to some of their houses, but not lately inhabited, yet could they not meet with any. As they came home, they shot at an eagle and killed her, which was excellent meat; it was hardly to be discerned from mutton.

Friday, the 5th of January. One of the sailors found alive upon the shore a herring, which the master had to his supper, *which put us in hope of fish, but as yet we had got but one cod; we wanted small hooks.*

Saturday, the 6th of January. Master Martin was very sick, and to our judgment no hope of life, so Master Carver was sent for to come aboard to speak with him about his accounts, who came the next morning.

Monday, the 8th day of January. Was a very fair day, and we went early to work. Master Jones sent the shallop, as he had formerly done, to see where fish could be got. They had a great storm at sea, and were in some danger; at night they returned with three great seals and an excellent good cod, which did assure us that we should have plenty of fish shortly.

Early colonists dig New England clams. Plymouth's location overlooking Cape Cod Bay enabled the Pilgrims to harvest shellfish—although their first such meal sickened some of them.

AMERICAN BOOK COMPANY

This day, Francis Billington, having the week before seen from the top of a tree on a high hill a great sea as he thought, went with one of the master's mates to see it. They went three miles and then came to a great water, divided into two great lakes, the bigger of them five or six miles in circuit, and in it an isle of a cable length square, the other three miles in compass; in their estimation they are fine fresh water, full of fish, and fowl. A brook issues from it; it will be an excellent help for us in time. They found seven or eight Indian houses, but not lately inhabited. When they saw the houses they were in some fear, for they were but two persons and one piece.

Tuesday, the 9th of January, was a remarkable fair day, and we went to labor that day in the building of our town, in two rows of houses for more safety. We divided by lot the plot of ground whereon to build our town. After the proportion formerly allotted, we agreed that every man should build his own house, thinking by that course men would make more haste than working in common. The common house, in which for the first we made our rendezvous, being near finished wanted only covering, it being about twenty feet square. Some should make mortar, and some gather thatch, so that in four days half of it was thatched. Frost and foul weather hindered us much, this time of the year seldom could we work half the week.

Thursday, the 11th, William Bradford being at work (for it was a fair day) was vehemently taken with a grief and pain, and so shot to his huckle-bone. It was doubted that he would have instantly died; he got cold in the former discoveries, especially the last, and felt some pain in his ankles by times,

"We agreed that every man should build his own house"

but he grew a little better towards night and in time, through God's mercy in the use of means, recovered.

Friday, the 12th, we went to work, but about noon it began to rain that it forced us to give over work. This day two of our people put us in great sorrow and care; there was four sent to gather and cut thatch in the morning, and two of them, John Goodman and Peter Brown, having cut thatch all the forenoon, went to a further place, and willed the other two to bind up that which was cut and to follow them. So they did, being about a mile and a half from our plantation. But when the two came after, they could not find them, nor hear anything of them at all, though they hallooed and shouted as loud as they could, so they returned to the company and told them of it. Whereupon Master Leaver and three or four more went to seek them, but could hear nothing of them, so they returning, sent more, but that night they could hear nothing

A Colonial Era woman plucks a goose. The Pilgrims quickly attempted to make a life in their new home, felling trees to build homes, and learning how to hunt and fish in the wilds—but their determined efforts were hampered by illness.

AMERICAN BOOK COMPANY

at all of them. The next day they armed ten or twelve men out, verily thinking the Indians had surprised them. They went seeking seven or eight miles, but could neither see nor hear anything at all, so they returned, with much discomfort to us all.

[As it turned out,] these two that were missed, at dinner time took their meat in their hands, and would go walk and refresh themselves. So going a little off they find a lake of water, and having a great mastiff bitch with them and a spaniel, by the water side they found a great deer; the dogs chased him, and they followed so far as they lost themselves and could not find the way back. They wandered all that afternoon being wet, and at night it did freeze and snow. They were slenderly appareled and had no weapons but each one his sickle, nor any victuals. They ranged up and down and could find none of the savages' habitations. When it drew to night they were much perplexed, for they could find neither harbor nor meat, but, in frost and snow, were forced to make the earth their bed and the element their covering. And another thing did very much terrify them; they heard, as they thought, two lions roaring exceedingly for a long time together, and a third, that they thought was very near them. So not knowing what to do, they resolved to climb up into a tree as their safest refuge, though that would prove an intolerable cold lodging; so they stood at the tree's root, that when the lions came they might take their opportunity of climbing up. The bitch they had to hold by the neck, for she would have been gone to the lion; but it pleased God so to dispose, that the wild beasts came not. So they walked up and down under the tree all night; it was an extremely cold night.

So soon as it was light they traveled again, passing by many lakes and brooks and woods, and in one place where the savages had burnt the space of five miles in length, which is a fine champion country, and even. In the afternoon, it

> "They lost themselves and could not find the way back"

pleased God, from a high hill they discovered the two isles in the bay, and so that night got to the plantation, being ready to faint with travail and want of victuals, and almost famished with cold. John Goodman was fain to have his shoes cut off his feet they were so swelled with cold, and it was a long while after that he was able to go; those on the shore were much comforted at their return, but they on the shipboard were grieved at deeming them lost.

But the next day, being the 14th of January, in the morning about six of the clock the wind being very great, they on shipboard spied their great new rendezvous on fire, which was to them a new discomfort, fearing because of the supposed loss of men, that the savages had fired them. Neither could they presently go to them, for want of water, but after three quarters of an hour they went, as they had purposed the day before to keep the Sabbath on shore, because now there was the greatest number of people. At their landing they heard good tidings of the return of the two men, and that the house was fired occasionally by a spark that flew into the thatch, which instantly burnt it all up but the roof stood and little hurt. The most loss was Master Carver's and William Bradford's, who then lay sick in bed, and if they had not risen with good speed, had been blown up with powder, but, through God's mercy, they had no harm. The house was as full of beds as they could lie one by another, and their muskets charged, but, blessed be God, there was no harm done.

Monday, the 15th day. It rained so much all day, that they on shipboard could not go on shore, nor they on shore do any labor but were all wet.

"And our people, so many as were in health, worked cheerfully"

Tuesday, Wednesday, Thursday, were very fair sunshiny
days, as if it had been in April, and our people, so many as
were in health, worked cheerfully....[3]

"That Which Was Most Sad and Lamentable"

Illness Kills the Pilgrims in Shocking Numbers

A young seventeenth-century mother mourns her loss. Illnesses ravaged the Pilgrim families during their first winter at Plymouth, killing almost half of those who had made the voyage to America.

RIJKSMUSEUM OF AMSTERDAM

Even as the Pilgrims worked to build their cottages, contagious illnesses swept through their ranks, striking down men, women, and children, and filling Plymouth's new common house with makeshift sickbeds occupied by the ailing. Many had sickened while in the cramped quarters of the *Mayflower*. Others fell ill from their exposure to the harsh New England winter. Some were stricken with scurvy, some apparently with tuberculosis or typhus, and others by what appears to have been pneumonia. Within a few months, scores were dead. It had begun even before Dorothy Bradford's drowning: one of the four More children sickened and died, and Mary Allerton, the third pregnant woman aboard the *Mayflower*, soon afterwards gave birth to a stillborn child. Seventeenth-century English people were accustomed to death: infant mortality, reduced life expectancy, and death by illnesses such as measles were common. But the amount of death that struck the Pilgrims in their first months in America shocked even them.

Most of the women died. Captain Standish lost his wife, Rose. Edward Winslow's wife Elizabeth died. So did Mary Allerton, who had endured the stillborn birth. Christopher Martin—the belligerent "governor" of the *Mayflower*—perished, followed by his widow, Mary. Governor Carver's wife Katherine died too, but the governor was not present to witness it—he died shortly before after being stricken in the field by an apparent sunstroke. Of the eighteen wives who had left England aboard the *Mayflower*, thirteen died. The single men among the Pilgrims did not fare much better: nineteen of twenty-nine died. Four entire families perished, and almost half the husbands and fathers died. Oddly, the small children experienced a better survival rate, including Peregrine White, the first child born in New England. Many were orphaned, however, and of the four More children—sent to America when their father learned they were not his—one survived. Approximately half of the *Mayflower*'s crew died too. The rough-and-tumble sailors took an every-man-for-himself attitude, offering little aid to each other even as one after another sickened and died.

"It was the Lord which upheld them"

The Pilgrims were different. Their faith sustained them when all else seemed to be crumbling. Again, they followed Pastor Robinson's advice to treat each other with biblical charity. As more fell ill or died, the numbers left to care for the others steadily dwindled, and at one point those who remained "healthy" were reduced to seven. The few served the many. "Greater love hath no man than this," declares the Scriptures, "that a man lay down his life for his friends." The few who were able nursed the ill and dying, and buried the dead on the hillside, lowering the bodies into unmarked graves lest the Indians count the crosses and realize how vulnerable the Pilgrims were to attack. Two who demonstrated true servants' hearts, according to William Bradford, were Elder

William Brewster and Captain Myles Standish. They and the few others who remained healthy "spared no pains night nor day," Bradford would recall, "but with abundance of toil and hazard of their own health, fetched them wood, made them fires, dressed them meat, made their beds, washed their loathsome clothes, clothed and unclothed them.... and all this willingly and cheerfully."

December, January, February, March, April—the death toll continued, finally dwindling to an occasional death after winter eased into spring. By summer, fifty would be dead—almost half the number of Pilgrims who had sailed to America on the

Mayflower. The village site that had become a graveyard for the Native Americans before them had also become a burial place for the Pilgrims. But Plymouth Colony somehow survived. Of the nineteen cottages that had been planned, only seven had actually been built by spring—but half the colonists had survived and so had their colony. Why did they not all die? Why did Plymouth Colony not cease to exist during that first, deadly winter? Perhaps the survivors were spared by the timely arrival of spring and warm weather. Perhaps they were saved by the critical care provided by the few who remained healthy. Or perhaps there was another reason. William Bradford believed so, concluding confidently that "it was the Lord which upheld them." Bradford, who was among those who survived a near-death illness, would later recount the story of that first killer winter:

The few among the Pilgrims who remained able-bodied nursed the ill and dying "with abundance of toil and hazard of their own health." The sacrifices they made, observed William Bradford, demonstrated "their true love unto their friends and brethren."

ABC BOOK COMPANY

"A rare example and worthy to be remembered"

Thirteen Pilgrim men were made widowers by killer illnesses during the deadly winter, and four entire families were wiped out.

LIBRARY OF CONGRESS

But that which was most sad and lamentable was that in two or three months' time, half of their company died, especially in Jan. and February, being the depth of winter, and wanting houses and other comforts, being infected with the scurvy and other diseases, which this long voyage and their [unaccommodating] condition had brought upon them. So as there died sometimes two or three of a day in the foresaid time, that of 100 and odd persons, scarce 50 remained. And of these in the time of most distress, there was but six or seven sound persons, who, to their great commendations be it spoken, spared no pains, night nor day, but with abundance of toil and hazard of their own health, fetched them wood, made them fires, dressed them meat, made their beds, washed their loathsome cloths, clothed and unclothed them. In a word, did all the homely and necessary offices for them which dainty and queasy stomachs cannot endure to hear named; and all this willingly and cheerfully, without any grudging in the least, showing herein their true love unto their friends and brethren: a rare example and worthy to be remembered.

Two of these seven were Mr. William Brewster, their reverend Elder, and Miles Standish, their Captain and military commander, unto whom myself and many others were much beholden in our low and sick condition. And yet the Lord so upheld these persons as in this general calamity they were not at all infected either with sickness or lameness. And what I have said of these, I may say of many others who died in this general visitation, and others yet living, that while they had health, yea, or any strength continuing, they were not wanting to any that had need of them. And I doubt not but their recompense is with the Lord....

The spring now approaching, it pleased God the morality began to cease among them, and the sick and lame recovered apace, which put as it were new life into them; though they had borne their sad affliction with as much patience and contentedness as I think any people could do. But it was the Lord which upheld them....[4]

"In two or three months' time, half of their company died"

"He Saluted Us in English and Bade Us Welcome"

The Surviving Pilgrims Are Befriended by Unlikely Allies

By mid-March of 1621, the New England weather hinted of approaching spring, when gentle rains and warm days would bring a rich green hue to the forests surrounding the tiny cluster of crude structures that marked the site of Plymouth Colony. The surviving Pilgrims doubtlessly yearned for the warm days ahead. As before, they did their daily chores and worked to improve their fledgling colony, but now there were so few of them. Almost half their number now lay in unmarked graves on the hillside above the double row of hand-hewn cottages. Buried there were the loved ones with whom they had planned to make a new life—husbands, wives, fathers, mothers, children. Yet, those who still lived were determined to see the original vision of a God-loving colony arise in the wilds of America. But with so few left, could they make that vision into a reality? They needed to

The Pilgrims who survived their deadly first winter at Plymouth were thankful the colony had survived. They realized, however, that their severely reduced numbers made the colony vulnerable to Indian attacks.

BOSTON PUBLIC LIBRARY

prepare garden plots and plant the crops that would ensure their survival—and how could the few survivors adequately protect themselves from Indian raids?

That was one of their greatest fears—that they would be slain in the wilderness by the Indians like so many before them. Over the winter they had repeatedly seen the smoke of distant Indian fires, and several times they had seen Indians at a distance. Once, a lone Pilgrim hid in the brush as an Indian hunting party passed just yards away, and on one occasion, Indians had stolen tools temporarily put aside by a Pilgrim wood-cutting party. A peace delegation led by Captain Standish had attempted to make contact, but failed to locate any inhabited Indian villages. One day in mid-February, two Indian men had appeared just outside Plymouth, but they retreated when some of the Pilgrims tried to meet with them. To improve security as their numbers were reduced by illness and death, the Pilgrims tried to strengthen their hilltop fortification, eventually mounting a half-dozen artillery pieces in the battery. Even so, they surely understood that the slow-firing firearms of the day, and even artillery, could be overrun by a rapid assault by a determined mass of enemies.

On Friday, February 16, 1621, the Pilgrim leaders met on the hilltop to review their defenses and to officially appoint Captain Standish as the colony's military commander. Midway through the meeting, they were shocked to see a lone Indian man approaching from the woods, clad only in a breechcloth, and carrying a bow and arrows. As the Pilgrim militiamen scrambled for their weapons in alarm, the Indian boldly walked up the dirt street between the rows of cottages until face to face with the surprised Pilgrim leaders. "Welcome, Englishmen!" he said. "Welcome, Englishmen!" His name was Samoset, or so it sounded to the Pilgrims. He was a sub-chief of the Abenaki tribe from the coast of modern-day Maine, where he had learned English from cod-fishing crews from England. For some reason, he had been picked up by Captain Thomas Dermer on his 1619 expedition and dropped in the Cape Cod region, where he was presently living as a guest of the Pokanoket.

Speaking in broken English, he asked for some beer, to which he had apparently been introduced by Europeans in Maine. The Pilgrims had none, but they did find some "strong water"—aqua-vitae, perhaps— which they served him, along with some cheese, butter, and pudding—"all which he liked well." Samoset then cheerfully began educating the Pilgrims, explaining that the site of their colony was known as "Patuxet" or "Little Bay" to the Indians, how its former inhabitants had died of a plague, and that the Pokanoket and other allied tribes were ruled by a leader named Massasoit or Ousamaquin. He also told them of another English-speaking Indian known as Tisquantum or Squanto. The Pilgrims treated Samoset as their guest, housing him for the night in one of their homes, and sending him away with gifts. Several days later, he returned with Squanto, who arranged a meeting with Chief Massasoit. When Massasoit arrived at Plymouth, the Pilgrim leaders

In February 1621, the Pilgrims were shocked to see a lone Indian man boldly walking up the street in Plymouth. "Welcome, Englishmen!" he called out.

STORIES OF THE PILGRIMS

treated Massasoit with the respect afforded a head of state. They seated him on a rug and pillows in one of the Pilgrim homes, and referred to him as the tribal "king." Their respect and diplomacy were successful: Chief Massasoit agreed to a peace treaty that would be rarely duplicated in the American Colonial Era—both sides would honor it for more than half a century.

Massasoit's decision to make peace with the Pilgrims would prove critical to the survival of Plymouth Colony. At the time of the treaty, the Pilgrims could muster barely twenty men to serve in the colony's militia. Despite their firearms and artillery, they were massively outnumbered by the Indians. Why did Massasoit not order a massacre of the Pilgrims and wipe out the weak, struggling colony in its infancy? Why was Plymouth spared the repeated attacks and bloodshed that marked the early history of Virginia's Jamestown Colony? Was it the Pilgrims' generally respectful attitude toward the Native Americans, or the diplomacy they afforded Massasoit? Or did Chief Massasoit simply decide to exercise restraint? Again, to William Bradford, it was all an act of divine grace, in which "the powerful hand of the Lord did protect them."

The English-speaking Indian whom Samoset introduced to the Pilgrims—Squanto—was in his own way equally important to the survival and success of Plymouth Colony. Squanto was believed to be the sole survivor of the Patuxet Indians who had inhabited the land on which the Pilgrims established their colony. In 1614, he was among the local Native

Americans kidnapped by the notorious Captain Hunt to be sold into slavery in Spain. There, however, sympathetic Catholic priests managed to free some of the slaves, and Squanto found himself living in London, where he became fluent in English. In 1619, he came back to the Cape Cod region as an interpreter and guide for Captain Thomas Dermer, whose expedition disintegrated under Indian attacks. Squanto thus found himself free and back home—only to discover that the 1617 epidemic had wiped out his people and their village. Taken in by the Pokanoket, he was called upon to use his English to interpret for Chief Massasoit and the Pilgrims.

In addition to his key role in the critical peace treaty, Squanto became a valuable and trusted friend and teacher for the Pilgrims. He trained them how to fish, taught them how to plant corn, served as a pilot and guide as they trapped beaver and developed the colony's fur trade, and he instructed them in the skilled tradecraft necessary to survive in the wilderness. He was, avowed William Bradford, "a special instrument sent of God for their good beyond their expectation." The story of Squanto, Samoset, Chief Massasoit, and their impact on the survival of the Pilgrims and Plymouth Colony was recounted in rich detail by Winslow and Bradford in *Mourt's Relation*:

* * *

Friday, [March] the 16ᵗʰ, a fair warm day towards; this morning we determined to conclude the military orders, which we had begun to consider before but were interrupted…for there presented himself a savage, which caused an alarm. He very boldly came all alone and along the houses straight to the rendezvous, where we intercepted him, not suffering him to go in, as undoubtedly he would, out of his boldness. He saluted us in English and bade us welcome, for he had learned some broken English among the Englishmen that came to fish at Monchiggon, and knew by name most of the captains, commanders, and masters that usually came.

He was a man free in speech, so far as he could express his mind, and of a seemly carriage. We questioned him of many things; he was the first savage we could meet withal. He said he was not of these parts, but of Moratiggon, and one of the sagamores or lords thereof, and had been eight months in these parts, it lying hence a day's sail with a great wind, and five days by land. He discoursed of the whole country, and of every province, and of their sagamores, and their number of men and strength. The wind beginning to rise a little, we cast a horseman's coat about him, for he was stark naked, only a leather about his waist, with a fringe about a span long or little more; he had a bow and two arrows, the one headed, and the other unheaded. He was a tall straight man, the hair of his head black, long behind, only short before, none on his face at all; he asked some beer, but we gave him strong water and biscuit, and butter, and cheese, and pudding, and a piece of mallard, all which he liked well, and had been acquainted with such amongst the English.

He told us the place where we now live is called Patuxet, and that about four years ago all the inhabitants died of an extraordinary plague, and there is neither man, woman, nor child remaining, as indeed we have found none, so as there is none to hinder our possession, or to lay claim unto it. All the afternoon we spent in communication with him; we would gladly have been rid of him at night, but he was not willing to go this night. Then we thought to carry him on shipboard, wherewith he was well content, and went into the shallop, but the wind was high and the water scant, that it could not return back. We lodged him that night at Stephen Hopkins' house, and watched him.... Saturday, in the morning we dismissed the savage, and gave him a knife, a bracelet, and a ring; he promised within a night or two to come again, and to bring with him some of the Massasoits, our neighbors, with such beavers' skins as they had to [trade] with us.

Saturday and Sunday, reasonable fair days. On this day came again the savage, and brought with him five other tall proper men; they had every man a deer's skin on him, and the principal of them had a wildcat's skin, or such like on the one arm. They had most of them long [leggings] up to their groins, close made; and above their groins to their waist another leather, they were altogether like the Irish-trousers. They are of a complexion like our English gypsies, no hair or very little on their faces, on their heads long hair to their shoulders, only cut before, some trussed up before with a feather, broad-wise, like a fan, another a fox tail hanging out. These left (according to our charge given him before) their bows and arrows a quarter of a mile from our town. We gave them entertainment as we thought was fitting them; they did eat liberally of our English

In this imaginary late nineteenth-century illustration, Chief Massasoit of the Pokanoket tribe offers a gesture of peace to Pilgrim governor William Carver. At the actual meeting in 1621, it was Massasoit who was seated—as a guest of honor by Governor Carver and the Pilgrim leaders.

LIBRARY OF CONGRESS

victuals. They made semblance unto us of friendship and amity; they sang and danced after their manner....

Thursday, the 22nd of March, was a very fair warm day. About noon we met again about our public business, but we had scarce been an hour together, but Samoset came again, and Squanto...with three others, and they [made signs] unto us that their great sagamore Massasoit was hard by, with Quadequina his brother, and all their men. They could not well express in English what they would, but after an hour the king came to the top of a hill over against us, and had in his train sixty men, that we could well behold them and they us. We were not willing to send our governor to them, and they unwilling to come to us, so [Squanto] went again unto him, who brought word that we should send one to parley with him, which we did, which was Edward Winslow, to know his mind, and to signify the mind and will of our governor, which was to have trading and peace with him. We sent to the king a pair of knives, and a copper chain with a jewel in it. To Quadequina we sent likewise a knife and a jewel to hang in his ear, and withal a pot of strong water, a good quantity of biscuit, and some butter, which were all willingly accepted.

Our messenger made a speech unto him, that King James saluted him with words of love and peace, and did accept of him as his friend and ally, and that our governor desired to see him and to [trade] with him, and to confirm a peace with him, as his next neighbor. He liked well of the speech and...Captain Standish and Master Williamson met the king at the brook, with half a dozen musketeers. They saluted him and he them, so one going over, the one on the one side, and the other on the other, conducted him to a house then in building, where we placed a green rug and three or four cushions. Then instantly came our governor with drum and trumpet after him, and some few musketeers. After salutations, our governor kissing his hand, the king kissed him, and so they sat down. The governor called for some strong water, and drunk to him, and he drunk a great draught that made him sweat all the while after; he called for a little fresh meat, which the king did eat willingly, and did give his followers. Then they treated of peace, which was:

1. That neither he nor any of his should injure or do hurt to any of our people.

2. And if any of his did hurt to any of ours, he should send the offender, that we might punish him.

3. That if any of our tools were taken away when our people are at work, he should cause them to be restored, and if ours did any harm to any of his, we would do the likewise to them.

4. If any did unjustly war against him, we would aid him; if any did war against us, he should aid us.

5. He should send to his neighbor confederates, to certify them of this, that they might not wrong us, but might be likewise comprised in the conditions of peace.

6. That when their men came to us, they should leave their bows and arrows behind them, as we should do our pieces when we came to them.

Lastly, that doing thus, King James would esteem of him as his friend and ally.

All which the king seemed to like well, and it was applauded of his followers; all the while he sat by the governor

A member of the Patuxet tribe, Tisquantum, or "Squanto" as the Pilgrims called him, became an invaluable instructor for the Pilgrims, teaching them how to plant corn and catch fish, and serving as an interpreter with other Native Americans. William Bradford considered him to be "a special instrument sent of God."

WIKIMEDIA COMMONS

257

he trembled for fear. In his person he is a very lusty man, in his best years, an able body, grave of countenance, and spare of speech. In his attire little or nothing differing from the rest of his followers, only in a great chain of white bone beads about his neck, and at it behind his neck hangs a little bag of tobacco, which he drank and gave us to drink; his face was painted with a [deep red color, like mulberry], and oiled both head and face, that he looked greasy. All his followers likewise, were in their faces, in part or in whole painted, some black, some red, some yellow, and some white, some with crosses, and other [clownish] works; some had skins on them, and some naked, all strong, tall men in appearance. So after all was done, the governor conducted him to the brook, and there they embraced each other and he departed....[5]

CHAPTER ELEVEN

"By the Goodness of God We Are So Far from Want"

T he *Mayflower*'s anchor rose glistening wet from the waters of Plymouth Harbor. Soon afterward, the ship turned seaward and set sail for England. It was April 5, 1621, and the *May- flower* was leaving for home. Aboard were the ship's commander, Mas-

ter Jones, and roughly half the ship's crew—the rest were dead. They had died from the same ailments that had killed so many of the Pilgrims. Enough crewmen survived to get the ship home, however, and Jones had decided that it was finally time to go. Remarkably, as the *Mayflower* sailed eastward in the direction of the rising sun, not a single Pilgrim was aboard. All of them—every survivor, men

On April 5, 1621, the *Mayflower* left Plymouth Colony to return to England. Despite the terrible toll the winter had taken on the ranks of the Pilgrims, none went back on the *Mayflower*. For the survivors, America was now their home.

LIBRARY OF CONGRESS

and women alike—had opted to remain at their new home: Plymouth Colony. Whatever awaited them in the future, they had chosen to face it in America.[1]

"God Be Praised, We Had a Good Increase of Indian Corn"

*Fish, Fowl, Game, and Bountiful Crops
Bring Health and Hope to Plymouth*

By late spring of 1621, the Pilgrims had endured the worst of the sickness and death, had built seven homes, and would soon build more. They had negotiated a truce with Massasoit's tribe, were learning from Squanto how to survive in the wilderness, and were planting the crops necessary to live through the fall and winter seasons.

When Governor Carver died of heat exhaustion soon after the *Mayflower*'s departure, they voted in a new governor—William Bradford, age thirty-one. The young leader easily could have declined the post: his wife had died just a few months earlier, and he had been critically ill himself. But abdicating his duty was not William Bradford's way: he assumed the post with the humble but capable manner in which he seemed to approach all responsibilities. In one of his first acts as Plymouth's governor, he dispatched Edward Winslow—guided by Squanto—on a successful

A Pilgrim couple converses at waterside. All was not grim in the early days of Plymouth Colony: in the spring of 1621, widower Edward Winslow married Susanna White, who had lost her spouse in the winter's great sickness.

BOSTON PUBLIC LIBRARY

New World Indians plant corn in this sixteenth-century engraving. Learning how to plant the crop may have spared the Pilgrims starvation. "We set the last spring some twenty acres of Indian corn," Edward Winslow wrote friends in England, ". . . and God be praised, we had a good increase."

LIBRARY OF CONGRESS

diplomatic mission to Chief Massasoit, which reinforced the relations established by the recent peace treaty. He dispatched another team on a mission that established a measure of peace with other tribes in the region, and he also reimbursed the Nausets for the corn that the Pilgrims had taken from them during their first days ashore.

In addition to his diplomatic duties, Bradford also oversaw a happy event which signaled the survival of Plymouth Colony—its first wedding. Susanna White and Edward Winslow had both lost their spouses in the great sickness of the winter, and on May 12, 1621, they were married to each other. Other events were anything but joyful—rabble-rouser John Billington was disciplined for disrespect toward Captain Standish, and two servants were punished for dueling with each other. Although unpleasant, both events were dealt with promptly and lawfully and demonstrated the stability and reliability of the fledgling colony's government. Equally important, the colonists had learned how to catch fish and hunt game—and by summer's end, their crops had produced a

Cape Cod Bay and offshore waters provided an abundant food source for the Pilgrims during much of the year. "For fish and fowl, we have great abundance," Edward Winslow reported, "fresh cod in the summer is but coarse meat with us [and] our bay is full of lobsters all the summer...."

HISTORY OF THE UNITED STATES

bountiful harvest. The corn that Squanto had shown them how to cultivate far outperformed the peas and barley they had brought from England, and promised to be the staple crop grown in America. "God be praised," Edward Winslow observed, "we had a good increase of Indian corn, and our barley indifferent good.... And although it be not always so plentiful as it was at this time with us, yet by the goodness of God we are so far from want." Winslow's joy at achieving survival and success in the New World wilderness was obvious in a letter he penned to friends in England:

You shall understand that in this little time that a few of us have been here, we have built seven dwelling-houses, and four for the use of the plantation, and have made preparation for [numerous] others. We set the last spring some twenty acres of Indian corn, and sowed some six acres of barley and peas, and according of the Indians, we manured our ground with herrings, or rather shad, which we have in great abundance,

> "God be praised, we had a good increase of Indian corn"

and take with great ease at our doors. Our corn did prove well, and God be praised, we had a good increase of Indian corn, and our barley indifferent good, but our peas [were] not worth the gathering, for we feared they were too late sown. They came up very well, and blossomed, but the sun parched them in the blossom....

We have found the Indians very faithful in their covenant of peace with us, very loving and ready to pleasure us. We often go to them, and them come to us; some of us have been fifty miles by land in the country with them.... Yea, it has pleased God so to possess the Indians with a fear of us, and love unto us, that not only the greatest king amongst them, called Massasoit, but also all the princes and peoples round about us, have either made suit unto us, or been glad of any occasion to make peace with us...and we for our parts walk as peaceably ad safely in the wood as in the highways of England. We entertain them familiarly in our houses, and they as friendly bestowing their venison on us. They are a people without any religion or knowledge of any God, yet very trusty, quick of apprehension, ripe-witted, just. The men and women go naked, only a skin about their middles.

For the temper of the air, here it agrees well with that in England, and if there be any difference at all, this is somewhat hotter in summer. Some think it to be colder in the winter, but I cannot out of experience so say; the air is very clear and not foggy, as has been reported. I never in my life remember a more seasonable year than we have here enjoyed, and if we have once but [cows], horses, and sheep, I make no question but that men might live as contented here as in any part of the world. For fish and fowl, we have great abundance; fresh

The peaceful relations that the Pilgrims nurtured with the area's Native Americans spared the colony the violence that beset other Europeans. "We entertain them familiarly in our houses," Winslow said of the Indians.

GENERAL SOCIETY OF MAYFLOWER DESCENDANTS

263

cod in the summer is but coarse meat with us; our bay is full of lobsters all the summer and affords variety of other fish; in September we can take a hogshead of eels in a night, with small labor, and can dig them out of their beds all the winter. We have mussels and [others] at our doors. Oysters we have none near, but we can have them brought by the Indians when we will; all the springtime the earth sends forth naturally very good [salad greens]. Here are grapes, white and red, and very sweet and strong also. Strawberries, gooseberries, raspberries, etc. Plums of three sorts, with black and red, being almost as good as a damson; abundance of roses, white, red, and damask; single, but very sweet indeed.

The country [needs] only industrious men to employ, for it would grieve your hearts if, as I, you had seen so many miles together by goodly rivers uninhabited, and withal, to consider those parts of the world wherein you live to be even greatly burdened with abundance of people. These things I thought good to let you understand, being the truth of things as near as I could experimentally take knowledge of, and that you might on our behalf give God thanks who has dealt so favorably with us.[2]

"The country [needs] only industrious men"

"Three Days We Entertained and Feasted"

The Pilgrims Celebrate Their First Thanksgiving in America

In gratitude for the Pilgrims' plentiful 1621 harvest, Governor Bradford called for a thanksgiving observance—the event that would inspire the American tradition of Thanksgiving. The Pilgrims were not the first Europeans to hold a thanksgiving event in the New World—

ESTELLE KERR.

After their brutal first winter at Plymouth, the Pilgrims were grateful to enjoy a bountiful harvest from the growing season of 1621. "Such was the bounty and goodness of our God," noted Edward Winslow.

AMERICAN BOOK COMPANY

although they appear to have been the first to do so in New England. In New Spain, Catholic colonists had assembled to give thanks to God for their survival, and so had the Anglican settlers at Jamestown. It was the Pilgrims of Plymouth, however, who would be credited with establishing America's distinctive Thanksgiving holiday—thanks to a joyful observance some time in the autumn of 1621.

The Christian tradition of observing a time of thanksgiving was based on the Jewish feast days recorded in the Old Testament. The Feast of Harvest—also called Firstfruits—and the Feast of Tabernacles—also known as Ingathering—celebrated God's grace and provision at harvest time. It was a time of rejoicing when all work ceased as on the Sabbath, and the people gathered in worship, offered the firstfruits of their labors to the Lord, extended mercy to the poor, and gave thanks to God. The New Testament called on believers to personally

Pilgrim women prepare for a feast. In gratitude for the Pilgrims' plentiful 1621 harvest, Governor Bradford called for a thanksgiving observance—the event that would inspire the American tradition of Thanksgiving.

STORIES OF THE PILGRIMS

maintain an attitude of thanksgiving, and the early Church observed times of thanksgiving. Later, on Lammas Day in Medieval England, churchgoers brought a loaf of bread or a lamb to Mass in thanksgiving for harvest time.

Following the Reformation, Protestants replaced the annual Catholic festivals with days of prayer, fasting, and thanksgiving. A typical seventeenth-century thanksgiving was described by Puritan theologian Thomas Wilson, an English pastor at Canterbury, in an influential work entitled *A Christian Dictionarie*. Published less than a decade before the Pilgrims established Plymouth Colony, the book recorded the meaning of a thanksgiving observance in the early 1600s. An authentic thanksgiving observance, it noted, included an "acknowledging and confessing, with gladness, of the benefits and deliverances of God, both toward ourselves and others to the praise of his Name." It also included "Remembrance of the good done to us…Confessing God to be the Author and giver of it…being glad of an occasion to praise him, and doing it gladly, with joy."

Although the famous 1621 celebration at Plymouth was the first of its kind for the Pilgrims in America, it was not their first thanksgiving observance. During their years in Holland, the Separatist Pilgrims had repeatedly witnessed Leiden's annual October third day of thanksgiving, when the city's Protestants gave thanks to God for Leiden's deliverance from a brutal 1574 siege by the Spanish army. The Separatists also celebrated their own thanksgiving observances in Holland, beginning soon after their arrival with an event designed to thank God for their escape from English persecution. They carried the practice to the New World, where they held thanksgiving observances in obedience to Scripture, such as Psalm 107:

> *O give thanks unto the LORD, for he is good: for his mercy endureth forever. Let the redeemed of the LORD say so, whom he hath redeemed from the hand of the enemy; and gathered them out of the lands.... They wandered in the wilderness in a solitary way; they found no city to dwell in. Hungry and thirsty, their soul fainted in them. Then they cried unto the LORD in their trouble, and he delivered them out of their distresses. And he led them forth by the right way, that they might go to a city of habitation. Oh that men would praise the LORD for his goodness, and for his wonderful works to the children of men!*

"O give thanks unto the LORD, for he is good"

To prepare for the colony's autumn thanksgiving observance, Governor Bradford dispatched a four-man hunting party to obtain game for the celebration. The hunters returned with a week's supply of "waterfowl" and "wild Turkeys." Added to the event's menu was a supply of venison, which was contributed by Pokanoket Indians. Chief Massasoit and more than ninety members of the tribe attended the celebration. Although they outnumbered the Pilgrims two to one, the Indians were "entertained and feasted" as honored guests by the Pilgrims, who now viewed the Pokanokets with little fear. Hosting the Pokanokets may have been more than simple friendship and diplomacy: the Pilgrims may also have felt biblically bound to extend hospitality to non-believers or "strangers"—as directed by the book of Deuteronomy: "And thou shalt rejoice in thy feast, thou, and thy son, and thy daughter, and thy servant, and thy maid, and the Levite and the stranger...." If the celebration featured other foods normally consumed by the Plymouth colonists, it would have also included beaver, baked clams, lobster, cod, bass and other fish, Indian corn, peas, beans, cabbage, onions, parsnips, English cheese, porridge, biscuits, and corn-based hasty pudding. Typical beverages would have been ale and spring water.

Thanksgiving, Pilgrim-style, was more than a simple meal—it was a three-day event. Like most seventeenth-century English people, Separatists and Puritans loved field sports, and the 1621 thanksgiving celebration featured sports activities—or "recreations," as Edward Winslow called them. If the festivities followed the usual Puritan pattern, they included wrestling, foot-races, and jumping contests. The festival's entertainment also included the use of firearms. Winslow reported that "we exercised our arms," which may have referred to target-shooting or a firing demonstration for Massasoit and his Pokanokets. The event's three-day length was unique: typical Puritan thanksgiving observances could go for a day or an entire week. It was normally preceded by a worship service, although Winslow made no reference to a service in his account of the 1621 event. It was very unlikely that his omission meant that the devout Pilgrims failed to worship; more likely, Winslow simply assumed that his readers understood Separatist practices. With their pastor, John Robinson, still in England, the thanksgiving worship service very likely would have been conducted by the Pilgrims' spiritual leader, Elder William Brewster.

The faith-based nature of the Pilgrims' 1621 event was clearly demonstrated by the pattern they would later establish with numerous other thanksgiving observances. Two years later, for example, when a prolonged drought threatened the colony's crops and survival, Plymouth's magistrates called for a day of prayer and fasting, which Winslow recorded:

To that end a day was set apart by public authority, and set apart from all other employments, hoping that the same God who had stirred us up hereunto, would be moved hereby in mercy to look down upon us, and grant the request of our dejected souls.... For though in the morning when we assembled together, the heavens were as clear and the drought as like to continue as ever it was; yet (our exercise continuing some eight or nine hours) before our departure the weather was over-cast, the clouds gathered together on all sides, and on the next morning distilled such soft, sweet, and mild showers of rain, continuing some fourteen days, and mixed with such seasonable weather as it was hard to say whither our weathered corn or drooping affections were most quickened or revived. Such was the bounty and goodness of our God.[3]

The famous 1621 celebration at Plymouth was not the first thanksgiving in the New World or the Pilgrims' first thanksgiving observance—but it was the first for the Pilgrims in America.

STEDELIJK MUSEUM

With similar sentiment, Winslow concluded his account of the Pilgrims' original 1621 thanksgiving observance:

Our harvest being gotten in, our governor sent four men on fowling, that so we might after a special manner rejoice together after we had gathered the fruit of our labors. They four in one day killed as much fowl as, with a little help beside, served the company almost a week. At which time, among other recreations, we exercised our arms, many of the Indians coming among us, and among the rest their greatest king Massasoit, with some ninety men, for whom three days we entertained and feasted; and they went out and killed five deer, which they brought to the plantation and bestowed on our governor and upon the captain and others. And although it be not always so plentiful as it was at this time with us, yet by the goodness of God, we are so far from want....[4]

"Three days we entertained and feasted"

Governor Bradford would also later describe that first Thanksgiving in Plymouth Colony:

They now began to gather in the small harvest they had, and to fit up their houses and dwellings against winter, being all well recovered in health and strength, and had all things in good plenty. For as some were employed in affairs abroad, others were exercised in fishing, about cod and bass and other fish of portion. All the summer there was no want, and now began to come in [a] store of fowl as winter approached, of which this place did about when they came first (but afterward decreased by degrees). And besides waterfowl, there was [a] great store of wild turkeys, of which they took many, besides venison, etc. Besides they had about a peck [of] meal a week to a person, or now since harvest, Indian corn to that proportion. [It] made many afterwards write so largely of their plenty here to their friends in England, which were not feigned but true reports.[5]

"The Dawning . . . of This New World"

New Arrivals Increase the Numbers at Plymouth Colony

The alarm spread quickly: a ship had appeared in Cape Cod Bay and was sailing straight for Plymouth Harbor. It was mid-November, 1621, and the Pilgrims feared they were under attack by a French warship. At Governor Bradford's order, an alarm gun was fired from Plymouth's hilltop artillery battery. In response, Plymouth's menfolk hurriedly abandoned their work, manned their body armor and took up their firearms. According to Edward Winslow, "every man, yea, boy, who could handle a gun, were ready, with full resolution...." Soon, however, they all stood down—to their joy and relief, the approaching vessel was an English ship. It was, they soon learned, the fifty-five-foot-ton *Fortune*, and it had been sent from England by the Merchant Adventurers with some thirty-five new settlers for Plymouth Colony, including some of the Separatists who had been unable to sail on the packed *Mayflower*.

Just as the Pilgrims had been shocked to see the approaching ship, so were the passengers aboard the *Fortune*—but for a different reason. Their first impression of the New England coast—as viewed from offshore—was sobering and disappointing: it was "a naked and barren place," in their estimation. If they felt reassured by the sight of two rows of crude wooden cottages that made up most of Plymouth, their burst of optimism faded quickly when they learned of the many deaths among the Pilgrims and nearby presence of a large Indian population. So dismayed and frightened were some of the newcomers that they considered confiscating the ship's sails to prevent it from leaving. They were eventually calmed by the Pilgrims' reassurances—and a promise by the *Fortune*'s captain to transport them to Virginia if New England failed to satisfy them.

Some two weeks later, the *Fortune* departed, leaving behind new colonists at Plymouth. They had to be temporarily housed with Pilgrim families, and the additional numbers sorely taxed Plymouth's winter rations, but their arrival not only added labor to Plymouth's thin ranks of survivors, it also reunited families. Among those reunited were William Brewster and his thirty-seven-year-old son Jonathan, and Edward Winslow with his younger brother John. Also aboard the *Fortune* was Robert Cushman, the Pilgrims' representative to the Merchant Adventurers, who had opted to remain in England the year before when the leaky *Speedwell* had to be abandoned.

Cushman would not be staying; he was there to check on the colony, report back to the investors, and to deliver a charge to the Pilgrims to remain true to the faith that had led them into the wilderness. He did so in a sermon that he personally delivered, and which was apparently received with humble acceptance by the survivors of the epic 1620 pilgrimage to America. It was reminiscent of the Bible-based advice given

In November of 1621, the Plymouth colonists were alarmed to see a distant ship approaching across Cape Cod Bay. Their fears soon turned to joy, however, when they realized that the ship—the *Fortune*—was bringing new colonists from England—along with old friends and relatives.

AMERICAN BOOK COMPANY

to them upon their departure for America by their beloved Pastor Robinson. It was entitled "the Sin and Dangers of Self-Love." In it, Cushman warned the Pilgrims that the "bird of self-love, which was hatched at home, if not looked to, will eat out the life of all grace and goodness...." In an obvious reference to the early Christian church as depicted in the second chapter of the book of Acts, he urged them to put aside self and serve one another:

If God see this disease of self-love so dangerous in us, then it stands us all in hand to suspect ourselves, and so to seek out the root of this disease so that it may be cured. If a learned physician shall see by our countenance and eye that we have some dangerous disease growing on us, then our hearts will smite us…and every man will bestir himself to get rid of it, and will prevent always that which feeds the disease and cherish all courses that would destroy it.

Now, how much more ought we to bestir ourselves for this matter of self-love, since God himself hast pronounced us all dangerously sick of this disease? Believe it. God cannot lie nor be deceived; He that has made the heart, does He not know it? Let every man's heart smite him, and let him fall to the examination of himself and see first whether he love not riches and worldly wealth too much…. So if thy lovest thine ease and pleasure, see whether thou can be content to…endure hard labor as [well as] to live at ease, and art as willing to go to the house of mourning as to the house of mirth….

Again, see if thy heart cannot be as merry and thy mind as joyful and thy countenance as cheerful with coarse fare…with bread and water (if God offer thee no better, nor the times afford

One of the passengers aboard the *Fortune* was Robert Cushman— the Pilgrims' representative to the Merchant Adventurers. While at Plymouth, Cushman preached a sermon to the assembled Plymouth colonists, urging them to put aside self-love.

AMERICAN BOOK COMPANY

no other) as if thou had the greatest dainties. So also whether thou can be content with the scorns of men when thou hast done well, as with their praises…for if thou be disheartened, discouraged and weakened in any duty because of man's disparagement, it is a sign thou lovest thyself too much….

Is this a time then, for men to begin to seek themselves? Paul saith that men in the last days shall be lovers of themselves. But it is here yet but the first days, the dawning (as it were) of this new world. It is now therefore no time for men to look to get riches, brave clothes, dainty fare, but to look to present necessities. It is now no time to pamper the flesh, live at ease, snatch, catch, scrape, and…hoard up, but rather to open the doors, the chests and the vessels and say, "Brother, neighbor, friend, what want ye? Anything that I have? Make bold with it; it is yours to command, to do you good, to comfort and cherish you, and glad I am that I have it for you."[6]

"Brother, neighbor, friend, what want ye? Anything that I have?"

While in Plymouth, Cushman also gave the Pilgrim leaders a letter sent to them from the bombastic Thomas Weston, the Merchant Adventurers' representative who had angrily stalked away from the Pilgrims at the docks in England after they rejected his proposed new terms. In his letter, Weston chastised the Pilgrims for not sending the *Mayflower* back to England loaded with furs, fish, and other New World commodities, completely ignoring their grievous loss of life. He faulted the Pilgrims for "a weakness in judgment," and chided them for "discoursing, arguing and consulting" instead of making a profit and submitting to the controversial agreement. Bradford, Brewster and others were rankled by Weston's accusations, but Cushman somehow convinced them that they were honor-bound to accept the Adventurers' terms, and so they did. Then—leaving his teenage son in the care of Governor Bradford—Cushman returned to England aboard the *Fortune.*

Although the arrival of the *Fortune* and its new colonists resurrected the conflict between the Pilgrims and their financial sponsors and put a severe strain on Plymouth's winter rations, it was also another key turning point in the survival of Plymouth Colony. When the *Mayflower* had departed for England, Pilgrim leaders had sent with it a request for a new patent to the recently formed Council for New England, which held jurisdiction for the region that included Cape Cod and the Plymouth colony—and it had been granted. The Plymouth colonists were expected to remain generally submissive to royal authority, but with their new patent approved and their financial backers placated for the time being, the Pilgrims would continue to govern themselves according to the principles of the Mayflower Compact. In reality, they would enjoy more freedom than most Englishmen back home, including the freedom of faith that they so ardently desired.

The arrival and departure of the *Fortune* also demonstrated the Plymouth Colony's potential for generating a profit. Aboard the *Fortune* when it departed for England was a fortune in products that the Pilgrims had wrestled from the American wilderness—split New England timber, a valuable harvest of wild sassafras, and an immense store of beaver pelts. With it, the Pilgrims hoped to pay off much of their indebtedness

On her return to England, the *Fortune* was raided by French privateers, who looted the ship of all the cargo the Pilgrims sent back to help repay their investors. The looters, however, missed one treasure —a priceless manuscript by Edward Winslow and William Bradford.

RIJKSMUSEUM OF AMSTERDAM

to Weston and his partners in the Merchant Adventurers. Although the cargo did prove that the Pilgrims had the potential to produce income, it would not help repay their debt to the Merchant Adventurers. To their great consternation, the *Fortune* was hijacked by French privateers en route to England, and its cargo was hijacked.

The loss was substantial, but one bright spot in the cloud of disappointment: the French privateers missed one important "treasure"—a manuscript carried by Robert Cushman. It was *Mourt's Relation*—the account of Plymouth Colony's earliest days, co-authored by Edward Winslow and William Bradford. Despite the hijacking, Cushman somehow managed to get the manuscript safely to England. There, in 1622, it was published by a London printer under the rambling title *A Relation or Journal of the Beginning and Proceedings of the English Plantation Settled at Plimoth in New England*—which, for uncertain reasons, would be shortened eventually to *Mourt's Relation*. The book landed in London bookstores during the peak of an English reading fad. So did a later work by Edward Winslow, *Good News from New England*, which was published in London two years later.

Reading was the rage in early seventeenth-century England, and the colorful account of English colonists building a new life in the American wilderness was well-timed to recruit like-minded colonists to Plymouth. Most future colonists would settle elsewhere in America, but some would come to Plymouth—with the *Fortune* being the first of many ships to follow. They would bring new colonists to Plymouth and ferry goods back and forth to England. Although they would not be free of hardships and serious danger, never again would the Pilgrims stand as close to the edge of destruction as they had during their first year. Plymouth Colony would survive, and modestly but steadily it would develop as the first successful colony in New England.

"They Are Friends with All Their Neighbors"

The Pilgrims Survive and Succeed in America

As the years unfolded, the Pilgrims settled into the routines of life at Plymouth Colony, and as the colony and its population slowly grew, they saw their vision for America unfold. Homes were built. Couples were married. Crops were raised. Trades were pursued. Children were born. And the faith for which they had given so much was followed in freedom. As governor of the colony, William Bradford eliminated a socialistic, common-store system that the Plymouth colonists had initially followed. It had allowed everyone equal rations from a common storehouse regardless of how much they worked, and—in Bradford's words—it bred "confusion and discontent, and retarded much employment that would have been to their benefit and comfort." Following the New Testament admonition that "if any would not work, neither should he eat," he replaced the common-store policy with the free enterprise system and allowed the private ownership of land. "This had very good success," he would later report, "for it made all hands very industrious...."

As the generations passed and scores of new colonists settled in New England, the Pilgrims generally retained their reputation for wholesomeness, fairness, and integrity, in many ways setting an example as the best of America's Colonial Era people. It was said of them by an objective observer, "they are friends with all their neighbors." A revealing glimpse into Plymouth Colony's formative years—and the activities of its Pilgrim founders—would be preserved in three early seventeenth-century eyewitness accounts. Two were recorded by English observers and the third

Under Governor William Bradford the Plymouth colonists abandoned a flirtation with a debilitating common-store system of socialism in favor of the more productive free enterprise system. "This had very good success," Bradford reported.

AMERICAN BOOK COMPANY

by a Dutch visitor. The earliest account, written in 1622, was penned by John Pory, an English scholar and former member of the English Parliament, who visited Plymouth Colony en route to England from a stint as a colonial administrator in Virginia:

First, the harbor is not only pleasant for air and prospect, but most sure for shipping both small and great, being landlocked on all sides. The town is seated on the ascent of a hill, which besides the pleasure of variable objects entertaining the unsatisfied eye, such is the wholesomeness of the place (as the Governor told me) that for the space of one whole year, of the two wherein they had been there, died not one man, woman, or child. This healthiness is accompanied with much plenty both of fish and fowl every day in the year, as I know no place in the world that can match it. In March the eels come forth out of places where they lie bedded all winter, into the fresh streams, and [from] there into the sea, and in their passages are taken in pots. In September they run out of the sea into the fresh streams to bed themselves in the ground all winter, and are taken again in pots as they return homewards. In winter the inhabitants dig them up, being bedded in gravel not above two or three foot deep, and all the rest of the year they may take them in pots in the salt water of the bay. They are sweet, fat and wholesome, having no taste at all of the mud, and are as great as ever I saw anywhere.

In April & May come up another kind of fish which they call herring, or old wives, in infinite schools.... Into another river some two miles to the northeast of Plymouth all the month of May the great smelts pass up to spawn likewise in troupes innumerable, which with a scoop or a bowl, or a piece of bark, a man may cast up upon the bank. About midway come into the harbor the main school of bass and bluefish, which they take with seines—some of 3 foot long, and with hooks those of 4 and 5 foot long. They enter also at [flood tide] up into the small creeks, at the mouths whereof the inhabitants, spreading their nets, have caught 500 and 700 at a time.... Now as concerning the bluefish, in delicacy it excels all kind of fish that ever I tasted, [including] the salmon of the Thames in his prime season....

In the same bay lobsters are in season in the 4 months, so large, so full of meat, and so plentiful in number that no man will

To provide greater security for the colony, the Pilgrims strengthened Plymouth's defenses with a palisade fence and additional artillery in their hilltop blockhouse.

AMERICAN BOOK COMPANY

New England colonists make soap from tallow. In Plymouth, crops were raised, trades were pursued, families grew, and daily routines became a meaningful life for the Pilgrims.

AMERICAN BOOK COMPANY

"Lobsters are . . . so plentiful in number that no man will believe that has not seen"

believe that has not seen. For a knife of 3 halfpence I bought 10 lobsters that would well have dined 40 laboring men, and the least boy in the ship, with an hour's labor, was able to feed the whole company with them for two days.... Mussels and clams they have all year long; which being the [most common] of God's blessings here, and such as these people fatten their hogs with [them] at low water....

The reasons of their continual plenty for those 7 months in the year may be the continual tranquility of the place, being guarded on all sides from the fury of the storms, as also the abundance of food they find at low water, the bottom of the bay then appearing as a green meadow, and lastly the number of [freshwater brooks] running into the bay, where...they may refresh and quench their thirst. And therefore this bay is such a pond for fowl as in any man's knowledge of our nation that has seen it.... Touching on their fruit, I will not speak of their [common] raspberries, cherries, gooseberries, strawberries, delicate plums and others, but they have commonly throughout the country several sorts of grapes, some whereof I tasted, being fairer and larger than any I ever saw in [Virginia].... In this land (as in other parts of the mainland), they have plenty of deer and turkeys as fat as in any other place.

Now as concerning the quality of the people, how happy were it for our people in [Virginia], if they were as free from wickedness and vice as these are in this place. And their industry is well [judging from] their buildings, as by a substantial palisade about their settlement of 2700 foot in compass, stronger than I have seen in Virginia, and lastly by a blockhouse which they have erected in the highest place of the town to mount their ordinance upon, from whence they may command all the harbor. As touching their correspondence with the Indians, they are friends with all their neighbors.[7]

"How happy
were it for
our people...
if they were
as free from
wickedness
and vice as
these are"

"They are
friends with
all their
neighbors"

By the time English businessman Emmanuel Altham visited Plymouth Colony in the summer of 1623, the colony had the benefit of two and a half years of growth. Altham was one of Plymouth Colony's financial backers, and he sailed to New England aboard the ship *Little James*, which he hoped to use for transporting New World products back to England. Even though the colony was not showing a great financial return on investment, Altham was enthusiastic about the colony's future. At the time of his arrival, he found Plymouth encircled by a protective palisade fence or "pale" and further protected by improvements to its hilltop artillery battery. The amount of English-held livestock had

Women and children tend a field of flax. As the years passed and the Pilgrims engaged in the activities of everyday life, they saw their vision for a new life in America slowly unfold.

AMERICAN BOOK COMPANY

increased, naturally and by importation, and Plymouth's hillside cluster of homes and buildings had expanded enough that Altham could refer to it as a "town":

"In this plantation are about twenty houses"

It is well situated on a high hill close to the seaside, and [is] very commodious for shipping to come unto them. In this plantation are about twenty houses, four or five of which are very fair or pleasant, and the rest (as time will serve) will be made better. And this town is in such great manner that it makes a street between the houses, and at the upper end of the street, there is a strong fort, both by nature and by art, with six pieces of reasonable good artillery mounted thereon; in which [the] fort is [in continuous] watch, so that no Indian can come near about but that he is presently seen.

This town is paled about with pale of eight feet long, or thereabouts, and in the pale are three great gates. Furthermore, here is belonging to the town six goats, about fifty hogs and also [various] hens. And, lastly, the town is furnished with a company of honest men....[8]

✦✦•━━━━━━•✦✦

Issack de Rasieres visited Plymouth Colony in the fall of 1627. He was an agent for the East India Trading Company and a government administrator for the new Dutch colony of New Netherland. The colony had been established in 1624, where the Pilgrims had originally intended to land—around the mouth of the Hudson River in the vicinity of what is now New York City. De Rasieres sailed to Plymouth to establish a trading agreement with the Pilgrim colonists, and met with Governor Bradford.

By the time of his visit in 1627, Plymouth was still a hillside village, but more houses had been built, others had been improved, and several public structures had been constructed. He noted Plymouth's fortifications—its stockade or palisade fence, its well-built blockhouse, and its formidable battery of artillery. He was also impressed by the orderliness of the town, with its private courtyards and produce gardens.

He observed the weekly procession to Sunday worship, which convened in Plymouth's hilltop blockhouse, noted the Pilgrims' democratic form of government, and commented on the colonists' high morals—which he contrasted, perhaps sardonically, with what he called the "barbarously" worldly lifestyle of the Dutch in New Netherland. He also credited the Pilgrims for developing peaceful and productive relations with the area's Native American population, and praised them for what he called their "prosperous and praiseworthy undertakings and government." His observations:

> "Their houses and courtyards are arranged in very good order"

New Plymouth lies on the slope of a hill stretching east towards the seacoast, with a broad street about a cannon shot of 800 feet long, leading down the hill; with a [lane] crossing in the middle.... The houses are constructed of hewn planks, with gardens also enclosed behind and at the sides with hewn planks, so that their houses and courtyards are arranged in very good order, with a stockade against a sudden attack; and at the ends of the streets there are three wooden gates. In the center, on the cross street, stands the governor's house, before which is a square stockade upon which four [swivel guns] are mounted, so as to enfilade the streets. Upon the hill they have a large square house, with a flat roof, made of thick sawn plank, stayed with oak beams, upon the top of which they have six cannon, which shoot iron balls of four and five pounds, and command the surrounding country.

The lower part [of the fortified blockhouse] they use for their church, where they preach on Sundays and the usual holidays. They assemble by beat of drum, each with his musket or firelock, in front of the captain's door; they have their cloaks on, and place themselves in order, three abreast, and are led by a sergeant without beat of drum. Behind comes the governor, in a long robe; beside him, on the right hand, comes the preacher with his cloak on, and on the left hand the captain with his side-arms, and cloak on, and with a small cane in his hand; and so they march in good order, and each sets his arms down near him. Thus they are constantly on their guard night and day.

Their government is after the English form. The governor has his council, which is chosen every year by the entire community, by election or prolongation of term. In inheritances they place all the children in one degree, only the eldest son has an

A Pilgrim mother plays with her children. Within a few decades, the Pilgrims of Plymouth Colony were surrounded by other colonies and colonists.

STORY OF THE PILGRIMS

acknowledgment for his seniority of birth. They have made stringent laws and ordinances upon the subject of fornication and adultery, which laws they maintain and enforce very strictly indeed, even among the tribes which live amongst them. They speak very angrily when they hear from the savages that we live so barbarously in these respects, and without punishment.

Their farms are not so good as ours, because they are more stony, and consequently not so suitable for the plough.... The maize seed which they do not require for their own use is delivered over to the governor, at three guilders the bushel, who in his turn sends it in sloops to the north for the trade in skins among the savages; they reckon one bushel of maize against one pound of beaver's skins; the profits are divided according to what each has contributed, and they are credited for the amount in the account of what each has to contribute yearly towards the reduction of his obligation. Then with the remainder they purchase what next they require, and which the governor takes care to provide every year.

They have better sustenance than ourselves, because they have the fish so abundant before their doors. There are also many birds, such as geese, herons and cranes, and other small-legged birds, which are in great abundance there in the winter. The tribes in their neighborhood...are better conducted than ours, because the English give them the example of better ordinances and a better life; and who also, to a certain degree, give them laws, in consequence of the respect they from the very first have established among them....[9]

In the seven years since Plymouth Colony's arduous and deadly beginning, the Pilgrims had achieved their vision of building a new home and a new life in the wilderness of America. Visitors, supporters, and neighboring colonists admired what they had achieved, and they would become the model for all that was good about the early forging of the American nation. Ironically, serving as a model would likely have caused discomfort for the typical humble-hearted Pilgrim of 1620, as noted by Pilgrim leader Edward Winslow later in life. Look not to us as a model for your life, he counseled, but instead look to the Lord:

And if any will take us for a precedent, I desire that they may really know what we do, rather than what others ignorantly or maliciously report of us, assuring myself that none will ever be losers by following us so far as we follow Christ. Which that we may do, and our posterities after us,

> "None will ever be losers by following us so far as we follow Christ"

the Father of our Lord Jesus Christ and our Father accept in Christ what is according to him; discover, pardon and reform what is amiss amongst us; and guide us and them by the assistance of the Holy Ghost, for time to come, till time shall be no more; that the Lord our God may still delight to dwell amongst his plantations and churches there by his gracious presence, and may go on blessing to bless them with heavenly blessings in these earthly places, that so by his blessing they may not only grow up to a nation, but become exemplary for good unto others.[10]

✤—————✤

And yet, despite human frailties and mistakes, the Pilgrims of Plymouth Colony would indeed establish important precedents and inspire generations of Americans in ages to come. Through faith, perseverance, courage, and much suffering, they had achieved their long-sought goal of worshipping in peace and freedom—"that their children after them might walk in the holy ways of the Lord." In so doing they had also established a model of faith-based democratic self-government. It had been a long, difficult, and sometimes tragic pilgrimage—from persecution in Scrooby and Gainsborough and grim English jails to hope and

As the generations passed, the Pilgrims were viewed with respect and good favor. Observed a visiting official from Virginia: "how happy were it for our people…if they were as free from wickedness and vice as these are in this place."

AMERICAN BOOK COMPANY

hardship in Holland, from frustrating false starts in Southampton and Dartmouth to a long, stormy voyage in the cramped quarters of the *Mayflower*, from illness and death in the untamed wilderness to hope and heroic determination as they forged their new lives at Plymouth Colony.

And they had succeeded. No one in America would be raiding their Sunday services to stop their worship. Neither would they be hauled off to jail because of their beliefs, nor ever again forced to flee their homes because of their faith. And the way of freedom they had blazed in the wilds of the New World would eventually become the path of liberty for countless people from around the world: people yearning for a new life, a new start, a new home—and who would find it as Americans.[11]

EPILOGUE

"One Small Candle"

I t only lasted for seventy-two years—a single lifetime. In 1692, Plymouth Colony ceased to exist. Inspired by the Pilgrims' perseverance
at Plymouth, England's mainstream Puritans established the much
larger Massachusetts Bay Colony next to Plymouth in 1630. Motivated
by the same desire for freedom of faith—and fear of increased persecution—increasing numbers of Puritan colonists spilled into their New
England colony: two hundred, seven hundred, eight hundred, and then
three thousand in a single year. They arrived not in a solitary ship like
the *Mayflower*, but in fleets of ships. Between 1630 and 1640, more than
twenty thousand English Puritans flooded Massachusetts Bay Colony—
so many that their exodus from England was known as the "Great
Migration."

Massachusetts Bay Colony did not experience the slow, modest growth
of neighboring Plymouth Colony—it boomed. And, in various ways, it
also produced the spinoff colonies of Connecticut, New Haven, and Rhode
Island, while an influx of Anglicans established nearby New Hampshire

289

Colony. For sixty years, Plymouth Colony remained in the shadow of its larger, more prosperous neighbor. After seventy years of existence, the entire population of Plymouth Colony numbered approximately seven thousand—the same number of people then living in the Massachusetts city of Boston. The population of New England at that time was approximately sixty thousand. In 1691, in the wake of a bloody Indian uprising—King Philip's War—the English government decided it would be strategically and politically prudent to fold Plymouth Colony into the larger, neighboring Massachusetts Bay Colony. It did so officially in 1692. "To everything there is a season," Scripture proclaims, "a time for every purpose under heaven." And Plymouth Colony's time had ended.

Plymouth Colony, however, was influential far beyond its limited population and brief lifetime—and so were its founders, the Pilgrims. Later immigrants and colonists lacked the faith and fervor of those *Mayflower* Pilgrims, and the colony's sense of community declined over time—but it was not so with those Separatist Pilgrims of 1620. They identified themselves with the Hebrew people of the Old Testament, who were led by God from Egyptian slavery into nationhood within the Promised Land. "Thou hast brought a vine out of Egypt," wrote the psalmist. "Thou preparedst room before it and didst cause it to take deep root, and it filled the land." Plymouth's Pilgrim founders were confident that they had been providentially placed in "New England" to become that biblical "vine"—to craft a culture that honored and reflected biblical truth. And, politically and culturally that Pilgrim "vine" did indeed "take deep root, and it filled the land."

The Pilgrims left a political, cultural, and theological legacy that would mold and motivate the American nation. In 1776, 156 years later, the foundation of the Declaration of Independence was the same foundation on which the Pilgrims built their colony in 1620, and they surely would have identified with and embraced its words:

*We hold these truths to be self-evident, that all men are cre-
ated equal, that they are endowed by their Creator with certain unalienable Rights, that among these are Life, Liberty
and the pursuit of Happiness.*

The treasured liberties championed by America's Founding Fathers
were in huge measure part of their heritage from the *Mayflower* Pilgrims.
Their biblically based values and principles would become the foundation
of the United States of America. "These same principles," the famed
eighteenth-century philosopher Alexis de Tocqueville would note,
"unknown to the European nations or despised by them, were proclaimed in the wilderness of the New World and became the future
symbol of a great people."

<hr />

William Brewster, the Pilgrims' beloved elder and former Scrooby
postmaster, continued to serve his people and his church until his death,
which likely occurred in 1644, at about age eighty-four. He outlived his
wife Mary and his children Patience, Wrestling, and Fear, but not Love.
William Bradford said of him: "He would labor with his hands in the
fields as long as he was able; yet when the church had no other minister,
he taught twice every Sabbath, and both powerfully and profitably, to
the great contentment of his hearers."

Edward Winslow, the printing assistant to William Brewster in Leiden, eventually became governor of Plymouth Colony. He co-authored
Mourt's Relation, which provided invaluable insight into Plymouth's
early days, and authored numerous other works. He returned to England
during the English Civil War and served in the government of Oliver
Cromwell, England's temporary Lord Protector. At age fifty-nine, he was
lost at sea.

Myles Standish earned fame as Plymouth Colony's military commander. He stirred controversy, however, when he killed several Indians whom he believed were a threat to the colony. Although Governor Bradford defended him, Pastor Robinson admonished him in a letter. "It is more glorious in men's eyes than pleasing in God's," he wrote, "to be a terror to poor, barbarous people." Even Robinson, however, commended Standish for his loyal and effective leadership as Plymouth's military leader. In the 1630s, he and his family helped establish the town of Duxbury. He died there in 1656, reportedly from a bout of kidney stones.

Robert Cushman went back to London aboard the *Fortune* in 1621 and never returned to Plymouth. His sermon, "The Sin and Danger of Self-Love" was published in England and became an enduring part of Pilgrim literature. From England, he continued to help the Plymouth colonists, notably in developing the fishing trade, but the agreement he persuaded them to sign with the Merchant Adventurers was a continued source of frustration. Four years after leaving Plymouth Colony, Cushman died in England. His son Thomas, whom he left in America in the care of William Bradford, grew up in Plymouth and succeeded William Brewster as the ruling elder of the Plymouth Congregation.

Squanto, or Tisquantum, the Patuxet Indian who did so much to assist the Plymouth colonists, developed a nosebleed and died in the winter of 1622. According to William Bradford, Squanto professed faith in Jesus Christ on his deathbed. Loyal to the last, in his final moments he asked Bradford to give his belongings to his friends at Plymouth.

Samoset, the Abenaki Indian leader who introduced the Pilgrims to Squanto, lived another thirty years in New England, and continued to distinguish himself as a Native American diplomat to the European newcomers. In 1625, he signed one of the first land deeds transacted between Native Americans and European colonists. Some claimed he died in what is now Maine in the 1650s, although there is no record of his death.

Massasoit, the chief of the Pokanoket or Wampanoag, remained a faithful friend to the Pilgrims and Plymouth Colony throughout his life. In 1623, he sent word that he was deathly ill. Edward Winslow led a party of Pilgrims to Massasoit's village, and successfully treated his illness, which may have been typhus. In gratitude, Massasoit warned the Pilgrims of an impending attack by the Massachusetts tribe. He is believed to have died in 1661, after establishing peaceful relations with the Plymouth colonists that would last for half a century. Ironically, his son Metacomet, better known as King Philip, led Native American forces in New England's bloodiest Indian conflict—King Philip's War.

Thomas Weston, the obnoxious agent of the Merchant Adventurers, continued to make trouble for the Plymouth colonists for years after the colony was established. Eventually, Plymouth's leaders negotiated a settlement with the Adventurers in exchange for a monopoly on certain trade opportunities. In an ill-fated money-making scheme, he helped establish a competing colony north of Plymouth in 1622, but it fell into disaster and its colonists had to be rescued by the Pilgrims. Weston showed up at Plymouth soon afterwards, begging for assistance from the Pilgrims. He was assisted by William Bradford and returned to England, where he reportedly died penniless.

John Billington, the profane belligerent "Stranger" who was so argumentative aboard the *Mayflower* continued to cause problems in Plymouth Colony. In 1630, he was hanged for murder.

Peregrine White, the first English child born in New England, lived a long and productive life in Plymouth Colony. He married colonist Sarah Bassett, fathered seven children, and died at the age of eighty-four.

Stephen Hopkins, the "Stranger" who may have provoked the mutinous mood aboard the *Mayflower* that led to the creation of the Mayflower Compact, became a leader in the earlier years of Plymouth Colony, even serving briefly as assistant governor. He lost his wife Elizabeth and several children to illness, however, and fell into repeated problems with alcohol. He died in 1644, after requesting to be buried near his wife.

Oceanus Hopkins, the child of Stephen and Elizabeth Hopkins who was born at sea aboard the *Mayflower*, somehow survived the great sickness that killed so many Pilgrims in Plymouth's first winter. He died of unknown causes, however, at about age six.

Richard More, the sole survivor of the four More children aboard the *Mayflower*, grew up to become a sea captain.

John Howland, the young servant to John Carver who was rescued after falling overboard on the *Mayflower*, received his freedom after Governor Carver's death—and may have also received a sizeable inheritance from the Carvers. He became a prominent citizen of Plymouth Colony, serving at one point as deputy governor of the colony. He married colonist Elizabeth Tilley, lived until his seventies, and fathered ten children. Among his descendants were three American presidents—Theodore Roosevelt, George Bush, and George W. Bush.

Christopher Jones, the master of the *Mayflower*, died soon after returning home to England in 1622—most likely as another victim of the illness that killed so many of the Pilgrims.

The *Mayflower* sat at anchor and unused after Jones's death. Four years after her historic voyage to America, she was found unseaworthy by her owners, and was probably scrapped.

The *Speedwell*, which turned back from the Pilgrims' voyage to America because of her many leaks, made numerous other voyages over the years without incident.

John Robinson, the Pilgrims' beloved pastor, managed to preach two more sermons in Leiden after falling mortally ill in the deadly plague of 1625. His death was a disheartening blow to the Pilgrims, and prevented the Separatists at Leiden from sending larger numbers of colonists to Plymouth as planned. "Fare you well in Him in whom you trust, and in whom I rest," Robinson wrote his flock in his final letter. Separatist pastor John Robinson did more for the Pilgrims and Plymouth Colony than any man who never came to America.

William Bradford served as governor of Plymouth Colony for more than thirty years. Two and a half years after his wife Dorothy drowned in Cape Cod Bay, Bradford married a widow named Alice Carpenter, who came to Plymouth with a new group of colonists aboard the ship *Anne* in 1623. His son John, whom he and Dorothy had left in the care of relatives in England, also came to Plymouth. William Bradford's second wife was a widow with two children, and together the Bradfords had three more. Bradford served Plymouth Colony faithfully and wisely, and no person came to be identified with the Pilgrims and Plymouth Colony more than he—largely due to his authorship of the Pilgrims' story in *Of Plymouth Plantation*, which he began in about 1630 and completed in 1651.

As a new generation of colonists migrated to Plymouth Colony, William Bradford worried about the loss of community caused in part by the spreading out of the colony's population. Even more, he worried about what he perceived as declining faith as younger colonists arrived and as Plymouth's residents became comfortable with a more prosperous lifestyle. "Do you not now see the fruits of your labors, O all ye servants of the Lord," he wrote to Plymouth's people in 1646. "You have not only had a seed time, but many of you have seen the joyful harvest; should you not

"Thou hast brought a vine out of Egypt," proclaimed Scripture familiar to the Pilgrims, "…and it filled the land." Far greater than their numbers might suggest, the Pilgrims of Plymouth Colony influenced the making of America.

LIBRARY OF CONGRESS

then rejoice? Yes, and again rejoice, and say Hallelujah!" Near the end of his life, he wrote a poem which reflected the Christ-centered heart he bore, and which he hoped would mark the lives of the newcomers to Plymouth Colony:

> *My days are spent, old age is come,*
> *My strength it fails, my glass near run.*
> *Now I will wait, when work is done,*
> *Until my happy change shall come,*
> *When from my labors I shall rest,*
> *With Christ above for to be blest.*

William Bradford died at age sixty-seven on May 9, 1657, and was buried in the hillside cemetery of his beloved Plymouth, overlooking the wide bay on which he had arrived so long before in 1620. Despite his worries about his people and his colony, he clearly understood that the Pilgrims of Plymouth had in a mighty way helped launch a nation. "Thus, out of small beginnings, greater things have been produced by his hand that made all things of nothing…," he wrote, "and as one small candle may light a thousand, so the light here kindled hath shone unto many…let the glorious name of Jehovah have all the praise."[1]

Acknowledgments

Authoring a book—especially a history book—is a team effort, and I am very grateful for the team members who helped produce *The Pilgrim Chronicles*. Special thanks are due to Executive Editor Harry Crocker and Publisher Alex Novak of Regnery History for suggesting this project. My editor, Maria Ruhl, did a phenomenal job of editing, especially in managing the inevitable final crunch. The superb layout is the masterful work of the very talented designer Amber Colleran, and the handsome jacket was done by Mark Bacon. Many thanks are due as well to Alive Communications' Joel Kneedler, who was my literary agent for this book. My thanks also to the administration of Coastal Carolina University and the CresCom Bank Center for Military & Veterans Studies for the opportunities to research and publish. Special thanks also to English Pilgrim authority Sue Allen for her suggestions, and for her splendid tour of the Pilgrim sites in Great Britain's East Midlands.

I'm very grateful to numerous research and archival institutions whose collections aided this work, including Pilgrim Hall Museum in Plymouth, Massachusetts, the British Library and British Museum in London, the Maritime Archaeology Trust in Southampton, the National Archives of Great Britain, the Rijksmuseum of Amsterdam, Boston Public Library, the Manuscripts Division and the Prints and Photographs Division at the Library of Congress, the National Archives, the David M. Rubenstein Rare Book & Manuscript Library at Duke University, the New England Historic Genealogical Society, the Massachusetts Historical Society, and Kimbel Library at Coastal Carolina University.

Thanks too are due to my friend and fellow historian Dr. John Navin. I owe a unique debt to my parents, Skip and Elizabeth Gragg, who sparked my lifelong love of history with many books and road trips, and to my brother Ted, who shared his heart for history with me at an early age. Thanks also to my cousins Bob, Charles, and Tony, and to "Aunty" Delores, who made history exciting for me as a child, and continues to share a love for it.

I'm also thankful for Connie, Sandra, Martha, Deborah, Margaret, Joe, Jackie, Doug, Tina, John, Gail, Jimmy, Newt, Irena, and Mama-O— and the next generations of history-lovers: Wendy, John, Eddie, Vaughn, Holly, Shelley, Meagan, Chris, Emerson, Riley, Caroline, William, Mary Catherine, Rachel Grace, Clayte, Will, Danielle, Christi, Tommy, Abbey, Shannon, Joseph, Margaret, Sam, and Caleb. I'm always thankful for the prayers and support of my own shipload of pilgrims: Faith, Troy, Rachel, Jay, Elizabeth, Jon, Joni, Penny, Ryan, Skip, Matt, and Miranda—and for Kylah, Sophia, Cody, Jaxon, Gracie, Ashlyn, and Jate. Always, my heartfelt love and appreciation for my book-widow wife, Cindy, who remains the love of my life. Lastly, I remain eternally grateful for the truth of Isaiah 53:5.

Rod Gragg
Conway, SC

Notes

Chapter One
"Who Shall Separate Us from the Love of Christ?"

1. Henry Martyn Dexter, ed., *Mourt's Relation or Journal of the Plantation at Plymouth* (Boston: John K. Wiggin, 1865), 2; William Bradford, *Of Plymouth Plantation, 1620–1647*, Samuel Eliot Morison, ed. (New York: Alfred A. Knopf, 2002), 3–14 (Hereafter referred to as Bradford/Morison, *Of Plymouth Plantation*); Nathaniel Philbrick, *Mayflower: A Story of Courage, Community, and War* (New York: Viking Penguin, 2006), 35–36.

2. Bradford/Morison, *Of Plymouth Plantation*, 3–14; David Chandler and Ian Beckett, *The Oxford History of the British Army* (Oxford: Oxford University Press, 1994), 28–29; Leslie Stephens, ed., *Dictionary of National Biography* (London: Smith, Elder, 1885–1900), 6:161–64; George Bancroft, "The Pilgrim Fathers," *Littell's Living Age* (April–June 1845), 5:73–75; Nick Bunker, *Making Haste from Babylon: The Mayflower Pilgrims and Their*

World (New York: Alfred A. Knopf, 2010), 187, 190–96; Statement of Thomas Elvish, May 1608, Her Majesty's State Papers 14:32:82, National Archives of Great Britain; William Cullen Bryant and Sidney Howard Gay, *A Popular History of the United States* (New York: Charles Scribner's Sons, 1878), 377; William Bradford, *Bradford's History of the Plymouth Settlement, 1608–1650*, Harold Paget, ed. (New York: E.P. Dutton, 1920), 10–13 (Hereafter referred to as Bradford/Paget, *Plymouth Plantation*).

3. Henry Martyn Dexter and Morton Dexter, *The England and Holland of the Pilgrims* (Boston: Houghton, Mifflin, 1905), 341; Christopher Durston and Jacqueline Eales, *The Culture of English Puritans, 1560–1700* (New York: Macmillan, 1996), 8, 11; Francis J. Bremer and Tom Webster, eds., *Puritans and Puritanism in Europe and America: A Comprehensive Encyclopedia* (Santa Barbara: Clio, 2006), 130, 320, 419; Martin Luther, *The Works of Martin Luther*, Adolph Spaeth, L. D. Reed, and Henry Jacobs, eds. (Philadelphia: J. Holman, 1915), 29–38; Thomas Lindsey, *A History of the Reformation* (New York: Charles Scribner's Sons, 1906), 207; Crane Brinton, John B. Christopher, and Robert Lee Wolfe, *A History of Civilization* (Englewood Cliffs: Prentice-Hall, 1955), 1:203–5; Elias B. Sanford, *A History of the Reformation* (Hartford: S.S. Scranton, 1917), 80; Jeremy C. Jackson, *No Other Foundation: The Church Through Twenty Centuries* (Westchester: Cornerstone, 1980), 127–29; Frank Leslie Cross, ed., *Oxford Dictionary of the Christian Church* (New York: Oxford University Press, 1974), 752–53, 1051; Arthur G. Dickens, *The English Reformation* (New York: Scribner & Armstrong, 1873), 324; Daniel Neal, *The History of the*

Puritans or Protestant Non-Conformists (Boston: Charles Ewer, 1817), 179–80; Ira M. Price, *The Ancestry of Our English Bible: An Account of Manuscripts, Texts and Versions of the Bible* (New York: Harper & Brothers Publishers, 1956), 240–51; F. L. Cross, ed., *The Oxford Dictionary of the Christian Church* (Oxford: Oxford University Press, 1997), 752–54, 1051; Edward Been Underhill, ed., *Tracts on Liberty of Conscience and Persecution, 1614–1661* (London: J. Haddon, 1846): Lii; John Richard Green, *History of the English People* (London: Macmillan, 1885), 4:191; *The Prayer Book of Queen Elizabeth, 1559* (Edinburgh: Grant, 1911).

4. Mandel Creighton, *The Story of Some English Shires* (London: Religious Tract Society, 1897), 281; 9–10; Henry Gee and William John Hardy, eds., *Documents Illustrative of English Church History* (New York: Macmillan, 1896), 460–61; John Gordon Palfrey, *History of New England (*Boston: Little and Brown, 1899), 1:111–14, 5:61–67; John Hastings, ed., *The Encyclopedia of Religion and Ethics* (New York: Charles Scribner's Sons, 1919): 10: 507; Perry Miller and Thomas H. Johnson, *The Puritans: A Sourcebook of Their Writings* (New York: Harper & Row, 1963), 6–7; Stephen Monganiello, ed., *The Concise Encyclopedia of the Revolutions and Wars of England, Scotland* (Oxford: Scarecrow Press, 2004), 252; Romans 8:28–39, 10:9–15.

5. Price, *Ancestry of the English Bible*, 260–70; Brinton, Christopher and Wolff, *History of Civilization*, 1:591–92; F. F. Bruce, *The Books and the Parchments* (Westwood: Fleming H. Revell, 1963), 224–25; Bill R. Austin, *Austin's Topical History of Christianity* (Wheaton: Tyndale House,1983), 280–83; *Oxford Dictionary of*

the Christian Church, 859–60 90–120; *Dictionary of National Biography*: 20: 141–50; John Foxe, *Foxe's Book of Martyrs* (Philadelphia: E. Claxton, 1881), 271–81

Chapter Two
"Rather than Turn, They Will Burn"

1. Leslie Stephen, ed., *Dictionary of National Biography* (London: Macmillan, 1880), 50:5–6, 61:131–35; Geoffrey Treasure, *Who's Who in British History* (London: Fitzroy Dearborn, 1998), 1:972; William Ames, *The Marrow of Theology* (Grand Rapids: Baker Books, 1997), 155–58.

2. Gerald Bray, ed., *Documents of the English Reformation* (Cambridge: James Clarke, 1994), 550–53; *Dictionary of National Biography*, 7:57–61; Bunker, *Making Haste from Babylon*, 80–93; William Bradford, *A Dialogue: Or, Third Conference between Some Young Men Born in New England and Some Ancient Men Who Came Out of Holland and Old England*, John Wilson, ed. (Boston: John Deane, 1870), 51–53; Alexander Young, *Chronicles of the Pilgrim Fathers* (Boston: Little and Brown, 1841), 427–28; Ephesians 5:22–33, Proverbs 22:6; John Waddington, *John Penry: The Pilgrim Martyr*, 1553–1593 (London: W.F.G. Cash, 1854), 35–48, 171–77, 205–10, 282; Benjamin Hanbury, *Historical Memorials Relating to the Independents or Congregationalists* (London: Fisher and Son, 1839), 1:86.

3. J. R. Tanner, ed., *Constitutional Documents of the Reign of James I* (London: Bentley House, 1930), 58-65; Pauline Croft, *James I* (London: Palgrave Macmillan, 2003), 100–3, 156–59; George Punchard, *History of Congregationalism* (Boston: Tappan and Dennet, 1841), 279.

4.   Tanner, ed., *Constitutional Documents of the Reign of James I*, 58–65; Croft, *James I*, 100–3, 156–59; Ralph Anthony Houlbrook, ed., *James I and VI: Ideas, Authority and Government* (Hampshire: Ashgate, 2006), 77–78, 87–91; Anthony Weldon, ed., *The Court and Times of James I* (London: Henry Colburn, 1849), 2:227–28.

5.   Charles A. Beard, *An Introduction to the English Historians* (New York: Macmillan, 1908), 337–40; William Barlow, *Sum and Substance of the Hampton Court Conference* (London: Vance, 1604), 3–4, 7–10, 21–30; *Dictionary of National Biography*, 3:110–12; Dexter and Dexter, *England and Holland of the Pilgrims*, 370–73; Henry Morley, *A Miscellany Containing Richard of Bury's Prohibition, the Basilikon Doron of James I* (London: George Routledge, 1888).

Chapter Three
"They Resolved to Get Over into Holland"

1.   Green, *History of the English People*, 3:49–53; Alan Haynes, *The Gunpowder Plot: Faith in Rebellion,* (Dover: Alan Sutton, 1994), 10, 85, 92; Mark Nicholls, *Investigating the Gunpowder Plot* (Manchester: University of Manchester Press, 1991), 21, 41; Henry Garnett, *Guy Fawkes: An Experiment in Biography* (Madison: University of Wisconsin Press, 1962), 79, 100, 174; *Dictionary of National Biography*: 9:282–84; 18:165–68.

2.   Haynes, *Gunpowder Plot*, 18, 92; Nicholls, *Investigating the Gunpowder Plot*, 21, 41; Garnett, *Guy Fawkes*, 79, 100, 174; *Dictionary of National Biography*, 9:282–84; 18:165–68; "Civil and Religious Liberty Not Obtained by the Reformation," *Catholic Monthly Intelligencier* (January 1817) 5:44:3–5.

3. William H. Burgess, *John Robinson: Pastor of the Pilgrim Fathers* (London: Williams and Norgate, 1920): 47–48, 60–63; *Dictionary of National Biography*, 49:19–22; Dexter and Dexter, *England and Holland of the Pilgrims*:, 257, 399–400; Bunker, *Masking Haste from Babylon*, 100–5, 169–73; Patrick Collinson, *Richard Bancroft and Elizabethan AntiPuritanism* (Cambridge: Cambridge University Press, 2013), 6–10; George Stevens, *Three Centuries of a City Library* (Norwich: Public Library Committee, 1917), ii; George F. Willson, *Saints and Strangers: Lives of the Pilgrim Fathers* (Kingsport: Kingsport Press, 1945), 55–56, 492; Ephesians 5: 1–2, 11; John Robinson, *The Works of John Robinson, Pastor of the Pilgrim Fathers* (Boston: Doctrinal Tract and Book Society, 1851), 2:252, 259–75.

4. Burgess, *John Robinson*, 60–63; *Dictionary of National Biography*, 49:19–22; Bradford/Morison, *Of Plymouth Plantation*, 14; Robert Tracy McKenzie, *The First Thanksgiving: What the Real Story Tells Us About Loving God and Learning From History* (Downers Grove: IVP Academic, 2013), 50–51; Charle Garside, *The Origins of Calvin's Theology of Music, 1536–1543* (Philadelphia: American Philosophical Society, 1979), 7–8; Timothy George, *John Robinson and the English Separatist Tradition* (Macon: Mercer University Press, 1982), 148–51; J.C. Addison, *The Romantic Story of the Mayflower Pilgrims* (Boston: L.C. Page, 1911), 25; Augustus J. C. Hare, *The Story of My Life* (London: George Allen, 1900), 5:260; Joseph Hunter, *Collections Concerning the Church or Congregation of Separatists Formed at Scrooby in North Nottinghamshire in the Time of King James I* (London: John Russell Smith, 1854), 163–73; Benjamin Handbury, *Historical Memorials Relating to the Independents or Congregationalists* (London: Fisher and Son, 1839), 1:376.

5. Allen Johnson, ed., *Dictionary of American Biography* (New York: Charles Scribner's, 1929), 3:29–30; "Scrooby Manor Houses/Farm Houses," English Heritage Building I.D. 417777, Britishlistedbuilding.co.uk; Jeremy Dupertuis Bangs, *Strangers and Pilgrims, Travelers and Sojourners: Leiden and the Foundations of Plymouth Plantation,* (Plymouth: General Society of Mayflower Descendants, 2009), 30–33; Eugene Aubrey Stratton, *Plymouth Colony: Its History & People, 1620–1691* (Salt Lake City: Ancestry Publishing, 1986), 251–52; Burgess, *John Robinson,* 72–76, 80–81; Bunker, *Making Haste from Babylon,* 101–3; Caleb Johnson, ed., *Of Plymouth Plantation* (Bloomington: Xlibris, 2006), 197; Acts 5:27–29; Dexter and Dexter, *England and Holland of the Pilgrims,* 288–89.

6. Bunker, *Making Haste from Babylon,* 181–88; *Dictionary of American Biography,* 3:29–30; *Dictionary of National Biography,* 37:61–67; Alexander Young, ed., *Chronicles of the Pilgrims Fathers* (Boston: A.C. Little, 1834), 23–24, 32: Robert William Dale, *History of English Congregationalism* (London: Hodder and Stoughton, 1907), 192.

Chapter Four
"Butter-Mouths," "Lubbers," and "Manifold Temptations"

1. Cotton Mather, *Magnalia Christi Americana: An Ecclesiastical History of New England* (Hartford: Silas Andras, 1855), 1:109–11; Dictionary of American Biography: 2:559; Gary D. Schmidt, *William Bradford: Plymouth's Faithful Pilgrim* (Grand Rapids: William B. Eerdmans, 1999), 3–9; Peggy M. Baker, "Searching for the Promised Land: The Travels and Travails of Richard Clyfton," Pilgrim Hall Museum website, http://www.pilgrimhallmuseum.

org; I Peter 2:11; Dexter and Dexter, *England and Holland of the Pilgrims*, 423–30, 446–48; Keith L. Sprunger, *Dutch Puritanism: A History of English and Scottish Churches in the Netherlands in the 16th and 17th Centuries* (Leiden: E.J. Brill, 1982), 123–25, 134; William Bradford, *Bradford's History of the Plymouth Settlement, 1606–1659*, Harold Paget, ed. (New York: E.P. Dutton, 1909), 19–21 (Hereafter referred to as Bradford/Paget, *Bradford's History*).

2.   William Brereton, *Travels in Holland, England, the United Provinces, Scotland and Ireland* (London: Richard Pliner, 1634), 38–48: Dexter and Dexter, *England and Holland of the Pilgrims*, 491; *Dictionary of American Biography*, 2:29; Sprunger, *Dutch Puritanism*, 123–25, 134; *Encyclopedia Britannica*, 11:375; Register of Decisions of the Burgomasters and Aldermen, 30 October 1608–4 August 1609, Leiden City Archive, Record 501A, Leiden Regional Archive; Bradford, *Of Plymouth Plantation*, 16–18.

3.   John Abott Goodwin, *The Pilgrim Republic: An Historic Review of the Colony of New Plymouth* (Boston: Tichnor, 1888), 34, 44; Maaten Prak, *The Dutch Republic in the Seventeenth Century: The Golden Age* (Cambridge: Cambridge University Press, 2005), 15–18; Bradford/Morison, *Of Plymouth Plantation*, 18; I Corinthians 2:2; Conveyance from William Bradford to Jan Des Obrys, 19 April 1619, Register of Conveyances, Judicial Archive of Leiden, record number 508; A. J. Barnouw, "Echoes of the Pilgrim Fathers' Speech," *The Weekly Review*, vol. 4, no. 105 (14 May 1921): 466–67; D. Plooij and J. Rendel Harris, eds., *Leyden Documents Relating to the Pilgrim Fathers* (Leiden: E.J. Brill, 1920) 2–14; A. Eekhof, ed., *Three Unknown Documents Relating to the Pilgrim Fathers in Holland* (The Hague: Martinus Nijhoff, 1920), 30; *The Mayflower*

Descendant: A Quarterly Magazine of Pilgrim Genealogy, History and Biography (1907) 9:1:116.

4. Bradford/Morison, *Of Plymouth Plantation*, 25; *Dictionary of National Biography*, 39:172–73; Fynes Moryson, *An Itinerary: Containing His Ten Years Travel Through the Twelve Dominions of Germany, Bohemia, Switzerland, Netherland, Denmark, Poland, Italy, Turkey, France, England, Scotland and Ireland* (Glascow: MacLahose, 1908), 3:455, 4:469; Gervase Markham, *The English Housewife: Containing the Inward and Outward Vertues Which Ought to be in a Compleet Woman* (London: Richard Rogers, 1615), 8–16.

5. Goodwin, *Pilgrim Republic*, 32-45; Bangs, *Strangers and Pilgrims*, 527–42; William Bradford, *History of Plymouth Plantation, 1620–1647*, Worthington Chauncey Ford, ed. (Boston: Massachusetts Historical Society, 1912), 53–55 (Hereafter referred to as Bradford/Ford, *History of Plymouth Plantation*).

6. Goodwin, *Pilgrim Republic*, 38–42; Bunker, *Making Haste from Babylon*, 212–17; Bradford/Paget, *Bradford's History*; Bradford/Paget, *Plymouth Plantation*, 368–71; Burgess, *John Robinson*, 803, 253–56.

Chapter Five
"They Knew They Were Pilgrims"

1. Dexter and Dexter, *England and Holland of the Pilgrims*, 423–30, 446–48, 491; Brereton, *Travels in Holland, England*, 38–48; *Dictionary of American Biography*, 2:29; Sprunger, *Dutch Puritanism*, 123–25, 134; Bradford/Morison, *Of Plymouth Plantation*, 16–18:

2. John Navin, "Plymouth Plantation: The Search for Community on the New England Frontier," Dissertation (Brandeis University

Department of History, 1997),171–72; Goodwin, *The Pilgrim Republic*, 34, 44; Bradford/Morison, *Of Plymouth Plantation*, 18; Dexter and Dexter, *England and Holland of the Pilgrims*, 423–30, 446–48, 491; Bunker, *Making Haste from Babylon*, 37–42, 51; Philbrick, *Mayflower*, 24–26; Dillon, *Place of Habitation*, 116–17; Nathaniel Morton, *New England's Memorial* (Boston: Congregational Board of Publication, 1855), 267–69.

3. Bunker, *Making Haste from Babylon*, 37–42, 51; Philbrick, *Mayflower*, 24–26; Goodwin, *Pilgrim Republic*, 32–45; Bangs, *Strangers and Pilgrims*, 527–42; Bradford/Ford, *History of Plymouth Plantation*, 1:115–17.

4. Dexter and Dexter, *England and Holland of the Pilgrims*, 446–48, 491; Philbrick, *Mayflower*, 24–26; Dillon, *Place of Habitation*, 116–17; I Peter 1:9–11; Ezra 8:21; Arthur Stedman, ed., *A Library of American Literature from the Earliest Settlement to the Present time* (New York, NY: Charles Webster, 1888), 1:132; Young, *Chronicles of the Pilgrim Fathers*, 360–62.

5. Philbrick, *Mayflower*, 29–32; Goodwin, *The Pilgrim Republic*, 34, 44; Dexter and Dexter, *England and Holland of the Pilgrims*, 446–48, 491; Schmidt, *William Bradford: Plymouth's Faithful Pilgrim*; Dillon, *Place of Habitation*, 121–28; *Collections of the Massachusetts Historical Society* (Boston: W.P. Lewis, 1832), 9:30–32.

Chapter Six
"They Put to Sea Again with a Prosperous Wind"

1. Bernard B. Woodward, *A General History of Hampshire* (London: Virtue, 1861), 144–56; Henry John Englefield and John Bular, *A Walk Through Southampton: Including a Survey of its Antiquities*

(London: T. Baker, 1841), 14; Bradford/Morison, *Of Plymouth Plantation*, 54–55, 366.

2. Woodward, *General History of Hampshire:* 144-56; Bular, *Walk Through Southampton*, 14; Bunker, *Making Haste from Babylon*, 37–42, 51; Philbrick, *Mayflower*, 24–26; Robert Charles Anderson, *The Plymouth Migration: Immigrants to Plymouth Colony, 1620–1633* (Boston: New England Historic Genealogical Society, 2004), 2:159; Dillon, *The Pilgrims*, 119–22; The preferred spelling of the names in Bradford's passenger list can be found in the following: Charles Edward Bangs, *The English Ancestry and Homes of the Pilgrim Fathers* (New York: Grafton, 1929), 25–102; Caleb Johnson's MayflowerHistory.com; Bradford/Morison, *Of Plymouth Plantation*, 441–43; The basic list cited is found in Willlam T. Davis, ed., *William Bradford's History of Plymouth Plantation, 1606–1646* (New York: Charles Scribner's Sons, 1908), 407–9.

3. Bradford/Morison, *Of Plymouth Plantation*, 45–46, 52–53; Philbrick, *Mayflower*, 27–28; Richard Polwhele, *Historical Views of Devonshire* (London: Trewman and Son: 1793), 1:185; French, "Genealogical Research in England—Cushman," 68:181; Statton, *Plymouth Colony*, 275; Alan Heimert and Andrew Delbanco, *The Puritans in America: A Narrative Anthology* (Cambridge: Harvard University Press, 1985), 41; Robert Higham, ed., *Security and Defense in South-West England Before 1800* (Exeter: University of Exeter Press, 1987), 46; Robert Earl Cushman, Franklin P. Cole, and Judith Haddock Swan, *Robert Cushman of Kent: Chief Agent of the Plymouth Pilgrims* (Plymouth: General Society of Mayflower Descendants, 2005), 92–117; Joshua 6–7; Davis, ed., *William Bradford's History of Plymouth Plantation, 1606–1646*, 85–92.

4. Richard Nicholls Worth, *A History of Devonshire with Sketches of Its Worthies* (London: Elliot Stock, 1895), 203–10; Bradford/ Morison, *Of Plymouth Plantation*, 53–54; Philbrick, *Mayflower*, 25–32; Dillon, *Place of Habitation*, 121–28; John Smith; *The Generall Historie of Virginia, New England & the Summer Isles* (Glascow: James MacLeHose, 1907), 2:182; William Salters, "Captain John Smith, Governor of Virginia and Admiral of New England," *Annals of Iowa* (April 1908) 8:1:220–21; *Dictionary of National Biography*, 53:70–73; John Smith, *A Description of New England; or, Observations and Discoveries in the North of America* (Boston: William Veazie, 1865), *v*, 5–15.

5. Bradford/Morison, *Of Plymouth Plantation*, 51–53; Terrence Scully, *The Art of Cookery in the Middle Ages* (Woodbridge, UK: Boydell Press, 1995), 159; Richard W. Meade, *A Treatise on Naval Architecture and Shipbuilding* (Philadelphia: Lippincott,1869), 398; Michael V. Barry, ed., *Survey of English Dialects* (London: Routledge Press, 1994), 87; Gustav Eger, ed., *Technological Dictionary in the English and German Languages* (London: Trubner, 1884), 2:556; John Pinkerton, *A Collection of the Best and Most Interesting Voyages and Travels in All Parts of the World* (London: Longman Hurst, 1812), 250.

Chapter Seven
"They ... Encountered ... Many Fierce Storms"

1. Bradford/Morison, *Of Plymouth Plantation*, 58–59; Philbrick, *Mayflower:* 30–31; James Deetz and Patricia Scott Deetz, *The Times of their Lives: Life, Love and Death in Plymouth Colony* (New York: W.H. Freeman, 2000), 37–38; Bunker, *Making Haste from Babylon*, 55–59.

2. Bradford/Morison, *Of Plymouth Plantation*, 58–59; Philbrick, *Mayflower*, 30–31; James Deetz and Patricia Scott Deetz, *The Times of their Lives: Life, Love and Death in Plymouth Colony* (New York: W.H. Freeman, 2000), 37–38; Bunker, *Making Haste from Babylon*, 55–59; *Dictionary of National Biography*, 21: 327–29; Richard Hakluyt, *Divers Voyages Touching the Discovery of America* (London: Hakluyt Society, 1850), 3:135–48; Henry Burrage, ed., *Early English and French Voyages: Chiefly from Hakluyt* (New York: Charles Scribner's Sons, 1906, 178–222.

3. Bradford/Morison, *Of Plymouth Plantation*, 58–59; Nickerson, *Land Ho!*, 11; Dillon, *Place for Habitation*, 127–29; Philbrick, *Mayflower*, 29–32; Bunker, *Making Haste from Babylon*, 58–59; Thomas Secombe, ed., *Voyages and Travels Mainly in the 16th and 17th Centuries* (Westminster: Archibald and Constable, 1903), 1:157.

4. Dillon, *Place for Habitation*, 127–29; Philbrick, *Mayflower*, 29–32; Bradford/Morison, *Of Plymouth Plantation*, 58–59; Nickerson, *Land Ho!*, 11; Bunker, *Making Haste from Babylon*, 58–59; Thomas Sydenham, *The Whole Works of that Excellent, Practical Physician, Dr. Thomas Sydenham* (London: W. Feales, 1734), 117–18.

5. Caleb H. Johnson, *The Mayflower and Her Passengers* (Bloomington: 2006), 28–30; Bradford/Morison, *Of Plymouth Plantation*, 58–64, 441–47; Deetz and Deetz, *Times of Their Lives*, 36–37, 297–98; Caleb Johnson's Mayflowerhistory.com; Hugh Dunthorne, *Britain and the Dutch Revolt, 1560–1700* (Cambridge: Cambridge University Press, 2013), 76-77; *DNB*: 53:474–75, 9:236; Bangs, *English Ancestsry and Homes of the Pilgrim Fathers*, 30–31; William Bradford, *Governor William Bradford's Letter Book* (Boston: Massachusetts Society of Mayflower Descendants, 1906), 30–31; Bradford/Paget, *Plymouth Plantation*, 92–93.

6.   Bradford/Morison, *Of Plymouth Plantation:* 59; Harry Kelsey, *Sir John Hawkins: Queen Elizabeth's Slave Trader* (New Haven: Yale University Press, 2003), 270–71; *DNB:* 25:211–18,225; Myra Jehen and Michael Warner, eds., *The English Literature of America, 1500–1800* (London: Routledge, 1997), 51–52; Burrage, *Early English and French Voyages,* 127–28.

7.   Bradford/Morison, *Of Plymouth Plantation,* 25–26, 62; Richard James Hooker, *Food and Drink in America* (Indianapolis: Bobbs-Merrill, 1981), 6–8,82; *DNB* 61:54–55; Burrage, *Early English and French Voyages,* 290–91.

8.   Davis, *William Bradford's History of Plymouth Plantation, 1606–1646,* 30–31.

Chapter Eight
"They Fell upon Their Knees and Blessed the God of Heaven"

1.   Bradford/Morison, *Of Plymouth Plantation,* 59–60; Bunker, *Making Haste from Babylon,* 53–55.

2.   Philbrick, *Mayflower,* 31–42; Dillon, *A Place for Habitation,* 129–34; Bradford/Morison, *Of Plymouth Plantation,* 59–60; Bunker, *Making Haste from Babylon,* 53–55; Davis, *William Bradford's History of Plymouth Plantation, 1606–1646,* 123–24; Navin, *Plymouth Plantation,* 230–37.

3.   Winifred Cockshott, *The Pilgrim Fathers: Their Church and Colony* (New York: G.P. Putnam's Sons, 1909), 144–45, 288; James Thatcher, *History of the Town of Plymouth* (Boston: Marsh, Capen and Lyon, 1835), 261–62; Roland G. Usher, *The Pilgrims and Their History* (New York: Macmillan, 1980), 69, 144, 177–81; Ozara S. Davis, John Robinson: *The Pilgrim Pastor* (New York: Pilgrim Press, 1903), 144–45, 246–48; Nathaniel Morton, *New England's Memorial* (Boston: Congregational Board of Publication, 1855), 266; Bunker,

Making Haste from Babylon, 287; "Religion and the Founding of the American Republic," official exhibition website of the Library of Congress, 1988; Bradford/Morison, *Of Plymouth Plantation*, 75–75, 93, 370, 441–42; "Mayflower Compact, 1620," Avalon Project, Yale University, www.yale.edu/laweb/avalon/americandoc/mayflower.htm.

4. Morton, *New England's Memorial*, 27–28; Bradford/Morison, *Of Plymouth Plantation*, 64–66; Dwight B. Heath, ed., *Mourt's Relation: A Journal of the Pilgrims at Plymouth* (Bedford, MA: Applewood Books, 1963), 15–26; Cockshott, *Pilgrim Fathers*, 199–204; Henry David Thoreau, *The Writings of Henry David Thoreau* (Boston: Houghton Mifflin, 1906), 5:251–58; Lyon Sharman, ed., *The Cape Cod Journal of the Pilgrim Fathers: Reprinted from Mourt's Relation* (East Aurora, 1920), 12–27.

5. Cockshott, *Pilgrim Fathers*, 199–204; Morton, *New England's Memorial*, 27–28; Bunker, *Making Haste from Babylon*, 287; Bradford/Morison, *Of Plymouth Plantation*, 75–75, 93, 370, 441–42; Heath, ed., *Mourt's Relation*, 15–26

Chapter Nine
"The Best They Could Find"

1. Bradford/Morison, *Of Plymouth Plantation*, 68–70; Heath, ed., *Mourt's Relation*, 30–36.

2. Bradford/Morison, *Of Plymouth Plantation*: 68–70; Tom Iredale and Ellis Troughton, "The Correct Generic Name for the Grampus or Killer Whale, and the So-Called Grampus or Risso's Dolphin," *Records of the Australian Museum*, 19:1:36; Sharman, ed., *The Cape Cod Journal of the Pilgrim Fathers: Reprinted from Mourt's Relation*, 12–27.

3. Smith, *Description of New England*, 66; *DNB*: 60:393; Benjamin Eggleston, *The Wars of America* (Baltimore: Hazard and Bloomer,

1839), 80–82: Philbrick, *Mayflower*, 53–55; Bradford/Morison, *Of Plymouth Plantation*, 81; Henry VII to John Cabot, 5 March 1496, Public Records Office, London, UK, Plate 7, Series 2, C82/145:6; Thomas Dermer to "His Worshipful Friend," 27 December 1619, Letter of Thomas Dermer Describing His Passage from Maine to Virginia in A.D. 1619, Manuscript Division, Library of Congress; Harold S. Russell, *Indian New England Before the Mayflower* (Lebanon, N.H.: University Press of New England, 1980), 8–11, 22–33; William Moore, *Indian Wars of the United States* (Philadelphia: George Gorton, 1843), 113–15; Frederick W. Hodge, *Handbook of American Indians North of Mexico* (Washington, DC: Smithsonian Institution, 1907), 14, 40, 74, 98, 127; Katherine Donegan, *Seasons of Misery: Catastrophe and Colonial Settlement in Early America* (Philadelphia: University of Pennsylvania Press, 2014), 130; John Locke, *Two Treatises on Government: A Translation into Modern English* (Manchester, England: Industrial Systems Research, 2009), 130; Jeremy Dupertuis Bangs, *Indian Deeds: Land Transactions in Plymouth Colony, 1620–1691* (Boston: New England Historic Genealogical Society, 2002), 213–25; John Reed Swanton, *Indian Tribes of North America* (Washington, DC: Smithsonian Institution, 1952), 24–27; Barry Pritzker, *A Native American Encyclopedia: History, Culture and Peoples* (New York: Oxford University Press, 2001), 473; Dennis A. Cannole, *The Indians of the Nipmuck Country in Southern New England, 1630–1750: An Historical Geography* (Jefferson, NC: McFarland, 2001), 14–16; Burrage, ed., *Early English and French Voyages: Chiefly from Hakyluk*, 337–39; Christopher Tomlins, *Freedom Bound: Law, Labor and Civic Identity in Colonizing English America* (New York: Cambridge University Press, 2010), 148–49.

4. *Mourt's Relation*, 38–41; Bradford/Morison: *Of Plymouth Plantation*, 69–71; Morton, *New England's Memorial*, 32–36; Cockshott, *Pilgrim Fathers*, 201–6; Philbrick, *Mayflower*, 74–76; "Beyond the Pilgrim Story," http://www.pilgrimhallmuseum.org/plymouth_rock.htm; Deetz and Deetz, *Times of Their Lives*, 17; William Thomas Davis, *History of the Town of Plymouth: With a Sketch of the Origin and Growth of Separatism* (Philadelphia: J.W. Lewis, 1885), 21–23. Sharman, ed., *Cape Cod Journal of the Pilgrim Fathers, Reprinted from Mourt's Relation*, 52–66.

5. Davis, *William Bradford's History of Plymouth Plantation, 1606–1646*, 104.

Chapter Ten
"It Was the Lord Which Upheld Them"

1. Davis, *William Bradford's History of Plymouth Plantation, 1606–1646*, 76; Johnson, *Mayflower and Her Passengers*, 45; Philbrick, *Mayflower*, 76; Morton, *New England's Memorial*, 36; Cotton Mather, *Magnalia Christi Americana* (London: Thomas Parkhurst, 1702), 4.

2. Bradford/Morison, *Of Plymouth Plantation*, 444; Cockshott, *Pilgrim Fathers*, 204; Morton, *New England's Memorial*, 171–72; Bradford/Morrison, *Of Plymouth Plantation*, 72, 76, 87; Joseph Everett Chandler, *The Colonial House* (New York: Robert N. McBride, 1916), 330; Harold R. Shurtleff, *The Log Cabin Myth: A Study of the Early Dwellings of the English Colonists in North America* (Cambridge, Mass.: Harvard University Press, 1939), 43, 68, 104–10; William Cronon, *Changes in the Land: Indians, Colonists and the Ecology of New England* (New York: Macmillan, 1983), 4–5; Morton, *New England Memorial*, 360; John R. Swanton, *Indian Tribes of North America*, 25; Deetz and Deetz, *Times*

of Their Lives, 60–61; Increase Mather, *Early History of New England* (Boston: Samuel Drake, 1864), 67; Henry Martyn Dexter, ed., Edward Winslow and William Bradford, *Mourt's Relation: Or Journal of the Plantation at Plimouth* (Boston: John Kimball Wiggen, 1864), 66–77; Revelation 21:1–5, Hebrews 12:5–11.

3. Deetz and Deetz, *Times of Their Lives*, 60–61; Philbrick, *Mayflower*, 92–93; Bunker, *Making Haste from Babylon*, 288; Winslow and Bradford/Dexter, *Mourt's Relation*, 71–77.

4. Bradford/Morison, *Of Plymouth Plantation*, 76–78, 84; Morton, *New England Memorial*, 36–37; Dillon, *Place for Habitation*, 151–52; Philbrick, *Mayflower*, 76, 84–86; Deetz and Deetz, *Times of Their Lives*, 59–60, 298; John 15:13; William Bradford, *Bradford's History of Plymouth Plantation* (Boston: Wright and Potter, 1899), 111–19.

5. Bradford/Morrison, *Of Plymouth Plantation*, 79–84; Thomas Prince, *Chronological History of New England: In the Form of Annals* (Boston: Kneeland and Green, 1826), 185–88; Alvin Gardner Weeks, *Massasoit of the Wampanoags* (Norwood, MA: Plimpton, 1919), 126–32, 148; Deetz and Deetz, *Times of Their Lives*, 61–62; Prince, *Chronological History of New England*, 185–88; Philbrick, *Mayflower*, 92–93; Bunker, *Making Haste from Babylon*, 288; Lincoln N. Kinnicut, "The Plymouth Settlement and Tisquantam," Proceedings of the Massachusetts Historical Society (October 1914–June 1915), 48:109–117; DAB: 17:487; Winslow and Bradford/Dexter, *Mourt's Relation*, 84–95.

Chapter Eleven
"By the Goodness of God We Are So Far from Want"

1. Bradford/Morison, *Of Plymouth Plantation*, 86; Morton, *New England's Memorial*, 62; Deetz and Deetz, *Times of Their Lives*, 62–64.

2. Bradford/Morison, *Of Plymouth Plantation*, 86; Morton, *New England's Memorial*, 62; DNB: 6:162–63; Deetz and Deetz, *Times of Their Lives*, 60-61; Edward Winslow, *Good Newes from New England: A True Relation of Things Very Remarkable at the Plantation of Plimouth in New England* (London: William Bladen and John Bellamie, 1624), 29; Winslow and Bradford/Dexter, *Mourt's Relation: Or Journal of the Plantation at Plimouth* (Boston: John Kimball Wiggen, 1864), 134–37.

3. Francis J. Bremer and Tom Webster, eds., *Puritans and Puritanism in Europe and America: A Comprehensive Encyclopedia* (Santa Barbara, CA: Clio, 2006), 562, 642; Deetz and Deetz, *Times of Their Lives*, 60–61; Exodus 23:16; Numbers 18:8–32; Leviticus 23:20–21; Deuteronomy 16:11–12; 2 Chronicles 8:12–13; Philippians 4:6; John D. Davis, ed., *A Dictionary of the Bible* (Philadelphia: Westminster, 1917), 800–1, 856; John Brand, *Observations on Popular Antiquities* (London: Chatto and Windus, 1900), 189–90; Paul Bradshaw, ed., *New Webster Dictionary of Liturgy* (Louisville, KY: John Knox, 2002), 233–34; Austin Allibone, *A Critical Dictionary of English Literature and American Authors* (Philadelphia: Lippincott, 1899), 2:2784; John McLintock and James Strong, *Cyclopedia of Biblical, Theological and Ecclesiastical Literature* (New York: Harper Brothers, 1891), 10:301; Christine Kooi, *Liberty and Religion: Church and State in Reformation Leiden* (Boston: Brill, 2000), 34–37; Carrie B. Adams, "Thanksgiving," *The Inland Educator: A Journal for the Progressive Teacher* (August 1895): 1:248–49; George P. Cheever, *The Pilgrim Fathers* (London: William Collins, 1849), 231–34; John Gordon Palfrey, *History of New England* (Boston: Little and Brown, 1858), 1:213–14; Usher, *Pilgrims and Their History*, 90–94; Frederick A. Noble, *The Pilgrims* (Boston: Pilgrim, 1907), 309; James Thatcher, *History of the Town*

of Plymouth (Boston: Marsh, Capen and Lyon, 1835), 59, 261–62; Winslow, *Good News from New England*, 29; Psalms 107:1–8; Deuteronomy 16:13–14; Winslow and Bradford/Dexter, *Mourt's Relation*, 60, 71–77, 133.

4. Winslow and Bradford/Dexter, *Mourt's Relation*, 84–95.

5. William Bradford, *Bradford's History of Plymouth Plantation*, (Boston: Wright and Potter, 1899), 111–19.

6. Bradford/Morison, *Of Plymouth Plantation*, 92–96; Winslow and Bradford/Heath, *Mourt's Relation*, 84–85; Bunker, *Making Haste from Babylon*, 311–13; Thatcher, *History of the Town of Plymouth*, 262–65; Young, *Chronicles of the Pilgrim Fathers*, 265–67.

7. Bradford/Morison, *Of Plymouth Plantation*, 92–96; Winslow and Bradford/Heath, *Mourt's Relation*, 84–85; Bunker, *Making Haste from Babylon*, 311–13; Thatcher, *History of the Town of Plymouth*, 262–65; Usher, *Pilgrims and Their History*, 90–98; Sydney V. James Jr., ed., *Three Early Visitors to Plymouth: Letters About the Pilgrim Settlement in New England in its First Seven Years* (Bedford, MA: Applewood Books, 1963), 3–4; Champlin Burrage, ed., *John Pory's Lost Description of Plymouth Colony* (Boston: Houghton Mifflin, 1918), 37–38, 42.

8. "Letters of John Bridge and Emmanuel Altham," *Proceedings of the Massachusetts Historical Society* (October 1910–September 1911): 44:178–80; Sydney James, ed., *Three Early Visitors to Plymouth*, 3–12.

9. Bradford/Morison, *Of Plymouth Plantation*, 111, 202, 378; James, ed., *Three Early Visitors to Plymouth*, 63–64; *Narratives of New Netherland, 1609–1664*, J. Franklin Jameson, ed. (New York: Charles Scribner's Sons, 1909), vol. 8:102–15.

10. Dillon, *A Place for Habitation*, 220–22: Young, *Chronicles of the Pilgrim Fathers*, 408.

11. William Brigham, ed., *The Compact with the Charter and Laws of the New Colony of Plymouth* (Boston: Dutton and Wentworth, 1836), 242–43; Godfrey Hodgson, *A Great & Godly Adventure* (New York: Public Affairs, 2006), 192–93; Dillon, *A Place for Habitation*, 220–22.

Epilogue

1. Stratton, *Plymouth Colony*, 130–36, 245, 249–50, 308, 311, 324; Navin, *Plymouth Plantation*, 621, 785–87; Dillon, *Place for Habitation*, 222; Allen Weinstein and David Rubel, *The Story of America: Freedom and Crisis from Settlement to Superpower* (New York, NY: DK Publishing, 2002), 61–65; Stedman, ed., *A Library of American Literature from the Earliest Settlement to the Present Time*, 114; Ecclesiastes 3:1; Peter C. Herman, *A Short History of Early Modern England* (Oxford: John Wily, 2011), 112–18; DNB 60:374–75, 49:21, 2:560–61; Stratton, *Plymouth Colony*, 245; Deetz and Deetz, *Times of Their Lives*, 111; Philbrick, *Mayflower*, 101, 230–31; Rod Gragg, *Forged in Faith: How Faith Shaped the Birth of the Nation* (New York: Simon and Schuster, 2009), 35–37; Morison, *Plymouth Plantation*, 353, 785.

Bibliography

Adams, Carrie B. "Thanksgiving." *The Inland Educator: A Journal for the Progressive Teacher*, vol. 7 (August–January 1898).

Addison, J. C. *The Romantic Story of the Mayflower Pilgrims*. Boston: L.C. Page, 1911.

Alibone, Austin. *A Critical Dictionary of English Literature and American Authors*. Philadelphia: Lippincott, 1899.

Allan, Sue. *Steps Along the Mayflower Trail*. Burgess Hill: Domtom Publishing, 2011.

Ames, William. *The Marrow of Theology*. Grand Rapids: Baker Books, 1997.

Anderson, Robert Charles. *The Plymouth Migration: Immigrants to Plymouth Colony, 1620–1633*. Boston: New England Historic Genealogical Society, 2004.

Austin, Bill R. *Austin's Topical History of Christianity*. Wheaton: Tyndale House, 1983.

Baker, Peggy M. "Searching for the Promised Land: The Travels and Travails of Richard Clyfton." Pilgrim Hall Museum, http://www.pilgrimhallmuseum.org.

Bancroft, George. "The Pilgrim Fathers." *Littell's Living Age*, vol. 5 (April–June 1845).

Bangs, Charles Edward. *The English Ancestry and Homes of the Pilgrim Fathers*. New York: Grafton, 1929.

Bangs, Jeremy Dupertuis. *Indian Deeds: Land Transactions in Plymouth Colony, 1620–1691*. Boston: New England Historic Genealogical Society, 2002.

———. *Strangers and Pilgrims, Travelers and Sojourners: Leiden and the Foundations of Plymouth Plantation*. Plymouth: General Society of Mayflower Descendants, 2009.

Barlow, William. *Sum and Substance of the Hampton Court Conference*. London: Vance, 1604.

Barnouw, A. J. "Echoes of the Pilgrim Fathers' Speech." *The Weekly Review*, vol. 4, no. 105 (14 May 1921).

Barry, Michael V., ed. *Survey of English Dialects*. London: Routledge Press, 1994.

Beard, Charles A. *An Introduction to the English Historians*. New York: Macmillan, 1908.

"Beyond the Pilgrim Story." Pilgrim Hall Museum, http://www.pilgrimhallmuseum.org/plymouth_rock.htm.

Bradford, William. *Bradford's History of Plymouth Plantation*. Boston: Wright and Potter, 1899.

———. *A Dialogue: Or, Third Conference Between Some Young Men Born in New England and Some Ancient Men Who Came Out of Holland and Old England.* Boston: John Deane, 1870.

———. *Governor William Bradford's Letter Book.* Boston: Massachusetts Society of Mayflower Descendants, 1906.

Bradshaw, Paul, ed. *New Webster Dictionary of Liturgy.* Louisville: John Knox, 2002.

Brand, John. *Observations on Popular Antiquities.* London: Chatto and Windus, 1900.

Bray, Gerald, ed. *Documents of the English Reformation.* Cambridge: James Clarke, 1994.

Bremer, Francis J. and Tom Webster, eds. *Puritans and Puritanism in Europe and America: A Comprehensive Encyclopedia.* Santa Barbara: Clio, 2006.

Brereton, William. *Travels in Holland, England, the United Provinces, Scotland and Ireland.* London: Richard Pliner, 1634.

Brigham, William, ed. *The Compact with the Charter and Laws of the New Colony of Plymouth.* Boston: Dutton and Wentworth, 1836.

Brinton, Crane, John B. Christopher, and Robert Lee Wolfe. *A History of Civilization.* Englewood Cliffs: Prentice-Hall, 1955.

Bruce, F. F. *The Books and the Parchments.* Westwood: Fleming H. Revell, 1963.

Bryant, William Cullen and Sidney Howard Gay. *A Popular History of the United States.* New York: Charles Scribner's Sons, 1878.

Bunker, Nick. *Making Haste From Babylon: The Mayflower Pilgrims and Their World.* New York: Alfred A. Knopf, 2010.

Burgess, William H. *John Robinson: Pastor of the Pilgrim Fathers*. London: Williams and Norgate, 1920.

Burrage, Champlin, ed. *Early English and French Voyages: Chiefly from Hakluyt*. New York: Charles Scribner's Sons, 1906.

———, ed. *John Pory's Lost Description of Plymouth Colony*. Boston: Houghton Mifflin, 1918.

Calloway, Colin G., ed. *Dawnland Encounters: Indians and Europeans in Northern New England*. Hanover: University Press of New England, 1991.

Cannole, Dennis A. *The Indians of the Nipmuck Country in Southern New England, 1630–1750: An Historical Geography*. Jefferson, NC: McFarland, 2001.

Chandler, David and Ian Beckett. *The Oxford History of the British Army*. Oxford: Oxford University Press, 1994.

Chandler, Joseph Everett. *The Colonial House*. New York: Robert N. McBride, 1916.

Cheever, George P. *The Pilgrim Fathers*. London: William Collins, 1849.

"Civil and Religious Liberty Not Obtained by the Reformation." *Catholic Monthly Intelligencier*, vol. 5 (January 1817).

Cockshott, Winifred. *The Pilgrim Fathers: Their Church and Colony*. New York: G.P. Putnam's Sons, 1909.

Collections of the Massachusetts Historical Society. Boston: W.P. Lewis, 1832.

Collinson, Patrick. *Richard Bancroft and Elizabethan Anti-Puritanism*. Cambridge: Cambridge University Press, 2013.

Conveyance from William Bradford to Jan Des Obrys, 19 April 1619. Register of Conveyances. Record number 508. Judicial Archive of Leiden.

Creighton, Mandel. *The Story of Some English Shires.* London: Religious Tract Society, 1897.

Croft, Pauline. *James I.* London: Palgrave Macmillan, 2003.

Cronon, William. *Changes in the Land: Indians, Colonists and the Ecology of New England.* New York: Macmillan, 1983.

Cross, Frank Leslie, ed. *Oxford Dictionary of the Christian Church.* New York: Oxford University Press, 1974.

Cushman, Robert Earl, Franklin P. Cole, and Judith Haddock Swan. *Robert Cushman of Kent: Chief Agent of the Plymouth Pilgrims.* Plymouth: General Society of Mayflower Descendants, 2005.

Dale, Robert William. *History of English Congregationalism.* London: Hodder and Stoughton, 1907.

Davis, John D., ed. *A Dictionary of the Bible.* Philadelphia: Westminster, 1917.

Davis, Ozara S. *John Robinson: The Pilgrim Pastor.* New York: Pilgrim Press, 1903.

Davis, William T. *History of the Town of Plymouth: With a Sketch of the Origin and Growth of Separatism.* Philadelphia: J.W. Lewis, 1885.

Davis, William T., ed. *William Bradford's History of Plymouth Plantation, 1606–1646.* New York: Charles Scribner's Sons, 1908.

Deetz, James and Patricia Scott Deetz. *The Times of Their Lives: Life, Love and Death in Plymouth Colony.* New York: W.H. Freeman, 2000.

Dermer (Thomas) Papers. Manuscript Division. Library of Congress.

Dexter, Henry Martyn, ed. *Mourt's Relation or Journal of the Plantation at Plymouth.* Boston: John K. Wiggin, 1865.

Dexter, Henry Martyn and Morton Dexter. *The England and Holland of the Pilgrims.* Boston: Houghton Mifflin, 1905.

Dickens, Arthur G. *The English Reformation.* New York: Scribner & Armstrong, 1873.

Donegan, Katherine. *Seasons of Misery: Catastrophe and Colonial Settlement in Early America.* Philadelphia: University of Pennsylvania Press, 2014.

Dunthorne, Hugh. *Britain and the Dutch Revolt, 1560–1700.* Cambridge: Cambridge University Press, 2013.

Durston, Christopher and Jacqueline Eales. *The Culture of English Puritans, 1560–1700.* New York: Macmillan, 1996.

Eekhof, A., ed. *Three Unknown Documents Relating to the Pilgrim Fathers in Holland.* The Hague: Martinus Nijhoff, 1920.

Eger, Gustav, ed. *Technological Dictionary in the English and German Languages.* London: Trubner, 1884.

Eggleston, Benjamin. *The Wars of America.* Baltimore: Hazard and Bloomer, 1839.

Elvish (Thomas) Collection. Her Majesty's State Papers. National Archives of Great Britain.

Englefield, Henry John and John Bular. *A Walk through Southampton: Including a Survey of Its Antiquities.* London: T. Baker, 1841.

Fleming, Thomas J. *One Small Candle: The Pilgrims' First Year in America.* New York: W.W. Norton, 1964.

Ford, Worthington Chauncey, ed. *History of Plymouth Plantation, 1620–1647.* Boston: Massachusetts Historical Society, 1912.

Foxe, John. *Foxe's Book of Martyrs.* Philadelphia: E. Claxton, 1881.

French, Elizabeth. "Genealogical Research in England—Cushman." *New England Historical and Genealogical Register,* vol. 68 (1914).

Garnett, Henry. *Guy Fawkes: An Experiment in Biography.* Madison: University of Wisconsin Press, 1962.

Garside, Charles. *The Origins of Calvin's Theology of Music, 1536–1543.* Philadelphia: American Philosophical Society, 1979.

Gee, Henry and William John Hardy, eds. *Documents Illustrative of English Church History.* New York: Macmillan, 1896.

George, Timothy. *John Robinson and the English Separatist Tradition.* Macon: Mercer University Press, 1982.

Goodwin, John Abott. *The Pilgrim Republic: An Historic Review of the Colony of New Plymouth.* Boston: Tichnor, 1888.

Gragg, Rod. *Forged in Faith: How Faith Shaped the Birth of the Nation.* New York: Simon & Schuster, 2010.

———. *By the Hand of Providence: How Faith Shaped the American Revolution.* New York: Simon & Schuster, 2011.

Green, John Richard. *History of the English People.* London: Macmillan, 1885.

Hakluyt, Richard. *Divers Voyages Touching the Discovery of America.* London: Hakluyt Society, 1850.

Hanbury, Benjamin. *Historical Memorials Relating to the Independents or Congregationalists.* London: Fisher and Son, 1839.

Hare, Augustus. *The Story of My Life.* London: George Allen, 1900.

Hastings, John, ed. *The Encyclopedia of Religion and Ethics.* New York: Charles Scribner's Sons, 1919.

Haynes, Alan. *The Gunpowder Plot: Faith in Rebellion.* Dover: Alan Sutton, 1994.

Heath, Dwight B., ed. *Mourt's Relation: A Journal of the Pilgrims at Plymouth.* Bedford: Applewood Books, 1963.

Heimert, Alan and Andrew Delbanco. *The Puritans in America: A Narrative Anthology.* Cambridge: Harvard University Press, 1985.

Henry VII to John Cabot, 5 March 1496. Plate 7, series 2. Public Records Office, London.

Herman, Peter C. *A Short History of Early Modern England.* Oxford: John Wily, 2011.

Higham, Robert, ed. *Security and Defense in South-West England Before 1800.* Exeter: University of Exeter Press, 1987.

Hodge, Frederick W. *Handbook of American Indians North of Mexico.* Washington, DC: Smithsonian Institution, 1907.

Hodgson, Godfrey. *A Great & Godly Adventure.* New York: Public Affairs, 2006.

Hooker, Richard James. *Food and Drink in America.* Indianapolis: Bobbs-Merrill, 1981.

Houlbrook, Ralph Anthony, ed., *James I and VI: Ideas, Authority and Government.* Hampshire: Ashgate, 2006.

Hunter, Joseph. *Collections Concerning the Church or Congregation of Separatists Formed at Scrooby in North Nottinghamshire in the Time of King James I.* London: John Russell Smith, 1854.

Iredale, Tom and Ellis Troughton. "The Correct Generic Name for the Grampus or Killer Whale, and the So-Called Grampus or Risso's Dolphin." *Records of the Australian Museum*, vol. 19, no. 1 (1933).

Jackson, Jeremy C. *No Other Foundation: The Church through Twenty Centuries*. Westchester: Cornerstone, 1980.

Jameson, J. Franklin, ed. *Narratives of New Netherland, 1609–1664*. New York: Charles Scribner's Sons, 1909.

James, Sydney V., Jr., ed. *Three Early Visitors to Plymouth: Letters about the Pilgrim Settlement in New England in Its First Seven Years*. Bedford: Applewood Books, 1963.

Jehen, Myra and Michael Warner, eds. *The English Literature of America, 1500–1800*. London: Routledge, 1997.

Johnson, Allen, ed. *Dictionary of American Biography*. New York: Charles Scribner's, 1929.

Johnson, Caleb. "Passenger Lists." MayflowerHistory.com. http://mayflowerhistory.com/mayflower-passenger-list.

Johnson, Caleb, ed. *Of Plymouth Plantation*. Bloomington: Xlibris, 2006.

Kelsey, Harry. *Sir John Hawkins: Queen Elizabeth's Slave Trader*. New Haven: Yale University Press, 2003.

Kinnicut, Lincoln N. "The Plymouth Settlement and Tisquantam." *Proceedings of the Massachusetts Historical Society*, series 3, vol. 8 (October 1914–June 1915).

Kooi, Christine. *Liberty and Religion: Church and State in Reformation Leiden*. Boston: Brill, 2000.

Kupperman, Karen Odahl. *Indians and English: Facing Off in Early America*. Ithaca: Cornell University Press, 2000.

Leach, Douglas Edward. *Flintlock and Tomahawk: New England in King Philip's War*. East Orleans: Parnassus Imprints, 1992.

"Letters of John Bridge and Emmanuel Altham." *Proceedings of the Massachusetts Historical Society*, vol. 44 (October 1910–June 1911).

Lindsey, Thomas. *A History of the Reformation*. New York: Charles Scribner's Sons, 1906.

Locke, John. *Two Treatises on Government: A Translation into Modern English*. Manchester: Industrial Systems Research, 2009.

Markham, Gervase. *The English Housewife: Containing the Inward and Outward Vertues Which Ought to be in a Compleat Woman*. London: Richard Rogers, 1615.

Mather, Cotton. *Magnalia Christi Americana: An Ecclesiastical History of New England*. Hartford: Silas Andras, 1855.

Mather, Increase. *Early History of New England*. Boston: Samuel Drake, 1864.

"Mayflower Compact." Avalon Project. Yale University Library, www.yale.edu/laweb/avalon/americandoc/mayflower.htm.

Mayflower Descendant: A Quarterly Magazine of Pilgrim Genealogy, History and Biography, vol. 9, no. 1 (1907).

McKenzie, Robert Tracy. *The First Thanksgiving: What the Real Story Tells Us about Loving God and Learning from History*. Downers Grove: IVP Academic, 2013.

McLintock, John and James Strong. *Cyclopedia of Biblical, Theological and Ecclesiastical Literature*. New York: Harper Brothers, 1891.

Meade, Richard W. *A Treatise on Naval Architecture and Shipbuilding*. Philadelphia: Lippincott, 1869.

Miller, Perry. *Errand into the Wilderness*. Cambridge: Harvard University Press, 1956.

———. *The New England Mind: From Colony to Province*. Cambridge: Harvard University Press, 1953.

———. *The New England Mind: The Seventeenth Century*. New York: Macmillan, 1939.

Miller, Perry and Thomas H. Johnson. *The Puritans: A Sourcebook of Their Writings*. New York: Harper & Row, 1963.

Monganiello, Stephen, ed. *The Concise Encyclopedia of the Revolutions and Wars of England, Scotland, and Ireland, 1639–1660*. Oxford: Scarecrow Press, 2004.

Moore, William. *Indian Wars of the United States*. Philadelphia: George Gorton, 1843.

Morison, Samuel Eliot, ed. *Of Plymouth Plantation, 1620–1647*. New York: Alfred A. Knopf, 2002.

———. *The Story of the "Old Colony" of New Plymouth, 1620–1692*. New York: Alfred A. Knopf, 1960.

Morley, Henry. *A Miscellany Containing Richard of Bury's Prohibition, the Basilikon Doron of James I*. London: George Routledge, 1888.

Morton, Nathaniel. *New England's Memorial*. Boston: Congregational Board of Publication, 1855.

Moryson, Fryes. *An Itinerary: Containing His Ten Years Travel through the Twelve Dominions of Germany, Bohemia, Switzerland, Netherland, Denmark, Poland, Italy, Turkey, France, England, Scotland and Ireland*. Glascow: MacLahose Publishing, 1908.

Navin, John. "Plymouth Plantation: The Search for Community on the New England Frontier." Dissertation. Brandeis University Department of History, 1997.

Neal, Daniel. *The History of the Puritans or Protestant Non-Conformists*. Boston: Charles Ewer, 1817.

Nicholls, Mark. *Investigating the Gunpowder Plot*. Manchester: University of Manchester Press, 1991.

Nickerson, W. Sears. *Land Ho! 1620: A Seaman's Story of the Mayflower, Her Construction, Her Navigation, and Her First Landfall*. East Lansing: Michigan State University Press, 1997.

Noble, Frederick A. *The Pilgrims*. Boston: The Pilgrim Press, 1907.

Paget, Harold, ed. *Of Plymouth Plantation*. New York: E.P. Dutton, 1920.

Palfrey, John Gordon. *History of New England*. Boston: Little and Brown, 1899.

Philbrick, Nathaniel. *Mayflower: A Story of Courage, Community, and War*. New York: Viking Penguin, 2006.

Pinkerton, John. *A Collection of the Best and Most Interesting Voyages and Travels in All Parts of the World*. London: Longman Hurst, 1812.

Plooij, D. and J. Rendel Harris, eds. *Leyden Documents Relating to the Pilgrim Fathers*. Leiden: E.J. Brill, 1920.

Polwhele, Richard. *Historical Views of Devonshire*. London: Trewman and Son: 1793.

Prak, Maaten. *The Dutch Republic in the Seventeenth Century: The Golden Age*. Cambridge: Cambridge University Press, 2005.

Prayer Book of Queen Elizabeth, 1559. Edinburgh: Grant, 1911.

Price, Ira M. *The Ancestry of Our English Bible: An Account of Manuscripts, Texts and Versions of the Bible.* New York: Harper & Brothers Publishers, 1956.

Prince, Thomas. *Chronological History of New England: In the Form of Annals.* Boston: Kneeland and Green, 1826.

Pritzker, Barry. *A Native American Encyclopedia: History, Culture and Peoples.* New York: Oxford University Press, 2001.

Punchard, George. *History of Congregationalism.* Boston: Tappan and Dennet, 1841.

Register of Conveyances. Record number 508. Judicial Archive of Leiden.

Register of Decisions of the Burgomasters and Aldermen, 30 October 1608–4 August 1609. Leiden City Archive Record 501A. Leiden Regional Archive.

"Religion and the Founding of the American Republic." Official exhibition website of the Library of Congress, 1988, http://www.loc.gov/exhibits/religion.

Robinson, John. *The Works of John Robinson, Pastor of the Pilgrim Fathers.* Boston: Doctrinal Tract and Book Society, 1851.

Russell, Harold S. *Indian New England before the Mayflower.* Lebanon: University Press of New England, 1980.

Salisbury, Neal. *Manitou and Providence: Indians, Europeans, and the Making of New England, 1500–1643.* Oxford: Oxford University Press, 1982.

Salters, William. "Captain John Smith, Governor of Virginia and Admiral of New England." *Annals of Iowa*, vol. 8 (April 1908).

Sanford, Elias B. *A History of the Reformation*. Hartford: S.S. Scranton, 1917.

Schmidt, Gary D. *William Bradford: Plymouth's Faithful Pilgrim*. Grand Rapids: William B. Eerdmans, 1999.

"Scrooby Manor Houses/Farm Houses." English Heritage Building I.D. 417777. Britishlistedbuilding.co.uk.

Scully, Terrence. *The Art of Cookery in the Middle Ages*. Woodbridge: Boydell Press, 1995.

Secombe, Thomas, ed. *Voyages and Travels Mainly in the 16ᵗʰ and 17ᵗʰ Centuries*. Westminster: Archibald and Constable, 1903.

Sharman, Lyon, ed. *The Cape Cod Journal of the Pilgrim Fathers*. East Aurora: The Advocate, 1920.

Shurtleff, Harold R. *The Log Cabin Myth: A Study of the Early Dwellings of the English Colonists in North America*. Cambridge: Harvard University Press, 1939.

Smith, John. *A Description of New England or Observations and Discoveries in the North of America*. Boston: William Veazie, 1865.

———. *The Generall Historie of Virginia, New England & the Summer Isles*. Glasgow: James MacLeHose Publishing, 1907.

Spaeth, Adolph Spaeth, L. D. Reed, and Henry Jacobs, eds. *The Works of Martin Luther*. Philadelphia: J. Holman, 1915.

Sprunger, Keith L. *Dutch Puritanism: A History of English and Scottish Churches in the Netherlands in the 16th and 17th Centuries*. Leiden: E.J. Brill, 1982.

Stedman, Arthur, ed. *A Library of American Literature from the Earliest Settlement to the Present Time*. New York, NY: Charles Webster, 1888.

Stephens, Leslie, ed., *Dictionary of National Biography*. London: Smith and Elder, 1885–1900.

Stevens, George. *Three Centuries of a City Library*. Norwich: Public Library Committee, 1917.

Stratton, Eugene Aubrey. *Plymouth Colony: Its History & People, 1620–1691*. Salt Lake City: Ancestry Publishing, 1986.

Swanton, John Reed. *Indian Tribes of North America*. Washington, DC: Smithsonian Institution, 1952.

Sydenham, Thomas. *The Whole Works of That Excellent, Practical Physician, Dr. Thomas Sydenham*. London: W. Feales, 1734.

Tanner, J. R., ed. *Constitutional Documents of the Reign of James I*. London: Bentley House, 1930.

Thatcher, James. *History of the Town of Plymouth*. Boston: Marsh, Capen and Lyon, 1835.

Thoreau, Henry David. *The Writings of Henry David Thoreau*. Boston: Houghton Mifflin, 1906.

Tomlins, Christopher. *Freedom Bound: Law, Labor and Civic Identity in Colonizing English America*. New York: Cambridge University Press, 2010.

Treasure, Geoffrey. *Who's Who in British History*. London: Fitzroy Dearborn, 1998.

Underhill, Edward B., ed. *Tracts on Liberty of Conscience and Persecution, 1614–1661*. London: J. Haddon, 1846.

Usher, Roland G. *The Pilgrims and Their History*. New York: Macmillan, 1918.

Waddington, John. *John Penry: The Pilgrim Martyr, 1553–1593*. London: W.F.G. Cash, 1854.

Weeks, Alvin Gardner. *Massasoit of the Wampanoags*. Norwood, MA: Plimpton, 1919.

Weinstein, Allen and David Rubel. *The Story of America: Freedom and Crisis from Settlement to Superpower*. New York: DK Publishing, 2002.

Weldon, Anthony, ed. *The Court and Times of James I*. London: Henry Colburn, 1849.

Willson, George F. *Saints and Strangers: Lives of the Pilgrim Fathers*. Kingsport: Kingsport Press, 1945.

Winslow, Edward. *Good Newes from New England: A True Relation of Things Very Remarkable at the Plantation of Plimouth in New England*. London: William Bladen and John Bellamie, 1624.

———. *Hypocrisie Unmasked: A True Relation of the Proceedings of the Governor and Company of the Massachusetts against Samuel Gorton of Rhode Island*. New York: Burt Franklin, 1968.

Winthrop, John. *The History of New England from 1630 to 1649*. New York: Scribner's Sons, 1908.

Woodward, Bernard B. *A General History of Hampshire*. London: Virtue, 1861.

Worth, Richard Nicholls. *A History of Devonshire with Sketches of Its Worthies*. London: Elliot Stock, 1895.

Young, Alexander. *Chronicles of the Pilgrim Fathers*. Boston: Little and Brown, 1841.

Index